The ider of Sexuality

THE GENDER LENS:
A Sage Publications / Pine Forge Press Series

Series Editors

Judith A. Howard
University of Washington

Barbara Risman
North Carolina State University

Mary Romero
Arizona State University

Joey Sprague
University of Kansas

Books in the Series

Yen Le Espiritu, *Asian American Women and Men: Labor, Laws, and Love*

Judith A. Howard and Jocelyn A. Hollander, *Gendered Situations, Gendered Selves: A Gender Lens on Social Psychology*

Michael A. Messner, *Politics of Masculinities: Men in Movements*

Judith Lorber, *Gender and the Social Construction of Illness*

Scott Coltrane, *Gender and Families*

Pepper Schwartz and Virginia Rutter, *The Gender of Sexuality*

Books Forthcoming

Francesca Cancian and Stacy Oliker, *A Gendered View of Care*

Patricia Yancey Martin and David Collinson, *The Gendered Organization*

The Gender of Sexuality

Pepper Schwartz
University of Washington

Virginia Rutter
University of Washington

PINE FORGE PRESS

Thousand Oaks ■ London ■ New Delhi

For information:

 Pine Forge Press
A Sage Publications Company
2455 Teller Road
Thousand Oaks, California 91320
E-mail: sales@pfp.sagepub.com

SAGE Publications Ltd.
6 Bonhill Street
London EC2A 4PU
United Kingdom

SAGE Publications India Pvt. Ltd.
M-32 Market
Greater Kailash I
New Delhi 110 048 India

Printed in the United States of America

Library of Congress Cataloging-in-Publication Data

Schwartz, Pepper.
    The gender of sexuality / by Pepper Schwartz and Virginia Rutter.
        p.   cm. — (Gender lens)
    Includes bibliographical references and index.
    ISBN 0-8039-9042-1 (pbk.: alk. paper)
        1. Sex. 2. Sex (Psychology) 3. Sex differences (Psychology)
    4. Sex role. 5. Gender identity. I. Rutter, Virginia.
    II. Title. III. Series.
    HQ21.S328   1998
    306.7—dc21   97-33723

98 99 00 01 02 03 10 9 8 7 6 5 4 3 2 1

Production Editor:	Sanford Robinson
Production Assistant:	Karen Wiley
Typesetter:	Rebecca Evans
Indexer:	Molly Hall
Cover Designer:	Ravi Balasuriya
Print Buyer:	Anna Chin

CONTENTS

CHAPTER 1

Sexual Desire and Gender   1

CHAPTER 2

Sexual Behavior and Gender   35

It is now over 20 years since feminist sociologists have identified gender as an important analytic dimension in sociology. In the intervening two decades, theory and research on gender have grown exponentially. With this series, we intend to further this scholarship, as well as ensure that theory and research on gender become fully integrated into the discipline as a whole.

Beth Hess and Myra Marx Ferree, in *Analyzing Gender* (1987), identified three stages in the study of women and men since 1970. Initially, the emphasis was on sex differences and the extent to which such differences might be based in biological properties of individuals. In the second stage, the focus shifted to individual-level sex roles and socialization, exposing gender as the product of specific social arrangements, although still conceptualizing it as an individual trait. The hallmark of the third stage is the recognition of the centrality of gender as an organizing principle in all social systems, including work, politics, everyday interaction, families, economic development, law, education, and a host of other social domains. As our understanding of gender has become more social, so has our awareness that gender is experienced and organized in race- and class-specific ways.

In the summer of 1992, the American Sociological Association (ASA) funded a small conference, organized by Barbara Risman and Joey Sprague, to discuss the evolution of gender in these distinctly sociological frameworks. The conference brought together a sampling of gender scholars working in a wide range of substantive areas with a diversity of methods to focus on gender as a principle of social organization. The discussions of the state of feminist scholarship made it clear that gender is both pervasive in society and operates at multiple levels. Gender shapes identities and perception, interactional practices, and the very forms of social institutions, and it does so in race- and class-specific ways. If we did not see gender in social phenomena, we were not seeing clearly.

The participants in this ASA-sponsored seminar recognized that although these developing ideas about gender were widely accepted by feminist sociologists and many others who study social inequalities, they were relatively unfamiliar to many who work within other sociological paradigms. This book series was conceived at that conference as a means to introduce these ideas to sociological colleagues and students and to help further develop gender scholarship.

As series editors, we feel it is time for gender scholars to speak to our colleagues and to the general education of students. Many sociologists and scholars in other social sciences want to incorporate scholarship on gender and its intersections with race, class, and sexuality into their teaching and research but lack the tools to do so. For those who have not worked in this area, the prospect of the bibliographic research necessary to develop supplementary units, or to transform their own teaching and scholarship, is daunting. Moreover, the publications necessary to penetrate a curriculum resistant to change and encumbered by inertia have simply not been available. We conceptualize this book series as a way of meeting the needs of these scholars and thereby also encouraging the development of the sociological understanding of gender by offering a *Gender Lens.*

What do we mean by a gender lens? It means working to make gender visible in social phenomena, asking if, how, and why social processes, standards, and opportunities differ systematically for women and men. It also means recognizing that gender inequality is inextricably braided with other systems of inequity. Looking at the world through a gendered lens thus implies two seemingly contradictory tasks. First, it means unpacking the taken-for-granted assumptions about gender that pervade sociological research and social life more generally. At the same time, looking through a gender lens means showing just how central assumptions about gender continue to be to the organization of the social world, regardless of their empirical reality. We show how our often-unquestioned ideas about gender affect the worlds we see, the questions we ask, the answers we can envision. The *Gender Lens* series is committed to social change directed toward eradicating these inequalities. Our goals are consistent with initiatives at colleges and universities across the United States that are encouraging the development of more diverse scholarship and teaching.

The books in the *Gender Lens* series are aimed at different audiences and have been written for a variety of uses, from assigned readings in introductory undergraduate courses to graduate seminars and as professional resources for our colleagues. The series includes several different styles of books that address these goals in distinct ways. We are excited about this series and anticipate that it will have an enduring impact on the direction of both pedagogy and scholarship in sociology and other related social sciences. We invite you, the reader, to join us in thinking through these difficult but exciting issues by offering feedback or developing your own project and proposing it to us for the series.

About This Volume

The current volume presents a gendered analysis of a field often thought to be inseparable from gender, that is, human sexuality. Pepper Schwartz and Virginia Rutter offer a sociological framework for understanding this most complex and charged of human experiences.

Schwartz and Rutter begin their analysis by defining the key terms in this discussion: sex, gender, sexuality, and explaining the distinctions among them. They turn to a presentation of major theoretical understandings of sexuality, offering what they call an *integrative* perspective on sexuality that draws on the most useful of both biological and sociological perspectives on human sexuality. This integrative perspective shapes their subsequent discussion of the actual details of sexual behavior—who does what, how often, with whom, and in what circumstances—and their analysis of the dynamics of sexuality, both among those who are not married and within the institution of marriage. Schwartz and Rutter locate their analyses in the historical context of views of sexuality in the United States, including an in-depth analysis of changes—and stabilities—in sexual prescriptions and proscriptions over the past 30 years. They evaluate as well the possibilities for sexual relationships in the future, exploring the dynamics among peer marriages between equals as one model for the future. The volume closes with two powerful chapters that present contemporary debates about defining the boundaries and the possibilities of sexual experiences, as well as the highly politicized, and highly gendered, nature of these experiences, manifested in struggles over defining and regulating teenage sexuality, sexual harassment and assault, and the institutionalization of nonnormative forms of sexual expressions, as evident in the debates about gay marriage. Throughout this volume, Schwartz and

Rutter offer a nuanced analysis of the ways in which human sexuality is structured not only by gender but also by race, economic circumstances, and especially by moral and political approaches to same-sex sexual expressions and relationships.

We hope this book, together with others in the *Gender Lens* series, will help the reader develop her or his own "gender lens" to better and more accurately understand our social environments and relationships. As sociologists, we believe that an accurate understanding of human sexual desires and practices, a domain that is currently the target of heated political and social debates, is vital. Pepper Schwartz and Virginia Rutter take the reader a long way toward that understanding.

Judith A. Howard
Barbara Risman
Mary Romero
Joey Sprague
Series Editors

Why did we write this book? There are probably no two areas—gender and sexuality—with more taken-for-granted stereotypes and more arm-chair experts to expound upon them. This makes these topics a great challenge for students and teachers of sociology. In writing this book we sought to take the hot air out of a lot of unquestioned positions about gender and sexuality, especially all those deeply held "incorrigible" propositions that men and women are fundamentally and essentially different when it comes to sexuality.

Readers of this book will gain useful explanations for why the notion that "men are from Mars, women are from Venus" is misleading and sometimes downright silly. A good example of this was relayed to us recently by a colleague. The other night, our friend was channel surfing and *Love Line,* a cable television talk show about sex and relationships, caught her eye. On it, the "relationship expert" host claimed that when a woman's estrogen (a sex-related hormone) is high, she is at her most loving, passive, and receptive for her partner's vigorous sexual atten-tion. In other words, the speaker was suggesting that love and passivity are physiologically linked for a woman. Put another way, a woman's emotional and sexual response is dictated by her ovulation cycle. The result: the more sexually passive a woman is, the more she really loves you. We wonder, did the host (who was a guy) mean that if a woman is active or aggressive during sex, she really isn't in love or receptive? And what about when both sex partners are women, and both are high on estrogen? How in the world do these "naturally passive" women bring themselves to actually get any sexual activity done? Did the speaker have data to indicate women who have higher-than-average estrogen levels are more loving and receptive than other women are? Of course not. Not only is the biological information about estrogen incorrect in this case (the story is complicated, but estrogen appears to stimulate aggression, not passivity, as we discuss in Chapter 1), but this account relies on biological sex differences to interpret sexual behavior. There are much better data that indicate that our culture's social scripts, not estrogen levels, control women's sexual behavior and dictate passivity under some circumstances. We assure you that "receptivity" increases when sexual partners are skillful at making love to a woman, not when estrogen reaches some magical level.

What distressed our friend most while watching the show was the camera's pan of the audience. It revealed women and men alike nodding in agreement with the remarks of the speaker. Indeed, the show and its "talk" about estrogen and women's sexual passivity are another contribution to our culture's sexual scripts. What may be more evident after reading this book is how such talk about women's sexuality also defines and constrains sexual expression for men. It is all too commonplace to think of men and women as fundamentally different and to use biology to account for social behaviors.

We've noticed that it is hard to find books on gender that address sexuality, or to find human sexuality texts that locate gender as a fundamental explanation of how people learn and interpret sexuality. With this book, we hope to make the importance (and usefulness) of combining these topics in both gender and human sexuality classes irresistible. Gender and sexuality are an exciting and entertaining combination, but also a serious area of study. There are important human consequences that follow from the ways in which sexuality is organized around gender. Consequences range from how some people get punished for unusual behavior, while others do not; to how medical advice and research proceeds or how social resources are spent; to how much men and women are willing to bend themselves out of shape so as to fit in to social norms.

Take a recent news story about a 63-year-old California woman who, through the miracle of modern technology, gave birth to a baby. Certainly the story provoked gossip and curiosity in both mainstream media and the tabloids. But the issues around the debate are serious and zero in on the link between gender and sexuality. The most obvious issue is, Why was this woman sanctioned so intensely for having a baby at her mature age? Why do men who father children after age 60 receive, at best, a bit of congratulatory nudging to the effect of "We didn't know you still had it in you!" while women are labeled "sick" or "selfish"? The double standard is fairly obvious, and it is a valuable jumping-off point for thinking about gender and sexuality. A less obvious issue that we would invite students to consider is what produces in people, like this particular mother and her partner, the desire to reproduce (again) so much so that she is willing to go to extraordinary effort and expense to produce this child? This aspect of the case reminds us of the rather remarkable intersection between biological capacity for producing children and a socially constructed strong preference for motherhood as an identity-confirming role. So powerful is the appeal of motherhood—from a social perspective—that this woman lied about her age to her doctor and paid big bucks so that she could override nature and social convention to enact what must have been for her a central affirming role in her life. Was her act a product of "nature" or of "culture"?

Although instructors and students who read this book will enjoy the feminist perspectives we take, this book is not about feminism per se, but about analytic tools for understanding gender and sexuality. We owe a tremendous debt to the intellectual contributions of feminism to the area of gender and sexuality. Feminism has brought personal, everyday experiences to the political world and has drawn attention to logically inconsistent arguments, such as the argument that it is okay for men but not for women to have children after age 60. Feminism has served as a guidepost for improving (and raising questions about) a variety of theoretical approaches to social behavior, including social constructionism, symbolic interactionism, conflict theory, functionalism, exchange theory, and rational choice theory. Feminism has challenged the assumptions about gender and sexuality that are either implicit or explicit in explanations of social phenomena. This skepticism enables us and many other social scientists to think about how—and why—gender and sexuality have been constructed.

Sexuality and gender studies have been advanced, also, by the study of gay and lesbian experiences. Same-sex relationships involve doing sex that is, by definition, for nonprocreative reasons or, in other words, for pleasure only. Public arguments against homosexuality are influenced by negative attitudes toward sex that is only an act of intimacy and pleasure. In many ways, the fight for civil rights undertaken by gay and lesbian rights organizations and others has highlighted our cultural ambivalence about sex for pleasure. It also has highlighted the different social response to gay men on the one hand and lesbians on the other (which we address in our book). Homosexuality, like all other sexualities, is caught up with and complicated by different societal attitudes about men's and women's sexualities.

How did we write this book? As sociologists and journalists we integrated evidence and anecdote, theory and experience to engage students. We provide students with questions about where images of gendered sexual differences come from, in whose interest they operate, and how social context influences the performance of gender in sexual settings, and we offer ways for students to consider how else they might think about gender. We remind the reader with data and examples that the social construction of sexuality is a part of men's and women's experience. We wrote this book with our own students in mind—undergraduates we've encountered in general sociology courses as well as in more specialized courses on gender, on family, and on sexuality. We have sought to aid students in thinking like sociologists about gender and sexuality.

What were our personal motivations for getting involved in this area? While we have presented our professional reasons for writing about gender and sexuality, quite honestly, a couple of things in our personal backgrounds also helped shape us into scholars interested in sex and gender. When we were children—Pepper in the early 1960s and Virginia in the 1970s—we both discovered that talking about sex was fun and a sure-fire way to capture people's attention. Pepper had one of the youngest consciousness-raising reading groups ever, as she and a bunch of 10-year-old girls would gather in her parents' basement and discuss and study her mother's books on human sexuality. Virginia was schooled early in her aunt and uncle's irreverence about sex and what today would be called their "sex positivity." No subject was off limits around their breakfast table. Virginia loved for her mother to read to her from the biography of Madame Pompadour, courtesan to King Louis the XVI, and she was eager to tell school friends and their parents' driving carpool all she had learned about the sexual habits of the French aristocracy. As adults, we still love to talk about sex—it is so provocative, so personally meaningful, and there are so many unanswered questions to explore. It never escapes us that getting paid to talk about orgasms in public is an unusual job. It is a pleasure, therefore, to put some of these observations and studies on paper and to share them with you. We hope that you, our readers, will share our curiosity and enthusiasm, and it is with those high expectations that we submit this book to you.

ACKNOWLEDGMENTS

This book has the benefit of great care and attention from a number of wonderful and generous readers, editors, and commentators. Our *Gender Lens* series editors, Judy Howard and Barbara Risman, provided enormous challenges to our thinking (and improved our book), and for their cooperative, collaborative, and detailed attention we are grateful. Judy's 1996 SIGNS seminar at the University of Washington is just one of the many indirect ways she provided assistance in addition to her direct guidance as primary editor or *madrina* of this book.

Steve Rutter, Pine Forge Press publisher, provided patience, good humor, and support, and he kept us buoyed with his confidence in this book.

We thank other colleagues who read manuscripts, talked with us, and provided valuable ideas and insights: Deirdre Bowen, Julie Brines, Joanna Fox, Michael Heller, Jocelyn Hollander, Beth Jackson, Neil Jacobson, Diane Lye, Hara Marano, Jodi O'Brien, Tom Linneman, Davis Patterson, Frank Pittman, Tina Pittman-Wagers, and Diane Sollee. We are thankful for the *Gender Lens* series roundtable discussions sponsored by Pine Forge at the ASA meetings in 1994 and 1995, and those who participated in it; and the four readers of the early chapters of this manuscript, including Mary Ertel (Central Connecticut State University), Pamela Format (University of California-Davis), Val Jenness (Washington State University), and Susan Sprecher (Illinois State University). We would like to thank Becky Smith for her efficient and correct editing.

We would also like to thank The Department of Sociology at the University of Washington, which has provided valuable support to both authors in their creative endeavors as sociologists.

Finally, and perhaps most important, we are grateful for each other as collaborators, friends, and curious participants and voyeurs into the gender of sexuality.

Few books are without intellectual or emotional mentors. Pepper offers a special thanks and dedication to her late co-author Philip Blumstein, her husband Art Skolnik, and her friends Janet Lever and Nancy Mee for their stalwart support. Virginia would like to thank her partner Neil Jacobson for understanding the gender of sexuality and learning the difference between gender and sex.

CHAPTER 1

Sexual Desire and Gender

The gender of the person you desire is a serious matter seemingly fundamental to the whole business of romance. And it isn't simply a matter of whether someone is male or female; how well the person fulfills a lover's expectations of masculinity or femininity is of great consequence, as two examples from the movies illustrate.

In the movie *The Truth about Cats & Dogs* (1996), a man (Brian, played by Ben Chaplin) falls in love with a woman (Abby, played by Janeane Garofalo) over the phone, and she with him. They find each other warm, clever, charming, and intriguing. But she, thinking herself too plain, asks her beautiful friend (Noelle, played by Uma Thurman) to impersonate her when the man and woman are scheduled to meet. The movie continues as a comedy of errors. Although the man becomes very confused about which woman he really desires, in the end the telephone lovers are united. The match depended on social matters far more than physical matters.

In the British drama *The Crying Game* (1994), Fergus, an Irish Republican Army underling, meets and falls in love with the lover (Dil) of Jody, a British soldier whom Fergus befriended prior to being ordered to execute him. The movie was about passionate love, war, betrayal, and, in the end, loyalty and commitment. Fergus seeks out Jody's girlfriend in London out of guilt and curiosity. But Fergus's guilt over Jody's death turns into love, and the pair become romantically and sexually involved. In the end, although Fergus is jailed for terrorist activities, Fergus and Dil have solidified their bond and are committed and, it seems, in love. The story of sexual conquest and love is familiar, but this particular story grabbed imaginations because of a single, crucial detail. Jody's girlfriend Dil, Fergus discovers, turns out to be (physically) a man. Although Fergus is horrified when he discovers his lover is biologically different from what he had expected, in the end their relationship survives.

These movies raise an interesting point about sexual desire. Although sex is experienced as one of the most basic and biological of activities, in human beings it is profoundly affected by things other than the body's urges. Who we're attracted to and what we find sexually satisfying is not just a matter of the genital equipment we're born with. This chapter explains why.

Before we delve into the whys and wherefores of sex, we need to come to an understanding about what sex is. This is not as easy a task as it may seem, because sex has a number of dimensions.

On one level, sex can be regarded as having both a biological and a social context. The biological (and physiological) refers to how people use their genital equipment to reproduce. In addition, as simple as it seems, bodies make the experience of sexual pleasure available— whether the pleasure involves other bodies or just one's own body and mind. It should be obvious, however, that people engage in sex even when they do not intend to reproduce. They have sex for fun, as a way to communicate their feelings to each other, as a way to satisfy their ego, and for any number of other reasons relating to the way they see themselves and interact with others.

Another dimension of sex involves both what we do and how we think about it. **Sexual behavior** refers to the sexual acts that people engage in. These acts involve not only petting and intercourse but also seduction and courtship. Sexual behavior also involves the things people do alone for pleasure and stimulation and the things they do with other people. **Sexual desire,** on the other hand, is the motivation to engage in sexual acts. It relates to what turns people on. A person's **sexuality** consists of both behavior and desire.

The most significant dimension of sexuality is **gender.** Gender relates both to the biological and social contexts of sexual behavior and desire. People tend to believe they know whether someone is a man or a woman not because we do a physical examination and determine that the person is biologically male or biologically female. Instead, we notice whether a person is masculine or feminine. Gender is a social characteristic of individuals in our society that is only sometimes consistent with biological sex. Thus, animals, like people, tend to be identified as male and female in accordance with the reproductive function, but only people are described by their gender, as a man or a woman.

When we say something is **gendered** we mean that social processes have determined what is appropriately masculine and feminine and that gender has thereby become integral to the definition of the phenomenon. For example, marriage is a gendered institution: The definition of marriage involves a masculine part (husband) and a feminine part (wife). Gendered phenomena, like marriage, tend to appear "naturally" so. But, as recent debates about same-sex marriage underscore, the role of gender in marriage is the product of social processes and beliefs about men, women, and marriage. In examining how gender influences sexuality, moreover, you will see that gender rarely operates alone: Class, culture, race, and individual differences also combine to influence sexuality.

This book explores and takes issue with the assumptions that sexuality is naturally gendered and rooted in biology, that men and women are different sexually, and that this difference is consistent and universal across societies. Of course, what appears "natural" in one society may be very different in another. By calling the book *The Gender of Sexuality*, we challenge you to think about how even things that people tend to consider biological, like a woman's producing a baby, are influenced enormously by the social processes that determine what motherhood is all about and how motherhood is different from fatherhood.

As you can see, sexuality is a complex bit of business. The study of sexuality also presents methodological challenges. Sexual thoughts and behavior are typically private. Researchers must rely on what people say they want and do sexually, and these reports, as much as the desire and behavior itself, are influenced by what people believe they are supposed to feel and say. In this book, we will piece together this puzzle of acts, thoughts, and feelings with insights provided by survey research, physiological studies, ethnography, history, philosophy, and even art, cinema, and literature.

Desire: Attraction and Arousal

The most salient fact about sex is that nearly everybody is interested in it. Most people like to have sex, and they talk about it, hear about it, and think about it. But some people are obsessed with sex and willing to have sex with anyone or anything. Others are aroused only by particular conditions and hold exacting criteria. For example, some people will have sex only if they are positive that they are in love, that their partner loves them, and that the act is sanctified by marriage. Others view sex as not much different from eating a sandwich. They neither love nor hate the sandwich; they are merely hungry, and they want something to satisfy that hunger. What we are talking about here are differences in desire. As you have undoubtedly noticed, people differ in what they find attractive, and they are also physically aroused by different things.

Many people assume that differences in sexual desire have a lot to do with whether a person is female or male. In large representative surveys about sexual behavior, the men as a group inevitably report more frequent sex, with more partners, and in more diverse ways than the women as a group do. In Chapter 2, we will review that evidence. First, we should consider the approaches we might use to interpret it. Many observers argue that when it comes to sex, men and women have fundamentally different biological wiring. Others use the evidence to argue that culture has produced marked sexual differences among men and women. We believe, however, that it is hard to tease apart biological differences and social differences. As soon as a baby enters the world, it receives messages about gender and sexuality. In the United States, for example, disposable diapers come adorned in pink for girls and blue for boys. In case people aren't sure whether to treat the baby as masculine or feminine in its first years of life, the diaper signals them. The assumption is that girl babies really are different from boy babies and the difference ought to be displayed. This different treatment continues throughout life, and therefore a sex difference at birth becomes amplified into gender difference as people mature.

Gendered experiences have a great deal of influence on sexual desire. As a boy enters adolescence, he hears jokes about boys' uncontainable desire. Girls are told the same thing and told that their job is to resist. These gender messages have power not only over attitudes and behavior (such as whether a person grows up to prefer sex with a lover rather than a stranger) but also over physical and biological experience. For example, a girl may be discouraged from vigorous competitive activity, which will subsequently influence how she develops physically, how she feels about her body, and even how she relates to the adrenaline rush associated with physical competition. Hypothetically, a person who is accustomed to adrenaline responses experiences sexual attraction differently from one who is not.

What follows are three "competing" explanations of differences in sexual desire between men and women: a biological explanation, sociobiological and evolutionary psychological explanations, and an explanation that acknowledges the social construction of sexuality. We call these competing approaches because each tends to be presented as a complete explanation in itself, to the exclusion of other explanations. Our goal, however, is to provide a clearer picture of how "nature" and "nurture" are intertwined in the production of sexualities.

The Biology of Desire: Nature's Explanation

Biology is admittedly a critical factor in sexuality. Few human beings fall in love with fish or sexualize trees. Humans are designed to respond to other humans. And human activity is, to some extent, organized by the physical equipment humans are born with. Imagine if people had fins instead of arms or laid eggs instead of fertilizing them during intercourse. Romance would look quite different.

Although biology seems to be a constant (i.e., a component of sex that is fixed and unchanging), the social world tends to mold biology as much as biology shapes humans' sexuality. Each society has its own rules for sex. Therefore, how people experience their biology varies widely. In some societies, women act intensely aroused and active during sex; in others, they have no concept of orgasm. In fact, women in some settings, when told about orgasm, do not even believe it exists, as anthropologists discovered in some parts of Nepal. Clearly, culture—not biology—is at work, because we know that orgasm is physically possible, barring damage to or destruction of the sex organs. Even ejaculation is culturally dictated. In some countries, it is considered healthy to ejaculate early and often; in others, men are told to conserve semen and ejaculate as rarely as possible. The biological capacity may not be so different, but the way bodies behave during sex varies according to social beliefs.

Sometimes the dictates of culture are so rigid and powerful that the so-called laws of nature can be overridden. Infertility treatment provides an example: For couples who cannot produce children "naturally," a several billion dollar industry has provided technology that can, in a small proportion of cases, overcome this biological problem (Rutter 1996). Recently, in California, a child was born to a 63-year-old woman who had been implanted with fertilized eggs. The cultural emphasis on reproduction and parenthood, in this case, overrode the biological incapacity to produce children. Nevertheless, some researchers have focused on the biological foundations of sexual desire.

They have examined the endocrine system and hormones, brain structure, and genetics. Others have observed the mechanisms of arousal. What all biological research on sex has in common is the proposition that many so-called sexual choices are not choices at all but are dictated by the body. A prominent example comes from the study of the biological origins of homosexuality. However, contradictory and debatable findings make conclusions difficult.

The Influence of Hormones

Biological explanations of sexual desire concentrate on the role of hormones. **Testosterone,** sometimes called the male sex hormone, appears to be the most important hormone for sexual function. Numerous research studies identify testosterone as an enabler for male sexual arousal (Bancroft 1978; Masters, Johnson, and Kolodny 1995). But we cannot predict a man's sexual tastes, desires, or behavior by measuring his testosterone. Although a low level of testosterone in men is sometimes associated with lower sexual desire, this is not predictably the case. Furthermore, testosterone level does not always influence sexual performance. Indeed, testosterone is being experimented with as a male contraceptive (Wu et al. 1996), thus demonstrating that desire and the biological goal of reproduction need not be linked to sexual desire.

Testosterone has also been implicated in nonsexual behaviors, such as aggression. Furthermore, male aggression sometimes crosses into male sexuality, generating sexual violence. But recent research on testosterone and aggression in men has turned the testosterone-aggression connection on its head: Low levels of testosterone have been associated with aggression, and higher levels have been associated with calmness, happiness, and friendliness (Angier 1995).

Testosterone is also found in women, although at levels as little as one-fifth those of men. This discrepancy in levels of testosterone has incorrectly been used as evidence for "natural" gender differences in sex drives. However, women's testosterone receptors are simply more sensitive than men's to smaller amounts of testosterone (Kolodny, Masters, and Johnson 1979).

Estrogen, which is associated with the menstrual cycle, is known as the female hormone. Like testosterone, however, estrogen is found in both women and men. Furthermore, estrogen may be the more influential hormone in human aggression. In animal research, male mice whose ability to respond to estrogen had been bred out of them lost much of their natural aggressiveness. Researchers are currently investigating the

TABLE 1.1

Sexual Role of Hormones

Hormone	Influence	Weakness to theory
Testosterone (male hormone)	Triggers sexual arousal	Also present in women and also triggers women's sexual arousal; associated with calmness, not aggression
Estrogen (female hormone)	Triggers menstrual cycle	Also present in men; associated with aggression, not calmness

association between adolescents' moodiness and their levels of estrogen (Angier 1995). Of course, many social factors—such as changes in parental behavior toward their teenagers—help explain moodiness among adolescents (Rutter 1995).

Some biological evidence indicates that a woman's sexual desire may be linked to the impact of hormones as levels change during her reproductive cycle. (No evidence shows men's sexual desire to be cyclical.) Some scientists believe that women's sexual arousal is linked to the fertile portion of their cycle (Stanislaw and Rice 1988). They believe that sexual interest in women is best explained as the product of thousands of years of natural selection. Natural selection would favor for survival those women who are sexually aroused during ovulation (the time women are most likely to become pregnant). These women would be reproductively successful and therefore pass on to their children the propensity for arousal during ovulation. Neat though this theory is, it doesn't fit all the data. Other research (Bancroft et al. 1983; Bancroft 1984) finds no evidence of increased sexual interest among women who are ovulating. Instead, the evidence suggests that women's sexual interest actually tends to peak well before ovulation. Still other evidence finds no variation in sexual desire or sexual activity in connection to the menstrual cycle (Hoon, Bruce, and Kinchloe 1982; Meuwissen and Over 1992).

As Table 1.1 indicates, testosterone and estrogen are not clearly linked to either men's desire or women's. Research shows a complicated relationship between hormones and sexuality. Hormonal fluctuations may not be the central cause of sexual behavior or any social acts; instead, social circumstances may be the cause of hormonal fluctuation.

A famous series of experiments makes the point. One animal experiment took a dominant rhesus monkey out of his environment and measured testosterone level. It was very high, suggesting that he had reached the top of the monkey heap by being hormonally superior. Then the monkey was placed among even bigger, more dominant monkeys than himself. When his testosterone was remeasured, it was much lower. One interpretation is that social hierarchy had influenced the monkey's biological barometer. His testosterone level had adjusted to his social status. In this case, the social environment shaped physiology (Rose, Holaday, and Bernstein 1970).

The Mechanisms of Arousal

Biological explanations of gender differences in sexuality owe a great deal to the work of William Masters and Virginia Johnson, who studied the human sexual arousal system. Unlike other researchers, who had relied on self-reports, these pioneers actually hooked up their participants to machines that could provide information on physiological responses to sexual stimuli. They based their findings on laboratory observation of over 10,000 sexual episodes experienced by 382 women and 312 men (Masters and Johnson 1966). The research team photographed the inside of women's vaginas during arousal and observed circulatory and nipple response, and they observed the rise and fall of men's penises.

Notice that Masters and Johnson focused on bodies rather than the social and relationship contexts in which sex occurs. From the start, the research was limited to information about the mechanisms of sexuality. It's not hard to imagine that the responses of men and women hooked to machines and under observation might well be different from a loving couple's first (or 91st) sexual episode. In addition, the participants were far from "typical" or randomly selected. To the contrary, they were sexual extroverts such as prostitutes, who, as far as we can tell, were not really representative of the population.

Nevertheless, with this information Masters and Johnson created the new field of sex therapy, which sought to understand and modify the mechanisms of human sexual response or, as the case might be, nonresponse. The sexual therapies they developed were based on what they inferred from their data to be differences between male and female patterns of arousal.

One of Masters and Johnson's most important observations was a sexual difference between men and women in the timing of the excite-

FIGURE 1.1

Mismatched Sexual Responses of Women and Men

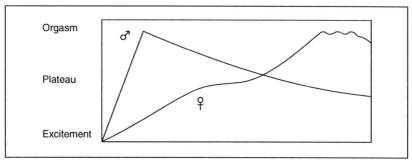

Source: Data from Masters and Johnson (1966).

♂ = men, ♀ = women.

ment cycle. The key difference is that male sexual physiology has a quicker trigger. Comparing men's and women's sexual responses is like comparing sprinters (men) to long-distance runners (women). Men are excited sooner, have an orgasm sooner, relatively quickly lose their erection, and require a "refractory" period before sexual excitation and erection can begin again. This refractory period among young or exceptional men could be very brief. But for the majority of men, 20 minutes, an hour, or even a day might be necessary.

The female cycle is, in general, a slower and more sustained proposition. The increase of blood to the genital area that accompanies arousal takes longer and remains longer after orgasm. This slower buildup may in part account for the longer time it typically takes women to be ready for sexual intercourse. Additionally, the longer time women take to reach and stay in the plateau phase theoretically makes orgasm less automatic than it is for men. However, the fact that blood leaves the genital area slowly after orgasm means that many women require little or no refractory period if restimulated. Consequently, Masters and Johnson described women as potentially "multi-orgasmic." In other words, some women can have more than one orgasm in fairly short succession.

These physiological findings were the basis for a theory about female and male mating styles. Masters and Johnson considered men's more quickly triggered mechanisms to be at odds with the slower mechanisms of women (see Figure 1.1). On the other hand, the ability of women to have more than one orgasm suggested that women might be the superior sexual athletes under certain conditions. Masters and

Johnson's followers work within a model that addresses sexual problems by matching male and female sexual strategies more closely than they believe nature has done. In fact, it might be argued that Masters and Johnson's general approach to sexual counseling was to teach men to understand and cope with the slower female sexual response and to modify their own sexual response so that they do not reach orgasm before their partner is fully aroused.

Sociobiology and Evolutionary Psychology

The past few decades of research on sexuality have produced a new school of human behavior—**sociobiology** and a related discipline, **evolutionary psychology**—that explains most gender differences as strategies of sexual reproduction. According to evolutionary psychologist David Buss (1995), "Evolutionary psychologists predict that the sexes will differ in precisely those domains in which women and men have faced different sorts of adaptive problems" (p. 164). By "those domains," Buss refers to reproduction, which is the only human function that depends on a biological difference between men and women.

The key assumption of sociobiological/evolutionary theory is that humans have an innate, genetically triggered impulse to pass on their genetic material through successful reproduction: This impulse is called **reproductive fitness.** The human species, like other species that sociobiologists study, achieves immortality by having children who live to the age of reproductive maturity and produce children themselves. Sociobiologists and evolutionary psychologists seek to demonstrate that almost all male and female behavior, and especially sexuality, is influenced by this one simple but powerful proposition.

Sociobiologists start at the species level. Species are divided into *r* and *K* **reproductive categories.** Those with *r* strategies obtain immortality by mass production of eggs and sperm. The *r* species is best illustrated by fish. The female manufactures thousands of eggs, the male squirts millions of sperm over them, and that is the extent of parenting. According to this theory, the male and female fish need not pair up to nurture their offspring. Although thousands of fertilized fish eggs are consumed by predators, only a small proportion of the massive quantity of fertilized eggs must survive for the species to continue. In the *r* species, parents need not stay together for the sake of the kids.

In contrast, humans are a *K*-strategy species, which has a greater investment in each fertilized egg. Human females and most female mammals have very few eggs, especially compared to fish. Moreover, offspring take a long time to mature in the mother's womb and are quite helpless after they are born, with no independent survival ability. Human babies need years of supervision before they are independent. Thus, if a woman wants to pass on her genes (or at least the half her child will inherit from her), she must take good care of her dependent child. The baby is a scarce resource. Even if a woman is pregnant from sexual maturation until menopause, the number of children she can produce is quite limited. This limitation was particularly true thousands of years ago. Before medical advances of the nineteenth and twentieth centuries, women were highly unlikely to live to the age of menopause. Complications from childbirth commonly caused women to die in their 20s or 30s. Where the food supply was scarce, women were less likely to be successful at conceiving, further reducing the possibility of generating offspring.

Sociobiologists and evolutionary psychologists say that men inseminate, women incubate. The human female's reproductive constraints (usually one child at a time, only so many children over a life cycle, and a helpless infant for a long period of time) shape most of women's sexual and emotional approaches to men and mating. According to their theory, women have good reason to be more selective than men about potential mates. They want to find a man who will stick around and continue to provide resources and protection to this child at least until the child has a good chance of survival. Furthermore, because a woman needs to create an incentive for a man to remain with her, females have developed more sophisticated sexual and emotional skills specifically geared toward creating male loyalty and commitment to their mutual offspring.

Sociobiologists and evolutionary psychologists say that differences in reproductive capacity and strategy also shape sexual desire. Buss asserts that reproductive strategies form most of the categories of desire: Older men generally pick younger women because they are more fertile; younger women seek older men who have more status, power, and resources (a cultural practice known as **hypergamy**) because such men can provide for their children. Furthermore, health and reproductive capacity make youth generally sexier, and even certain shapes of women's bodies (such as an "ideal" hip-to-waist ratio epitomized by an hourglass figure, which correlate with ability to readily reproduce), are widely preferred (Buss 1994)—despite varying standards of beauty across cultures. Likewise, men who have demonstrated their fertility by producing children are more sought after than men who have not (Buss 1994).

According to evolutionary psychologists, men's tastes for recreational sex, unambivalent lust, and a variety of partners are consistent with maximizing their production of children. Men's sexual interest is also more easily aroused because sex involves fewer costs to them than to women, and the ability for rapid ejaculation has a reproductive payoff. On the other hand, women's taste for relationship-based intimacy and greater investment in each sexual act is congruent with women's reproductive strategies.

In a field that tends to emphasize male's "natural" influence over reproductive strategies, evolutionary anthropologist Helen Fisher (1992) offers a feminist twist. Her study of hundreds of societies shows that divorce, or its informal equivalent, occurs most typically in the third or fourth year of a marriage and then peaks about every four years after that. Fisher hypothesizes that some of the breakups have to do with a woman's attempt to obtain the best genes and best survival chances for her offspring. In both agrarian and hunter-gatherer societies, Fisher explains, women breast-feed their child for three or four years—a practice that is economical and sometimes helps to prevent further pregnancy. At the end of this period, the woman is ready and able to have another child. She reenters the mating marketplace and assesses her options to see if she can improve on her previous mate. If she can get a better guy, she will leave the previous partner and team up with a new one. In Fisher's vision, unlike the traditional sociobiological view (see Table 1.2), different male and female reproductive strategies do not necessarily imply female sexual passivity and preference for lifelong monogamy.

Sociobiologists and evolutionary psychologists tell a fascinating story of how male and female reproductive differences might shape sexuality. To accept sociobiological arguments, one must accept the premise that most animal and human behavior is driven by the instinct to reproduce and improve the gene pool. Furthermore, a flaw of sociobiology as a theory is that it does not provide a unique account of sexual behavior with the potential to be tested empirically. Furthermore, other social science explanations for the same phenomena are supported by more immediate, close-range evidence.

Consider hypergamy, the practice of women marrying men slightly older and "higher" on the social status ladder than they are. Sociobiologists would say women marry "up" to ensure the most fit provider for

TABLE 1.2

Comparison of Traditional and Feminist Sociobiological Explanations of Gender Differences in Sexuality

Perspective	Gender difference	Explanation
Traditional	Men seek to maximize number of progeny by changing partners as often as possible. Women seek to maximize well-being of progeny by holding on to their partners as long as possible.	Men have biological capacity to inseminate many women in a short period of time; women's biological job is to incubate and nurture young.
Feminist	Men seek to maximize progeny; women seek to maximize well-being of progeny by exchanging partners when improved options are available.	Men and women both seek to maximize number of partners and quality of partners by exchanging when improved options are available.

their offspring. But hypergamy makes little sense biologically. Younger men have more years of resources to provide, and they have somewhat more sexual resources. Empirically, however, hypergamy is fact. It is also a fact that men, overall and in nearly every subculture, have access to more rewards and status than women do. Furthermore, reams of imagery—in movies, advertising, novels—promote the appeal of older, more resourceful men. Why not, when older, more resourceful men are generating the images? Social practice, in this case, overrides what sociobiologists consider the biological imperative.

The Social Origins of Desire

Your own experience should indicate that biology and genetics alone do not shape human sexuality. From the moment you entered the world, cues from the environment were telling you which desires and behaviors were "normal" and which were not. The result is that people who grow up in different circumstances tend to have different sexualities. Who has not had their sexual behavior influenced by their parents' or guardians' explicit or implicit rules? You may break the rules or follow them, but you can't forget them. On a societal level, in Sweden, for example, premarital sex is accepted, and people are expected to be sexually knowledgeable and experienced. Swedes are likely to associate sex with pleasure in this "**sex positive**" society. In Ireland, however, Catholics are supposed to heed the Church's strict prohibitions against sex outside of marriage, birth control, and the expression of lust. In Ireland the experience of sexuality is different from the experience of sexuality in Sweden because the rules are different. Certainly, biology in Sweden is no different from biology in Ireland, nor is the physical capacity to experience pleasure different. But in Ireland, nonmarital sex is clandestine and shameful. Perhaps the taboo adds excitement to the experience. In Sweden, nonmarital sex is acceptable. In the absence of social constraint, it may even feel a bit mundane. These culturally specific sexual rules and experiences arise from different **norms,** the well-known, unwritten rules of society.

Another sign that social influences play a bigger role in shaping sexuality than does biology is the changing notions historically of male and female differences in desire. Throughout history, varied explanations of male and female desire have been popular. At times, woman was portrayed as the stormy temptress and man the reluctant participant, as in the Bible story of Adam and Eve. At other times, women were seen as pure in thought and deed while men were voracious sexual beasts, as the Victorians would have it.

These shifting ideas about gender are the social "clothing" for sexuality. The concept of gender typically relies on a dichotomy of male versus female sexual categories, just as the tradition of women wearing dresses and men wearing pants has in the past made the shape of men and women appear quite different. Consider high heels, an on-again-off-again Western fashion. Shoes have no innate sexual function, but high heels have often been understood to be "sexy" for women, even though (or perhaps because) they render women less physically agile. (Of course, women cope. As Ginger Rogers, the 1940s movie star and dancing partner to Fred Astaire, is said to have quipped, "I did everything Fred did, only backwards and in high heels.") Social norms of femininity have at times rendered high heels fashionable. So feminine are high heels understood to be that a man in high heels, in some sort of visual comedy gag, guarantees a laugh from the audience. Alternatively, high heels are a required emblem of femininity for cross-dressing men.

Such distinctions are an important tool of society; they provide guidance to human beings about how to be a "culturally correct" male or female. Theoretically, society could "clothe" its members with explicit norms of sexuality that de-emphasize difference and emphasize similarity or even multiplicity. Picture unisex hairstyles and men and women both free to wear skirts or pants, norms that prevail from time to time in some subcultures. What is remarkable about dichotomies is that even when distinctions, like male and female norms of fashion, are reduced, new ways to assert an ostensibly essential difference between men and women arise. Societies' rules, like clothes, are changeable. But societies' entrenched taste for constructing differences between men and women persists.

The Social Construction of Sexuality

Social constructionists believe that cues from the environment shape human beings from the moment they enter the world. The sexual customs, values, and expectations of a culture, passed on to the young through teaching and by example, exert a powerful influence over individuals. When Fletcher Christian sailed into Tahiti in Charles Nordhoff's 1932 account, *Mutiny on the Bounty,* he and the rest of his nineteenth-century English crew were surprised at how sexually available, playful, guilt free, and amorous the Tahitian women were. Free from the Judeo-Christian precepts and straitlaced customs that inhibited English society, the women and girls of Tahiti regarded their sexuality joyfully and without shame. The English men were delighted and, small wonder, refused to leave the island. Such women did not exist in their own society. The women back in England had been socialized within their Victorian culture to be modest, scared of sex, protective of their reputation, and threatened by physical pleasure. As a result, they were unavailable before marriage and did not feel free to indulge in a whole lot of fun after it. The source of the difference was not physiological differences between Tahitian and English women; it was sexual **socialization** or the upbringing that they received within their differing families and cultures.

If we look back at the Victorian, nineteenth-century England that Nordhoff refers to, we can identify **social structures** that influenced the norms of women's and men's sexuality. A burgeoning, new, urban middle class created separate spheres in the division of family labor. Instead of sharing home and farm or small business, the tasks of adults in families became specialized: Men went out to earn money, women stayed home to raise children and take care of the home. Although this division of labor was not the norm in all classes and ethnicities in England at the time, the image of middle-class femininity and masculinity became pervasive. The new division of labor increased women's economic dependence on men, which further curbed women's sexual license but not men's. When gender organizes one aspect of life—such as men's and women's positions in the economy—it also organizes other aspects of life, including sex.

In a heterogeneous and individualistic culture like North America, sexual socialization is complex. A society creates an "ideal" sexuality, but different families and subcultures have their own values. For example, even though contemporary society at large may now accept premarital sexuality, a given family may lay down the law: Sex before marriage is against the family's religion and an offense against God's teaching. A teenager who grows up in such a household may suppress feelings of sexual arousal or channel them into outlets that are more acceptable to the family. Or the teenager may react against her or his background, reject parental and community opinion, and search for what she or he perceives to be a more "authentic" self. Variables like birth order or observations of a sibling's social and sexual expression can also influence a person's development.

As important as family and social background are, so are individual differences in response to that background. In the abstract, people raised to celebrate their sexuality must surely have a different approach to enjoying their bodies than those who are taught that their bodies will betray them and are a venal part of human nature. Yet whether or not a person is raised to be at ease with physicality does not always help predict adult sexual behavior. Sexual sybarites and libertines may have grown up in sexually repressive environments, as did pop culture icon and Catholic-raised Madonna. Sometimes individuals whose families promoted sex education and free personal expression are content with minimal sexual expression.

Even with the nearly infinite variety of sexuality that individual experience produces, social circumstances shape sexual patterns. For example, research shows that people who have had more premarital sexual intercourse are likely to have more extramarital intercourse, or sex with someone other than their spouse (Blumstein and Schwartz 1983). Perhaps early experience creates a desire for sexual variety and makes it harder for a person to be monogamous. On the other hand, higher levels of sexual desire may generate both the premarital and extramarital propensities. Or perhaps nonmonogamous, sexually active individuals are "rule breakers" in other areas also, and resist not only the traditional rules of sex but also other social norms they encounter. Sexual history is useful for predicting sexual future, but it does not provide a complete explanation.

To make explanations more useful, sociologists refer to societal-level explanations as the **macro** view and to individual-level explanations as the **micro** view. At the macrolevel, the questions pertain to the patterns among different groups. For example, we may note in our culture that some women wear skirts and all men do not. Why do women and men, generally speaking, differ in this way? **Social conflict theory,** which examines the way that groups gain and maintain power over resources and other groups, is often used to address macrolevel questions. One might ask: Whose interest does this custom serve, and how did it evolve? What does it constrain or encourage? If the custom changes, what social forces have promoted the change? What social forces resist change? Who has power over customs at any given time, and why?

Symbolic interactionism supplements this macrolevel view by looking at the microlevel: How does a particular custom gain its meaning through social interaction? For example, what is really happening when a man opens a door for a woman? **Symbolic interactionism** proposes that social rules are learned and reinforced through everyday interaction in both small acts, such as a man's paying for a woman's dinner, and larger enactments of male and female roles, such as weddings, manners and advice books, movies, and television. Through such everyday social interaction, norms are confirmed or resisted. When an adult tells a little girl "good girls don't do this," or when boys make fun of her for wanting to be on the football team, or when she observes people scorning or stoning women who venture forth in inappropriate garb (as in countries where women are required to wear a veil), or when she sees women joining a military school getting hazed and harassed, she is learning her society's rules of behavior.

When it comes to sexuality, all these social and behavioral theories hold that biological impulses are subservient to the influence of social systems. Consider high heels again. As anyone who has done so knows, wearing high heels has physical consequences, such as flexed calves while wearing them and aching feet at the end of an evening. But nothing in the physiology of women makes wearing high-heeled shoes necessary, and the propensity to wear high heels is not programmed into women's DNA. A sociobiologist might note that any additional ways a society can invent for women to be sexy accelerate reproductive success. A symbolic interactionist would counter that most rules of sexuality go way beyond what's needed for reproductive success. Footwear has never been shown to be correlated with fertility. Instead, society orchestrates male and female sexuality so that its values are served. A social conflict theorist would go a step further and note that the enactment of gendered fashion norms, individual by individual, serves the political agenda of groups in power (in this case men) at the macrolevel.

An astounding example of gender-based social control of sexuality was the practice of binding the feet of upper-class women in China starting around the tenth century. Each foot was bound so tightly that the last two toes shriveled and fell off. What was left was so deformed that the woman could barely walk and had to be carried. The function was to allow upper-class men to control the mobility of their women. Bound feet, which were thus associated with status and wealth, became erotically charged. Unbound feet were seen as repugnant. By the eighteenth and nineteenth centuries, even poor women participated in this practice. This practice was so associated with sexual acceptability and marriageability that it was difficult to disrupt, even when nineteenth-century missionaries from the West labeled the practice barbaric and unsafe. Only later, in the twentieth century, did foot binding become illegal (Greenhalgh 1977).

Social Control of Sexuality

So powerful are norms as they are transmitted through both social structures and everyday life that it is impossible to imagine the absence of norms that control sexuality. In fact, most images of "liberated" sexuality involve breaking a social norm—say, having sex in public rather than in private. The social norm is always the reference point. Because people are influenced from birth by the social and physical contexts of sexuality, their desires are shaped by those norms. There is no such thing as a truly free sexuality. For the past two centuries in North America, people have sought "true love" through personal choice in dating and mating (D'Emilio and Freedman 1988). Although this form of sexual liberation has generated a small increase in the number of mixed pairs—interracial, interethnic, interfaith pairs—the rule of **homogamy,** or marrying within one's class, religion, and ethnicity, still constitutes one of the robust social facts of romantic life. Freedom to choose the person one loves turns out not to be as free as one might suppose.

Despite the norm of true love currently accepted in our culture, personal choice and indiscriminate sexuality have often been construed across cultures and across history as socially disruptive. Disruptions to the social order include liaisons between poor and rich; between people of different races, ethnicities, or faiths; and between members of the same sex. Traditional norms of marriage and sexuality have maintained social order by keeping people in familiar and "appropriate" categories. Offenders have been punished by ostracism, curtailed civil rights, or in some societies, death. Conformists are rewarded with social approval and material advantages. Although it hardly seems possible today, mixed-race marriage was against the law in the United States until 1967. Committed same-sex couples continue to be denied legal marriages (discussed in Chapter 5), income tax breaks, and health insurance benefits; heterosexual couples take these social benefits for granted.

Some social theorists observe that societies control sexuality through construction of a dichotomized or gendered (male-female) sexuality (Foucault 1978). Society's rules about pleasure seeking and procreating are enforced by norms about appropriate male and female behavior. For example, saying that masculinity is enhanced by sexual experimentation while femininity is demeaned by it gives men sexual privilege (and pleasure) and denies it to women. Furthermore, according to Foucault, sexual desire is fueled by the experience of privilege and taboo regarding sexual pleasure. That is, the very rules that control sexual desire shape it and even enhance it. The social world could just as plausibly concentrate on how much alike are the ways that men and women experience sex and emphasize how broadly dispersed sexual conduct is across genders. However, social control turns pleasure into a scarce resource and endows leaders who regulate the pleasure of others with power.

Societies control sexuality in part because they have a pragmatic investment in it. Eighteenth-century economic theorist T. R. Malthus ([1798] 1929) highlighted the relationship between reproductive practices and economics in *The Principle of Population*. According to Malthus, excessive fertility would result in the exhaustion of food and other resources. His recommendation to curb the birth rate represents an intervention into the sexual behavior of individuals for the well-being of society. A more recent example is the one-child policy in modern China. Alarmed by the predictions of famine and other disastrous consequences of rapid population growth, Mao Tse-tung and subsequent Chinese leaders instituted a program of enforced fertility control, which included monitoring women's menstrual cycles, requiring involuntary abortions, and delaying the legal age for marriage. To this state, sexual behavior isn't really an intimate, private act at all; it is a social and even economically significant activity. Such policies influence society at large, but they influence private experience as well. In China, raising the legal age for marriage resulted in a shift toward tolerance regarding premarital sex, a practice that became more common. How does a society obtain the ideal number of healthy workers to create a thriving nation? How does a society produce enough people to create an army? How does it create a system in which parents control their offspring so that the state will not have to step into an expensive and impractical role? And how do such large-scale policies influence the everyday experiences and definitions of sexuality for individuals?

Society's interest in controlling sexuality is expressed in the debates regarding sex education. Debates about sex education in grade school and high school illustrate the importance to society of both the control of desire and its social construction. The debates raise the question, does formal learning about sex increase or deter early sexual experimentation? The point is, opponents and proponents of sex education all want to know how to control sexuality in young people. Those who favor sex education hold that children benefit from early, comprehensive information about sex, in the belief that people learn about sexuality from birth and are sexual at least from the time of puberty. Providing young people with an appropriate vocabulary and accurate information both discourages early sexual activity and encourages safe sexual practices for those teenagers who, according to the evidence, will not be deterred from sexual activity (Sexuality Information and Education Council of the United States [SIECUS] 1995). On the other hand, opponents of sex education are intensely committed to the belief that information about sex changes teenagers' reactions and values and leads to early, and what they believe are inappropriate, sexual behaviors (Whitehead 1994). Conservative groups hold that sex education, if it occurs at all, should emphasize abstinence as opposed to practical information.

These conflicting points of view about sex education are both concerned with managing adolescent sexual desire. Conservatives fear that education creates desire; liberals feel that information merely enables better decision making. So who is correct? In various studies, a majority of both conservative and liberal sex education programs have demonstrated little effect on behavior. Conservatives believe these results prove the programs' lack of worth. Liberals believe the studies prove that many programs are not good enough, usually because they do not include the most important content. Furthermore, liberals point out that sex education has increased contraceptive (including condom) use, which is crucial to public health goals of reducing sexually transmitted disease and unwanted pregnancy. Other research indicates that comprehensive sex education actually tends to delay the age of first intercourse and does not intensify desire or escalate sexual behavior. There is no evidence that comprehensive sex education promotes or precipitates early teen sexual activity (Kirby et al. 1994).

The passionate debate about sex education is played out with high emotions. Political ideology, parental fears, and the election strategies of politicians all influence this mode of social control. In the final analysis, however, teaching about sex clearly does not have an intense impact on the pupil. Students' response to sex education varies tremendously at the individual level. In terms of trends within groups, however, it appears that sex education tends to delay sexual activity and makes teenage sex safer when it happens.

To summarize, social constructionists believe that a society influences sexual behavior through its norms. Some norms are explicit, such as laws against adult sexual activity with minors. Others are implicit, such as norms of fidelity and parental responsibility. In a stable, homogeneous society, it is relatively easy to understand such rules. But in a changing, complex society like the United States, the rules may be in flux or indistinct. Perhaps this ambiguity is what makes some issues of sexuality so controversial today.

An Integrative Perspective on Gender and Sexuality

Social constructionist explanations of contemporary sexual patterns are typically pitted against the biology of desire and the evolutionary understanding of biological adaptations. Some social constructionists believe there is no inflexible biological reality; everything we regard as either female or male sexuality is culturally imposed. In contrast, **essentialists**—those who take a biological, sociobiological, or evolutionary point of view—believe people's sexual desires and orientations are innate and hard-wired and that social impact is minimal. Gender differences follow from reproductive differences. Men inseminate, women incubate. People are born with sexual drives, attractions, and natures that simply play themselves out at the appropriate developmental age. Even if social constraints conspire to make men and women more similar to each other (as in the 1990s, when the sensitive and nurturing new man is encouraged to get in touch with his so-called feminine, emotional side), people's essential nature is the same: Man is the hunter, warrior, and trailblazer, and woman is the gatherer, nurturer, and reproducer. To an essentialist, social differences, such as the different earning power of men and women, are the consequence of biological difference. In short, essentialists think the innate differences between women and men are the cause of gendered sexuality; social constructionists think the differences between men and women are the result of gendering sexuality through social processes.

Using either the social constructionist or essentialist approach to the exclusion of the other constrains understanding of sexuality. We believe the evidence shows that gender differences are more plausibly an outcome of social processes than the other way around. But a social constructionist view is most powerful when it takes the essentialist view into account. In Table 1.3, we describe this view of gender differences in sexual desire as **integrative.** Although people tend to think of sex as primarily a biological function—tab B goes into slot A—biology is only one part of the context of desire. Such sociological factors as family relationships and social structure also influence sex. A complex mix of anatomy, hormones, and the brain provides the basic outline for the range of acts and desires possible, but biology is neither where sexuality begins nor where it ends. Social and biological contexts link to define human sexual possibilities.

The integrative approach follows from a great deal that sexuality researchers have observed. Consider the following example: A research project, conducted over three decades ago, advertised for participants stating that its focus was how physical excitement influences a man's preference for one woman over another (Valins 1966). The researchers connected college men to a monitor that allowed them to hear their heartbeats as they looked at photographs of women models. The men were told that they would be able to hear their heartbeat when it surged in response to each photograph. A greater surge would suggest greater physical attraction. The participants were then shown a photograph of a dark-haired woman, then a blonde, then a redhead. Afterward, each man was asked to choose the picture that he would prefer to take home. In each case, the man chose the photograph of the woman who, as he believed from listening to his own speeding heartbeat, had most aroused him. Or at least the man thought he was choosing the woman who had aroused him most. In reality, the men had been listening to a

TABLE 1.3

Explanations of Male and Female Differences in Sexual Desire

Explanations	Causes of desire	Consequences
Essentialist: Desire is biological and evolutionary	Genetically prepro-grammed reproduc-tive functions specific to males and females	Male independence in reproduction and female-centered child-rearing practices and passivity are the cause, rather than the result, of gendered social institutions
Social constructionist: Desire is sociological and contextual	Social institutions and social interaction signal and sanction "male" and "female," gendered norms of behavior	Support for or oppo-sition to sex/gender-segregated repro-ductive and social practices depends on social definitions of men, women, and sexuality
Integrative: Desire is contextual and physical	Bodies, environments, relationships, families, governments shape sexualities	Policies address some biological differences (such as pregnancy and work); emphasize the impact of social forces, interaction, societal programs

faked heartbeat that was speeded up at random. The men thus actually chose the women whom they believed had aroused them most. In this case, the men's invented attraction was more powerful than their gut response. Their mind (a powerful sexual organ) told them their body was responding to a specific picture. The participants' physiological experience of arousal was eclipsed by the social context. When social circumstances influence sexual tastes, are those tastes real or sincere? Absolutely. The social world is as much a fact in people's lives as the biological world.

Now let us look at a case where the body's cues were misinterpreted by the mind. An attractive woman researcher stood at the end of a very stable bridge (Dutton and Aron 1974). She approached men after they had walked across the bridge, engaged them in conversation, and then gave the men her telephone number—in case they had further comments, she said. Then the researcher did the same thing with another group of participants, but at the end of an unstable, swinging bridge. People tend to feel a little nervous, excited, or even exhilarated when they make their way across such a bridge. The pulse rises. Adrenaline pumps. Indeed, the anxiety response of walking across the bridge is much like the arousal response caused by meeting a desirable new person. The question was, would that anxiety response confuse men into thinking that they were attracted to the woman at the end of the bridge, more so than the physiologically calm guys who met her on the stable bridge? Yes, a statistically significant, larger number of men from the swinging bridge called the woman. In this case, participants had interpreted an anxiety response as an attraction response, one compelling enough to warrant inviting a stranger on a date. The physical situation transformed the meaning of a casual meeting from anxiety to attraction, again showing the link between biological and social influences.

A very personal matter that seems to be utterly physical—penile erection, or more specifically a man's inability to get an erection—offers another example. How might an erection be socially constructed? It is more or less understood in the United States that a penis should be hard and ready when a man's sexual opportunity is available. And it is more or less understood that the failure to get or maintain an erection in a sexual situation has two meanings: The guy isn't "man enough," or the other person isn't attractive enough. But there are many other explanations, not the least of which has been poetically explained by Shakespeare (and scientifically documented):

> Lechery, sir, [alcohol] provokes and unprovokes: it provokes the desire, but it takes away the performance. Therefore much drink may be said to be an equivocator with lechery: it makes him, and it mars him; it sets him on, and it takes him off; it persuades him, and disheartens him; makes him stand to, and not stand to; in conclusion, equivocates him in a sleep, and, giving him the lie, leaves him. (*Macbeth*, Act II, Scene iii)

The Shakespearean speech refers to the way in which alcohol can undermine robust sexual desire by leaving the penis flaccid. The performance is not the intimate interaction of bodies in pursuit of pleasure; it is strictly focused on the penis, which ought to "stand to." The speech emphasizes the humiliation—the "mar"—for a man who fails to sustain an erection. Though the speech refers to the toll that alcohol takes on the circulatory system that assists penises in becoming erect, the discussion is about the social experience of a man failed by his penis.

Even in the absence of drinking, penises are not nearly so reliable as the mythology of masculinity and attraction would maintain. Erections appear to come and go with odd timing. For example, erections rise and fall on babies and young boys; men often wake up with erections. None of these instances has to do with machismo or sexual desire. Erections are not always evidence of romantic interest, though our culture tends to interpret them as such. But their absence or presence, which is a physical phenomenon, takes on great meaning thanks to Western culture's prevailing beliefs and norms. For example, men required to produce semen for in vitro fertilization who are unable to maintain an erection until orgasm report feeling humiliated; their partners also often report being stunned by this performance failure (Rutter 1996). Growing up in a culture that considers erectile unpredictability a problem influences the way men in that culture feel about themselves and about their sexual partners, and the way sexual partners feel about them.

Even biological research has supported the integrative perspective. A quarter century ago, one team of scientists found that homosexual men had lower testosterone levels than a matched group of heterosexual men (Kreuz, Rose, and Jennings 1972). The traditional interpretation at the time of the study was that homosexual men were less "masculine" than the comparison group and that their lower testosterone levels explained why they were gay. But a group of active military men were also measured and found to be low in testosterone. The researchers were loath to believe that an unusual number of military men were gay or that military men were below average hormonally, so they found an alternative explanation for low testosterone. The researchers speculated that stress, anxiety, and similar negative emotions had temporarily lowered hormone levels in both soldiers and homosexuals. The stressful social context—as either a gay man living in a straight world or as a military man being bossed around constantly—had shaped a biological response, the researchers concluded. Hormones were the cart, not the horse. Biology influences desire, but social context influences biology and gives meaning to bodily sensation.

What do these examples from research illustrate? Sexual desire—in fact, all sexuality—is influenced by the cultural, personal, and situational. But these examples also tell us that people can't escape the biological context of sex and sexuality—nor can they rely on it. Such an **integrative** approach—the intimate relationship between social context and biological experience—is central to understanding sexuality.

What are the implications of using an integrative approach to sexuality? First, an integrationist will raise questions about biology when social context is emphasized as cause, and will raise questions about social context when biological causes are emphasized. The point is, everything sexual and physical occurs and achieves meaning in a social context.

Sexual Identity and Orientation

Nowhere does the essentialist versus social constructionist argument grow more vehement than in the debate over **sexual identity** and **sexual orientation.** These terms are used to mean a variety of things. We use these terms to refer to how people tend to classify themselves sexually—either as **gay, lesbian, bisexual,** or **straight.** Sexual behavior and sexual desire may or may not be consistent with sexual identity. That is, people may identify themselves as heterosexual, but desire people of the same sex—or vice versa.

It is hard to argue with the observation that human desire is, after all, organized. Humans do not generally desire cows or horses (with, perhaps, the exception of Catherine the Great, the Russian czarina who purportedly came to her demise while copulating with a stallion). More to the point, humans are usually quite specific about which sex is desirable to them and even whether the object of their desire is short or tall, dark or light, hairy or sleek.

In the United States, people tend to be identified as either **homosexual** or **heterosexual.** Other cultures (and prior eras in the United States) have not distinguished between these two sexual orientations. However, our culture embraces the perspective that, whether gay or straight, one has an essential, inborn desire, and it cannot change. Many people seem convinced that homosexuality is an essence rather than a sexual act. For essentialists, it is crucial to establish the primacy of one kind of desire or another and to build a world around that identity. People tend to assume that the object of desire is a matter of the gender of the object. That is, they think even homosexual men desire someone who is feminine and that homosexual women desire someone who is masculine. In other words, even among gay men and lesbians, it is assumed that they will desire opposite-gendered people, even if they are of the same sex.

Historians have chronicled in Western culture the evolution of homosexuality from a behavior into an identity (e.g., D'Emilio and Freedman 1988). In the past, people might engage in same-gender sexuality, but only in the twentieth century has it become a well-defined (and diverse) lifestyle and self-definition. Nevertheless, other evidence shows that homosexual identity has existed for a long time. The distinguished historian John Boswell (1994) believes that homosexuals as a group and homosexuality as an identity have existed from the very earliest of recorded history. He used evidence of early Christian same-sex "marriage" to support his thesis. Social scientist Fred Whitman (1983) has looked at homosexuality across cultures and declared that the evidence of a social type, including men who use certain effeminate gestures and have diverse sexual tastes, goes far beyond any one culture. Geneticist Dean Hamer provides evidence that sexual attraction may be genetically programmed, suggesting that it has persisted over time and been passed down through generations.

On the other side of the debate is the idea that sexuality has always been invented and that sexual orientations are socially created. A gay man's or lesbian's sexual orientation has been created by a social context. Although this creation takes place in a society that prefers dichotomous, polarized categories, the social constructionist vision of sexuality at least poses the possibility that sexuality could involve a continuum of behavior that is matched by a continuum of fantasy, ability to love, and sense of self.

The jury is still out on the scientific origins of heterosexuality and homosexuality. One series of studies on the brain (LeVay 1993) identified some differences in the makeup of the brains of heterosexual and homosexual men. This research has been criticized because the brain samples for the homosexual population were taken from men who had died from AIDS, which may have systematically altered the brain structure of the men. Nevertheless, some researchers believe that sexual orientation is wired into the brain, perhaps even dictating the intensity and specificity of sexual tastes.

Dean Hamer, a researcher at the National Institutes of Health Cancer Research Center, became interested in the genetics of sexual attraction and orientation while he was studying the heritability of Kaposi's sarcoma, a type of skin cancer that some gay men with AIDS develop. Hamer looked further into the possibility that gay men (and, in separate research, lesbians) have a genetic makeup different from that of heterosexuals (Hamer and Copeland 1994). He found a specific gene formation, identified as $Xq28$, that appears to be inherited through the mother's line only in gay males. The lesbian research has not thus far established a genetic link, but the Hamer research is widely believed to be just the first attempt to find a link between genetic inheritance and sexual attraction and arousal.

Hamer himself makes no claim that all attraction or arousal is genetically programmed, but his research lends support to other studies on the genetics of sexuality. For example, genetics researcher Michael Bailey and colleagues looked at identical twins (who have identical genetic material) reared apart. The studies found a likelihood much greater than chance that if one male twin is homosexual, the other will also be homosexual (Bailey et al. 1993). Because the twins in the study did not share the same environment, this finding suggests that the twins' common genes made them similar in their sexual orientation. On the other hand, other recent genetic and twin studies have highlighted the fact that having a certain **genotype** (DNA coded for a particular characteristic, such as heart disease) does not always produce the corresponding **phenotype** (the physical expression of that characteristic, such as actually suffering from heart disease). Researchers speculate that environment and individual history influence the expression or suppression of genetic types (Wright 1995).

These are just a few of the studies that, in some people's opinions, support the idea that homosexuality is not a choice but a naturally occurring phenomenon in a predetermined proportion of births. By extension, they believe, much human sexual desire and behavior must be biologically determined. Of course, social constructionists would disagree. But if biology does not determine whether one is heterosexual or homosexual, is sexual orientation a choice? Not exactly. The notion that sexuality is a preference supposes a person goes to a sexuality bazaar and picks out what to be today. That is not the case either. Physical and social structures and individual biography join together to produce sexual desire and behavior in an individual that may vary over time. Because of powerful social norms regarding sexuality, people are more likely to sustain a single sexual orientation throughout adulthood. The overwhelming evidence supports the idea that biology is a player in the game of sexual orientation but is not the only player or even captain of the team.

FIGURE 1.2

The Sexual Continuum

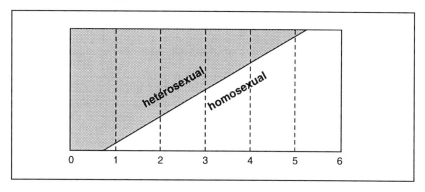

Source: Based on the Kinsey Heterosexual-Homosexual Rating Scale (Kinsey, Pomeroy, and Martin 1948).

Note: 0 = exclusively heterosexual desires and experiences; 3 = equally heterosexual and homosexual in desire and experience; 6 = exclusively homosexual desires and experiences.

The Continuum of Desire

Variation among people has been examined more than changes in sexual orientation within an individual. Alfred Kinsey (see Kinsey, Pomeroy, and Martin 1948), in his pioneering studies on human sexualities in the late 1940s and 1950s, introduced the Kinsey Heterosexual-Homosexual Rating Scale (see Figure 1.2). A person was coded using a zero for "completely heterosexual," a six for "completely homosexual," or a number in between to represent a more ambiguous orientation. Kinsey measured his participants' reports of interest in or attraction to and explicit past experiences with both same-sex and other-sex people and figured out where his participants fit on the continuum. However, his measurements were more of an art than a science. One cannot weigh or calibrate sexuality so finely. But Kinsey did examine actual behavior, fantasy, intensity of feeling, and other important elements that contribute to a person's sexuality.

Although such a rating scale may be an imperfect way of providing individuals with some sort of sex score, Kinsey made the point that a dichotomous vision of sexual orientation is even more inadequate and inaccurate. The Kinsey scale still defines the polarities of sexuality as heterosexuality and homosexuality, and in that sense it is essentialist. However, it provides alternatives beyond "yes," "no," or "in denial."

Kinsey opened the door to thinking in terms of the diversity of sexualities. People may use dichotomous terms in everyday life, but the idea that many people have the capacity to relate sexually to both males and females (at a single point in their life or intermittently over a lifetime) is part of the legacy of Kinsey's sex research.

By using a sexual continuum that blurs the edges of heterosexuality and homosexuality, Kinsey advanced the idea of bisexuality. The mere existence of **bisexuality** (the common term for some history of attraction to or sex with both men and women) is troubling for essentialists, who see sexuality as fixed and linked to procreation. However, biologists can show that bisexuality exists in the animal kingdom. Evolutionary psychologists and anthropologists hypothesize that bisexuality could be useful for a group's bonding and thus have survival value (Fisher 1992). The explanation is that adults who are like aunts and uncles to children—and who are intimate with parents—provide additional support for maintaining a family. But committed essentialists do not usually buy the idea that "true" bisexuality exists. Instead, they code men and women as "true" heterosexuals or homosexuals who have some modest taste in the other direction.

Given the evidence, it is possible to believe that the biological context tends to encourage an individual to acquire one sexual orientation or another but also to believe that society exerts greater influence than biology over behavior. Kinsey's data, as well as controversial data from a small gay and lesbian subsample from the National Health and Social Life Survey (NHSLS; Laumann, Michael, and Gagnon 1994), indicate that many more people report homosexual desire and behavior than those who claim homosexuality or bisexuality as their main sexual orientation or sexual identity (see Figure 1.3). Essentialists might say people who admit to homosexual behavior but deny being homosexuals are kidding themselves. Social constructionists say people are always kidding themselves; in other words, people acquire the desires and behaviors that are available and appealing. These choices will be based on personal history as well as social norms and will emerge in idiosyncratic and diverse ways across the continuum of sexuality. They will also be based on the costs and benefits in a given social system. How many people might code their fantasies differently if it were prestigious to be bisexual? Surely people's impulse to code themselves dichotomously is in part influenced by the social and emotional costs of doing otherwise.

FIGURE 1.3

Same-Sex Behavior and Homosexual Identity

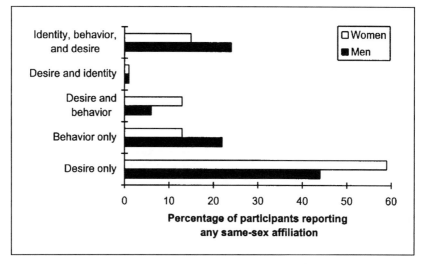

Source: Data from Laumann, Michael, and Gagnon (1994).
Note: N = 293 (143 men, 150 women).

An interesting issue that puzzles essentialists is how different male homosexuality seems to be from female homosexuality. Figure 1.3 demonstrates that more men than women identify as homosexual, but more women claim homosexual desire and/or behavior than men in those categories. In Lever's (1994a) *Advocate* survey, as well, more men than women identify themselves as homosexual. Indeed, much of the sexual attraction and behavior between women is not labeled as sexual. Women hug and kiss each other with impunity, and not necessarily with specific sexual intent. They can have extended sex play in their youth, or even in adulthood, without being instantly labeled as homosexual, as men who engaged in similar behavior would be. Women are also more likely to report that a same-sex sexual episode had less to do with sexual attraction than with love.

Historically, the waters are even murkier. As Lillian Faderman illustrates in *Surpassing the Love of Men* (1981), eighteenth- and nineteenth-century women were allowed such license to love each other that they could declare truly passionate feelings for one another without labels and identities being bandied about. For example, Faderman (1981) quotes Rousseau's eighteenth-century novel *La nouvelle Héloïse*, in which Julie writes to Clair: "The most important thing of my life has been to love you. From the very beginning my heart has been absorbed in yours" (p. 77). If these women expressed these sentiments today, observers would assume them to be homosexual. Are these the words simply of passionate friends? Essentialists would say these were lesbian lovers who did not have social permission to know who they really were. Historians and sociologists are divided as to whether these women experienced their love as sexual or romantic in the contemporary understanding of those feelings. It is difficult to label people's emotions for them after the fact and from a different historical and psychological vantage point. Just as beliefs and biases influence the way social science is conducted in the present, so such biases influence the views and interpretations of the past. We need to remember that sexual orientation, along with desire and other manifestations of sexuality, is socially constructed and culturally specific.

Gender as the Basis for Sexual Identity

Sexual orientation, as nearly everyone in Western culture has come to understand the phrase, signifies the identity one has based on the gender of the sexual partners one tends to pair with—either at a particular time or over a lifetime. In our culture, gender is the focus of sexual identity. But what if instead of discussing sexual identity in terms of one's preference for women or men, we referred to the various tastes one expresses for people who are funny or serious or tall or short or responsive or unresponsive to oral sex? For example, Virginia's sexuality would be "left-handed Jewish intellectual"—for this describes the people whom she tends to pair with. Pepper's sexuality would be "tall, high energy, sociable, and good looking." Instead, our culture zeroes in on which gender is doing what with which gender. Thus, the whole notion of sexual identity requires strict distinctions between male and female. The fact that the gender of sexual partners is of great social interest highlights yet again how gender organizes the definitions of sexuality.

Few can resist gendered distinctions. But a challenge comes from **transsexuals**, men and women who believe they were born in the wrong body. Although anatomically they are one sex, transsexuals experience themselves as the other sex, much the way we described Dil, in *The Crying Game* at the beginning of the chapter, who felt like a woman but was built like a man. Sometimes transsexuals "correct" their bodies with surgery or hormone treatments. And their sexual orientations are diverse. Some male-to-female transsexuals pair with men, some with women. The same is true for female-to-male transsexuals. One male-to-female person, speaking at a sexuality conference in the 1970s, declared, "Personally, I feel it is sexist to love on the basis of gender. You love the person, whatever their sex might be!"

Conclusion

There are, it seems, two arguments that help explain the way the genders express sexual desire. On the one hand are the images and statistics showing that men and women have distinct (albeit shifting) patterns of sexual expression, regardless of sexual orientation. On the other hand, the wide range of sexualities among men or among women also calls for an explanation. A continuum of passion, of desire, of sexual acts and feelings is a useful way to reconcile these phenomena. Furthermore, it helps to recognize that sexual phenomena are socially scripted but also highly individualized. Although sexual desire tends to be described in orderly and quantifiable terms, sexual desire is a chaotic playing field on which we, as sociologists, attempt to place some order to understand it better.

Biology or, more simply stated, bodies are the site for passionate experience, even if that experience is in the brain, in the absence of actual sensations in the skin or other sexual organs. In this sense, biology is a prominent context for sexuality. However, interpersonal, biographical, social, and political contexts influence sexuality and interact with biology in surprising ways. Thus, the continuum of sexuality we propose becomes even more diverse.

In the following chapters, we examine sexuality in various realms (dating and premarital relationships, marriage and long-term partnerships, teenage sexuality, same-sex marriage, sexual violence). We will remind you that we believe the differences between men and women are not any more important than the wide range of behavior and feelings that exist among men and among women. The social world, and even academic discussions of sexuality, seek to set up distinct categories for understanding sexuality. But individuals rarely fit into distinct categories.

Why do we take this precaution? Because of the inaccurate self-labeling that can happen as a reader sees, or doesn't see, himself or herself in the images we present. The woman who reads that women rarely have over 10 or so partners and has herself had 50 tempestuous love affairs or recreational encounters is not being told she is a man, nor is she being told that she is perverse because she is outside the middle range found in self-report survey data. Sexuality exists on a continuum. There are people whose experiences reflect either end of the continuum and people whose experiences reflect the middle. It is just as unfair to judge a sexually experienced woman as it is to judge a man who has had one sexual partner his whole life and seeks no more. Such a man is no less masculine than the man with 5 or 10 sexual partners.

Sociologists, who examine overall patterns, are often criticized because people assume that the statistics of the majority are being presented as proper conduct or that other conduct is by definition abnormal. But the social scientist makes no such assumption. In fact, diversity and change in behavior are at the center of social science. Sexuality is one of the most diverse, pervasive, and enigmatic of human experiences. Therefore, far from naming a single sexuality or a dichotomous sexuality (or even a trichotomous sexuality), we may more accurately say that there are as many sexualities as there are people. Yet detecting patterns within the diversity can advance an understanding of gender, sex, and society and show how differences and similarities among groups of men and women came into being and are sustained through social practices. The categorical language of sexuality is difficult to avoid. However, we will try to avoid categorizing people or acts, and we hope you will join us in that effort.

CHAPTER 2

Sexual Behavior and Gender

A scene from the Woody Allen movie *Annie Hall* (1977) provides a stereotype of gender differences in sexuality. A split screen shows Alvie Singer (played by Woody Allen) and Annie (played by Diane Keaton) as disenchanted lovers, each talking to their respective psychoanalysts about the relationship. Alvie gripes that the couple hardly has sex any more—maybe only three times per week. In the opposite frame, Annie complains that they have sex all the time, as much as three times per week.

As the writer of this scene, Allen apparently views sex as a chore for a woman, who reluctantly graces her partner with hardly enough sex to sustain him. He makes frequency of sex a surrogate for desire, something that women are often caricatured as having less of than men. That attitude is reflected in jokes such as "How do you get a woman to stop wanting sex?" (Answer: "Marry her"), which connote a shared cultural understanding that women consent to sex only as a way to land a husband. Men are thought to set the pace for sex in a relationship. In survey data, the myths of male and female sexual difference are, to a certain extent, borne out. The gendered frequency pattern suggested by the *Annie Hall* scene also exists among same-sex couples. Gay male couples, even nonmonogamous ones, have a higher sexual frequency than lesbian couples, who may end up having very infrequent genital sex. (And whatever kind of couple you look at, over time, sexual frequency declines.) How and why this is so is a complicated riddle.

In this chapter, we will explore the social sources of these differences and the ways these differences are exploited socially. We will also draw your attention to the more commonly occurring, though less often explored, sexual similarities between men and women.

The Challenge of Studying Sexual Behavior

When we look more carefully at situations like the one Woody Allen amusingly presents in *Annie Hall,* we might come up with some answers to questions about gender differences in sexuality. For example, maybe the reason that heterosexual couples with children have discrepant levels of sexual desire is biological: A new mother may feel more attached to her child than her spouse. Or maybe the reason is socially constructed: Mothers, who consistently do the lion's share of housework even when employed outside the home full-time (Brines 1994), have less sexual desire because the day-to-day reality of housework and child care is not much of an aphrodisiac and is also exhausting. Or maybe more wives than husbands suffer inequity in marriage, and the wives' anger interferes with desire.

These are all plausible explanations, but social scientists are reluctant to commit to any of them without methodically studying the behavior and attitudes of real people. In this chapter, we use many examples from the well-known National Opinion Research Center's National Health and Social Life Survey (NHSLS), as reported in Laumann, Michael, and Gagnon (1994). Based on personal interviews with a probability sample of 3,432 U.S. women and men between the ages of 18 and 59, the study explores the extent to which sexual conduct and general attitudes toward sexuality are influenced by gender, age, marital status, and other demographic characteristics. We also use many examples from the American Couples survey, published in *American Couples: Money, Work, and Sex* (Blumstein and Schwartz 1983). The American Couples study used survey data and in-depth interviews in a sample of 12,066 people that included married couples, heterosexual cohabitors, and gay and lesbian couples. The focus was on relationship quality and durability across all four couple types.

Because this is not a book about interpreting survey data or about conducting sex research, we will not go into great detail on those subjects. However, we caution students of sexuality to recognize the challenges of collecting and interpreting self-report data, particularly on the enigmatic topic of sexuality. Respondents may not tell the truth or remember the truth or even be sure that what they thought happened really did happen. For the healthy skeptic of sexual self-reporting, these survey data remain records of norms or values, if not precise accounts of deeds.

FIGURE 2.1

Overlapping Distributions of Men's and Women's Sexuality

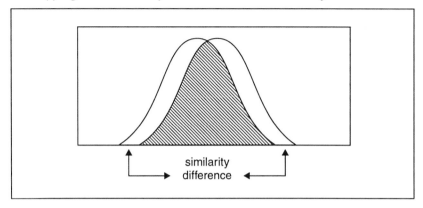

The Bell Curve of Women's and Men's Sexuality

The world makes much of gender difference: Difference between men and women is the theme on which movies, fashion, courtship, and even ideals about family structure are built. So much is made of gender difference that it is difficult to imagine, instead, the continuum of sexuality we discussed in Chapter 1. The great sociologist Erving Goffman (1977) made the point that much of what we think of as sex differences are illusions. Male and female characteristics are like two mostly overlapping distributions of physical characteristics. Think of it this way: Picture a **normal distribution,** also known as a **bell curve,** which represents the distribution of a particular characteristic in the general population. The units of a bell curve are characteristics—sexual frequency, for example—mathematically transformed into standard units. This is a good, though not perfect, tool for estimating norms and variations of those norms. Statistically, most people inhabit the fat, middle part of a bell curve. Some are a little above average, and some are a little below average. Little of the population is at either end.

Human sexuality can be displayed as a bell curve. Figure 2.1 shows one distribution for female sexuality and another for male sexuality. The line at the base of the chart, the x-axis, represents the continuum, or the range and diversity of the sexual phenomenon that has been charted onto the curve.

In Figure 2.1, note that a large portion of both female and male populations share much of the middle ground. This overlap is the case in almost every aspect of human experience, even sexual norms and practices. True, there are two separate distributions with two distinguishable averages (or pinnacles of the curves). However, only the small proportions of the population at either end of this double-jointed distribution are radically different from each other.

Sexual experience isn't all that different for men and women, but perhaps, like us, you wonder what causes men and women at one end of the continuum to be so different from other men and women at the middle or from members of the other sex at the opposite end of the continuum. You may even begin to wonder about the source of differences among women and among men—not simply differences between men and women. Finally, you may want to ask, as we do, why the world focuses on gender difference, rather than similarity.

Gender, Ethnicity, and Sexuality

This chapter is about differences and similarities in women's and men's sexual behavior. But before we address gender, remember that people's behavior is also influenced by many other variables, such as class, race, and ethnicity—both independently and as they intersect with gender.

As difficult as it is to get reliable population samples to examine overall patterns in sexuality, obtaining sufficient numbers of respondents within demographic subcategories is even more difficult. Thus, the examination of race, class, and ethnicity along with gender influences on sexuality is a challenge. And even when sufficient data exist, they should be interpreted with caution, because race, class, ethnicity, and gender as variables are poorly understood. Nevertheless, the distinctions that we do find among different groups illustrate a crucial sociological point: Social experience, more than biological inheritance, shapes sexuality. In some cases, gender overshadows other social categories; in other cases, gender combines with race, class, and ethnicity to produce variation in social and sexual norms of behavior.

Several very specific examples of sexual practices make the point. Figure 2.2 displays reported rates of masturbation by gender and by race/ethnicity, singling out white, black, and Hispanic respondents. Obviously, these divisions are very crude—whites, blacks, and Hispanics can be further divided by class, by region, by national origin, and so on. (Note that "Hispanics" is the category used in the Laumann et al.

FIGURE 2.2

Masturbation Practices and Attitudes

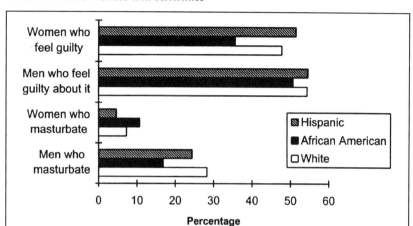

Source: Data from Laumann, Michael, and Gagnon (1994).

survey referred to in this section. Hispanic refers to people who identified as being of Spanish or Latin American origin.)

As you can see from Figure 2.2, there is a gender difference: Men
report more masturbation than women. This finding is consistent with
gendered norms of sexuality that persist across other categories of
experience, such as frequency or number of partners. But observe: Black
men are more similar to black, white, and Hispanic women in their
reported levels of masturbation than they are to white and Hispanic
men. That is, in the category of masturbation, black men and women
have a smaller gender difference than do men and women in other
racial/ethnic categories.

Now observe the sections that reflect how often people in different
groups feel guilty about masturbation. About half of all those surveyed
say they feel guilty about it, with one exception: Only a third of black
women, rather than half, say they feel guilty. The fact that black women
don't follow the general pattern may be the product of many cultural
influences.

Consider another aspect of sexual behavior: duration of most recent
sexual episode (see Table 2.1). Across ethnic groups, more men than
women claim that their last sexual episode lasted one hour or longer.
And across ethnic groups, more women than men claim that their last
sexual episode lasted 15 minutes or less. Does this finding make sense?
We think it suggests that men boast and women are demure when it

TABLE 2.1

Duration of Most Recent Sexual Episode, by Race, Ethnicity, and Gender (in percentages)

	One hour or more		Fifteen minutes or less	
Race/ethnicity	Men	Women	Men	Women
White	19.4	13.5	9.7	14.1
African American	24.0	21.5	15.2	17.5
Hispanic	15.9	15.6	13.3	18.2

Source: Data from Laumann, Michael, and Gagnon (1994).

comes to reporting sexual experience. This explanation is consistent with socially constructed norms that reward men, but not women, for sexual prowess. But of greater interest is the pattern of gender differences. Once again, black men and women have a smaller gender difference than the other racial/ethnic groups, suggesting that the sexual scripts among African Americans tend to be less gendered than the scripts for the other groups. Hispanics are split: there is no gender difference regarding 60-minute episodes, but fewer Latin men than women report the briefer, 15-minute episodes.

Finally, look at what men and women say about giving and receiving oral sex (see Figure 2.3). Whites have more oral sex than other groups; blacks report having oral sex less frequently than the other groups. Unlike duration of sex and masturbation, however, in this area blacks have a larger gender difference than whites or Hispanics. Black men are quite different from white men; black women are quite different from white women. And these groups are also different from Hispanics.

Figure 2.3 reveals something even more interesting about what people say about oral sex. Among whites, the rates that men and women report are quite similar for both giving and receiving oral sex. Among Hispanics and even more so among blacks, however, men and women both claim receiving oral sex more often than giving it. How could this be? It could be that they are having oral sex with same-sex as well as opposite-sex partners. We think these groups have different meanings associated with giving versus receiving oral sex. One hypothesis is that for Hispanics and blacks, giving oral sex is more of a taboo than receiving it.

But here is another explanation: Oral sex, more so than other sexual acts, can be viewed in terms of power. Even though partners may

FIGURE 2.3

Oral Sex in Three Race/Ethnic Categories

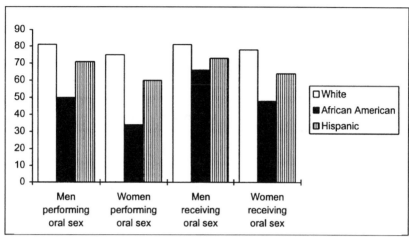

Source: Data from Laumann, Michael, and Gagnon (1994).

"return the favor," it tends to be a one-way experience when it is being done. The person receiving oral sex typically feels more powerful in the moment than the person giving oral sex, even though lying back and receiving it actually makes a person quite physically vulnerable. As the examples of masturbation and duration of sexual episodes suggest, the gender difference between black men and women is smaller than between whites. Thus, black women, like black men, will express their sense of entitlement—their sense of power in the relationship—by reporting being recipients of oral sex more often than being givers of oral sex.

Sex is always experienced in a context that is highly specific: It is within a relationship that may be intimate or fleeting; people having sex can be of different genders or the same, different races or the same. People having sex are influenced by all these factors, and more, in varying degrees. Although from time to time in this chapter and other chapters we examine the influence of social variables such as ethnicity and class, we encourage you to raise these sociological concerns yourself as you think about all the examples of gendered sexuality that we provide.

Gendered Patterns in Sexual Practices

What people think of as the "ideal man" or the "ideal woman" is often characterized by the behavior at the extreme ends of the bell curve.

Ironically, even where social forces work in concert to generate these "socially ideal" sexual norms and gender differences, few men or women achieve them: This shortfall is why so many men and women feel inadequate in the performance of feminine and masculine sexualities. Nevertheless, their expectations for gender-appropriate sexual behavior translate into many gender differences in sexual practice. As we explore below, however, men and women are generally far more alike than different.

Masturbation

We start our exploration of sexual practices with masturbation— where many of you may have started, too. As Woody Allen says, "Masturbation is sex with someone I love." It is strictly pleasure-focused, nonprocreative sex. Because it is fundamentally antisocial, societies tend to stigmatize it. Yet this we know: When it comes to sex, masturbation is the most common act, especially among people outside of committed relationships. It is the least dangerous, the most controllable by a person's own wishes, and the least likely to lead to misunderstandings. But masturbation is surely not the most socially acceptable sexual practice. Why not? The simple answer is religious taboo. Both Judaism and Christianity denounce "wasting seed," which refers to the nonprocreative character of male masturbation.

As late as the nineteenth and early twentieth centuries, doctors blamed masturbation for everything from insanity to baldness, and many of those myths live on. One woman recounted to us a story of a girlfriend from her youth in the late 1950s. The girl came over sobbing and shaking because her mother had caught her masturbating and told her she was going to go crazy and go to hell. The 12-year-old girl was relieved when she read a sex education book that said masturbation was natural, common, and harmless. In Philip Roth's novel *Portnoy's Complaint* (1967), Portnoy tells how he was obsessed with masturbation until the shame crept up on him one day.

> It was at the end of my freshman year of high school—and freshman year of masturbating—that I discovered on the underside of my penis, just where the shaft meets the head, a little discolored dot that has since been diagnosed as a freckle. Cancer. I had given myself *cancer*. All that pulling and tugging at my own flesh, all that friction, had given me an incurable disease. (P. 19)

These scenes of shame, however, continue in many households today. The stigma, particularly among those who take the Bible literally

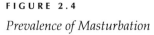

FIGURE 2.4

Prevalence of Masturbation

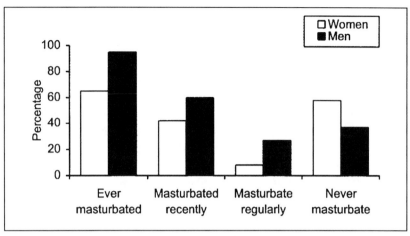

Source: Data from Laumann, Michael, and Gagnon (1994) and Hatfield and Rapson (1993).

and consider masturbation a sin, is powerful. In 1995, when President Clinton's Surgeon General, Joycelyn Elders, remarked that schools might teach teenagers about masturbation as a way to help them delay sexual involvement, the public uproar was so virulent that she was forced to resign. Sex without an emotional connection or with no procreative intent is still apparently frowned on in U.S. society, even after the sexual revolution of the 1960s (which will be discussed in Chapter 3).

Despite public ambivalence, in private, people continue to be quite fond of masturbation. Over 60 percent of men report masturbating (Laumann et al. 1994:81), and over 90 percent have tried it (Hatfield and Rapson 1993). They start at an early age and continue whether or not they are in a committed sexual relationship. Boys may learn to masturbate at an early age because of the fortuitous friction of bed sheets or because early erections cue children to the pleasures of their own bodies. Or masturbation may begin in adolescence with the onset of more adult attractions. Whatever the critical stimulus, masturbation for males is pretty common in America. Alternatively, although nearly half of all women report some level of masturbation (Laumann et al. 1994:81), they tend to masturbate less often than men. As people age, they also tend to masturbate less often. As Figure 2.4 shows, the NHSLS (Laumann et al. 1994:82) found that 58 percent of women—versus 37 percent of men—never touch themselves. Only 8 percent of women report masturbating once a week, as opposed to 27 percent of men. But 65 percent of women have at least tried masturbation (Hatfield and Rapson 1993).

Gender differences in frequency and prevalence of masturbation have been used by essentialists as evidence that the female sex drive is lower than the male sex drive. But social norms, including the idea that "nice girls don't touch themselves," have also been identified as the reason for the discrepancy. Think about how powerful social norms must be to convince women not to touch themselves, despite the intensely pleasurable sensation masturbation provides.

Men's and women's masturbation practices set the stage for their different approaches to sexuality in relationships. Masturbation is viewed as unavoidable for boys and men. But parents may be upset when their young daughter starts to touch herself, as if it is anomalous for a girl to explore the pleasure her body can provide. Girls may be discouraged from or punished for masturbation. They may be inculcated with the notion that sex for sex's sake is not appropriately female. Parents may teach their children that sex for pleasure and release is more dangerous for women than for men, because they believe that if a girl likes sex she may get pregnant or, in some locales, ruin her reputation. These worries are not passed on to men, except in the most conservative communities.

The lower rates of masturbation for women beg for explanation. Whatever the causes, however, less masturbation means that girls develop less sexual self-knowledge than boys do. Many single women, even in more recent years, enter their first relationship not having masturbated—and not having the vaguest idea about how their bodies should be touched or what thoughts are comfortable or arousing to them.

As women's desire for sexual equality has taken hold, their acceptance of masturbation has grown. Higher rates of masturbation are associated with higher rates of other sexual skills, including the ability to have orgasms. Feminist sex therapy and sex manuals for women who have been nonorgasmic teach them how to respond through masturbatory techniques. An orgasm is considered a woman's right, regardless of where and with whom she has it.

The focus on the individual and pleasure and the lack of concern for sex within relationships are major departures from the essentialist view of sex as procreative and properly confined to marriage. Not inconsequentially, a fairly extensive video and sex-toy business now exists, which is popular among middle- and upper-class women. Feminist sex shops sell a wide variety of vibrators for single women, women in pairs with men, or women paired with other women. Women learn to respond sexually by themselves, for themselves.

Rates of masturbation may still reveal a gender difference, but the absence of masturbation, rather than the presence of it, is more frequently being identified as a problem. In that respect, we are becoming more like the Scandinavians, who treat masturbation as a normal element of both men's and women's sexuality. To be sure, women more than men continue to be discouraged from sex for sex's sake, as the next section on relational and recreational sex observes. But women now have social permission to be sexual, and the change has little to do with the biology of sex. Instead, it has to do with social changes that influence the sex lives of men and women. Our prediction: Men's and women's rates of masturbation will become more similar over the next decade, as women's rates of masturbation increase.

Relational Sex versus Recreational Sex

The myth is that men want sex for fun, and women want sex for love. But it turns out that men and women both prefer sex in a relationship more than in a casual or anonymous setting. The difference is simply that casual sex, which may occur without any emotional connection, is more acceptable to men than women if relational sex is not an option. In many places, the normal setting for relational sex is marriage or committed cohabitation.

Nevertheless, among the most commonly observed gender differences in the United States and in many Western countries (e.g., Canada, Great Britain, France, Italy, and Scandinavia) is that women's sexual desire tends to be more "relational" than men's (Hatfield and Rapson 1996). That is, women's sexual desire focuses on a specific person and is ratified by love and mutual passion. Men's sexual desire is more likely to allow for sex just for fun. A woman's sexual desire increases when she is focused on a person who cares about her rather than a person who can simply fulfill an immediate sexual need.

The majority of men also prefer relational sex (Laumann et al. 1994), but more men than women seem to like recreational sex. For example, up until recent decades, many men's sexual initiation was with a prostitute (Kinsey, Pomeroy, and Martin 1948). And men would have sex with women who weren't the "marrying kind" or women they loved. Today, differences persist.

FIGURE 2.5

Attitudes toward Recreational and Relational Sex

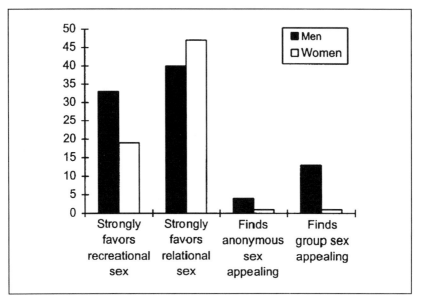

Source: Data from Laumann, Michael, and Gagnon (1994).

Figure 2.5 shows these differences, as well as men's and women's interest in two specific types of recreational sex. Although more men than women say that they find sex with a complete stranger appealing, and many more men than women say they find group sex appealing, only a very small proportion of the sample is interested in either. The proportion of men and women who prefer recreational sex may be small because of religious or personal values, family background, or a host of other reasons, not the least of which is a rational fear of sexually transmitted diseases, especially AIDS. The proportion interested in recreational sex may be larger among special subgroups of men and women, such as urban, educated, upper-middle-class professionals who have market-based incentives to delay marriage and whose advantages encourage them to feel secure about sex in uncommitted or fleeting liaisons.

Women's preference for relational sex shows up again in their limited use of prostitutes. Among those few women who have ever used a hired escort service (a hired date for the evening), if sex happens, it is rarely considered an exchange of sex for money. Instead, women see sex as an activity that was among the possibilities of the night out. The fee is for companionship, the sex is optional. Most women can hardly imagine even going so far as to hire an escort, much less pay for sex or seek sex in a totally anonymous format. It is extremely hard to imagine, say, someone like actress Emma Thompson being arrested on Hollywood's Sunset Boulevard for hiring a prostitute for a quick round of oral sex in the car, as happened to actor Hugh Grant in the summer of 1995. Both movie stars have a multitude of appealing sexual options; yet a woman is highly unlikely to count anonymous, quick sex among those options.

Gender differences in relational versus recreational sexuality is further illustrated by comparing lesbian to gay male couples. Homosexual partners, like heterosexuals, have been raised with male and female sexual norms. But unlike heterosexual couples, both partners bring similar, rather than different, gendered norms of sexuality to the situation. The contrast between recreational sex associated with men and relational sex associated with women therefore becomes quite vivid. Although gays and lesbians, like heterosexuals, prefer relationships, the sexual norms for gay men and for lesbians differ from each other and from heterosexuals. For example, in the 1970s and 1980s gay male magazines and subcultures touted recreational sex more than partnered sex. Since HIV and AIDS were discovered in the early 1980s, however, gay men may have shifted to preferring couplehood (Lever 1994a). There is some evidence that the popularity of gay couplehood preceded AIDS; the men of the **baby boom** generation (born between 1945 and 1962) were getting older and, like the rest of the country, more interested in "settling down" (Seidman 1992). Nevertheless, a significant number of gay men continue to approve of recreational sex and endorse nonmonogamy even within the context of a committed, lifetime relationship. Lesbians, on the other hand, tend to prefer sex in the context of love and relationship. Few lesbians approve of nonmonogamous recreational sex while in a committed relationship (Blumstein and Schwartz 1983). Recently, however, lesbian sex clubs have opened up that, like gay bars in their heyday, celebrate anonymous, recreational sex (Huston and Schwartz 1995). Yet this is a peripheral movement, at the "cutting edge" of female sexuality. For the most part, lesbians, like heterosexual women, prefer sex to complement relationship goals.

To sum up, the evidence suggests that men are more likely to see sex as fun for its own sake and that women are more likely to believe sex can be enjoyable only when it has meaning, affection, and, for some, love. Do women like quickies? Some do. As time marches on, women are at greater liberty to express lust, in such settings as male strip bars like Chippendale's. But the more impersonal sex is, the more likely it is that men will approve of it and women won't.

Although the differences in norms for men and women are striking, so are the differences between women today and women in previous eras, when women's sexual expression outside of marriage was more strictly constrained. Men today also differ from men in previous eras. In fact, men and women today are more similar to one another than men of today and men of previous eras or women of today and women of previous eras. And expectations for sexuality continue to change. The pressure on men to be more sensitive, less predatory, and less macho has been mounting for several decades. Legal challenges to what used to be unquestioned male sexual privilege (such as the freedom to touch or come on to women employees or co-workers, whether or not they have invited such attention) have put the sexes on more equal footing than they might have been just a few years ago. If we return to the image of the normal distribution, picture fewer and fewer men at the extreme "macho" end of the continuum and fewer women at the extreme "docile" end of the continuum. Male and female averages are still somewhat different, but over time the distributions have shifted toward a common center, and perhaps both continua have expanded to allow greater diversity in sexual expression regardless of gender.

Much of this change can be explained by social changes: Women have gained more economic power and social influence; therefore, women's privileges have shifted. Men and women also now have the everyday experience of encountering one another professionally, which has modified their approach toward each other. Although men and women have worked together in working-class settings, the change is that now middle-class professional positions have more women in them than ever before.

For a sign of changing norms, look at images of women in Hollywood movies and on MTV. Although some people consider them caricatures of greater sexual license, these media often show a new female sexual icon. Madonna in her videos is kinky and sexually voracious; Sharon Stone is dangerous in *Basic Instinct* (1992); Geena Davis and Susan Sarandon in *Thelma & Louise* (1991) are fun loving and pleasure seeking; Susan Sarandon is idiosyncratic, independent, and sexually wise in *Bull Durham* (1989). The list goes on. Of course, the alert movie fan can counter with as many conservative images of female sexuality. A woman's fate typically hinges on the man she is able to "catch"—as in *While You Were Sleeping* (1995), in which Sandra Bullock plays a down-and-out subway worker whose hopes for renewal hinge on making a match with a well-to-do man in a coma. Or a woman is a "whore with a heart of gold"—like Julia Roberts in *Pretty Woman* (1990), whose way out of street prostitution is to be the delightful playmate of an extremely rich benefactor and then to hold out for marriage. Perhaps the real story is that no single model of female sexuality prevails now so much as the possibility of a sexual entrepreneurship unknown to previous generations of women. Women have many more paths to take to gain a lover or to enjoy sex without gaining the obligation of a relationship.

It seems that men are also portrayed to be more loyal to their partners in some recent movies. Consider the new scruples of Pierce Brosnan's James Bond in *Golden Eye* (1996) (and his subtle mooning over the ever-faithful Miss Moneypenny). This character contrasts with Sean Connery's more promiscuous, womanizing portrayals of James Bond in the 1960s. Still, the '90s Bond has much sexual privilege.

The narrowing of the sexual gender gap between men and women today suggests the powerful influence of such social forces as media and the legal system. We are not saying that these forces have totally equalized the costs of sexual permissiveness for women and men or that women and men necessarily have the same emotional response to sex. However, the changes we have observed illustrate two important themes. First, the norms that govern women's sexuality are becoming less punitive or at least less effective (while norms for men have changed to a lesser degree). Second, this shift in rules and behavior supports the perspective that sexual desire is a social construction. Its expression varies widely according to time, place, and political climate.

Fantasy and Pornography

Another arena for examining gendered sexuality is sexual fantasy as portrayed in pornography and other material designed for sexual arousal. Here, too, there are some surprising patterns in gender differences and similarities, regardless of sexual orientation. Both heterosexual and gay men's pornography tends to be graphic and sexually straightforward. Certain acts, such as partners performing oral sex and swallowing the semen, seem to be de rigueur. Both written accounts and visual representations of sex often contain themes of power and submission. Heterosexual sado-masochistic material emphasizes the erotic power of either dominating a partner or being dominated. Although

FIGURE 2.6

Preferences for Pornography

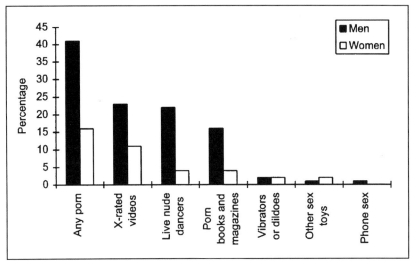

Source: Data from Laumann, Michael, and Gagnon (1994).

subspecialties of pornography cater to a great diversity of sexual tastes, mainstream male heterosexual pornography involves very little story telling. Instead, it gets into "hard, fast action" right away and almost never portrays a relationship between the sexually involved actors.

Many fewer women than men say they like to use pornography for arousal (Laumann et al. 1994), as Figure 2.6 shows. Even women who have used it complain that most pornography is designed for men and therefore is not usually arousing for them. They report being disgusted by the negative imagery of women, including the use of physical power and domination by men against women. In contrast, erotic material that appeals to women often emphasizes emotional as well as physical foreplay rather than intercourse. Depictions of romance and growing desire serve to make the sex more interesting. (Indeed, this is the stuff Hollywood movies are made of.) Explicit anatomical pictures are infrequent. The minimal availability of such pornography designed by women or for women may help explain gender differences in its popularity.

It is not that women cannot be visually aroused by images of nudity and explicit sexual acts. One study found that men reported more arousal than women in response to visual images, but that men's and women's actual responses (measured physiologically) were more similar than dissimilar (Schmidt and Sigusch 1970). By using a plethysmograph (a gauge attached to a penis or inserted into a vagina that monitors the amount of blood flowing to the genitals and thereby measures levels of sexual arousal), Heiman (1977) tracked the impact of erotic material. Volunteers were asked to watch sexually explicit movies and provide a self-report of their arousal. When self-reports were compared to physiological feedback, women had underreported their level of arousal as it was measured by the genital monitor. Men provided a more accurate report. Were the women not conscious of their own physiological experience? Do men and women operate with different definitions of what constitutes arousal? Or were they reluctant to admit an "improper" sexual response? In this case, men and women were physically similar, but their responses were completely consistent with social norms and stereotypes of sexuality. This finding supports social constructionist theories of sexuality.

Although women may respond to garden-variety pornography more than they let on, women's sexual response is generated by different kinds of stimuli, as indicated by the kinds of romance books they buy or movies they order. Women's preferences seem to suggest a somewhat more relational and less mechanical approach to sexual experience than men's. A recent series of studies supports this notion. Ellis and Symons (1990), evolutionary psychologists who emphasize that behavior evolves to maximize reproductive capability, systematically compared men's and women's sexual fantasies. They found that women's fantasies were generally relationship oriented, focused on someone they were dating or had experienced sexually. The fantasies were full of details about the partner and the environment of the encounter. The pace was typically slow and sensual, with lots of caressing and emotional exchange. Women concentrated on foreplay rather than intercourse. In contrast, men's fantasies were more impersonal, more focused on specific sexual acts, and more likely to be populated with strangers or multiple partners. Symons (1979) thinks that for men, sex is sheer lust and physical gratification. In their fantasies, sex is devoid of encumbering relationships, emotional elaboration, complicated plot lines, flirtation, courtship, and extended courtship, and women are easily aroused and willing. Although Ellis and Symons use their findings to support the notion that women and men are sociobiologically different, we think it illustrates simply that women and men continue to behave differently. This behavior may have biological features associated with it, but the preponderance of cues in the environment teach men and women that different things are sexy.

Not only are men's and women's sexual fantasies different in kind, but they appear to be different in number as well. In the NHSLS, the researchers found that 54 percent of men fantasized daily, compared to only 19 percent of women (Laumann et al. 1994). Male and female college students are a little more comparable. Jones and Barlow (1990) found that college men reported on average about seven fantasies per day and that college women reported about four and a half. We suspect these numbers would be more similar if romantic as well as strictly sexual fantasies were coded. Furthermore, self-reports may be influenced by social norms that discourage women from admitting or even recognizing sexual impulses.

Because the inner world of an individual is created largely, if not completely, by the external world, it stands to reason that men and women, living lives differentiated by their gender, would dream and fantasize in different ways. Some more embedded reason may explain why women's fantasies are different from men's, but the proximal reasons are quite "man made." External social constraints, such as what seems properly feminine or masculine, influence imagination and behavior. To be a proper lady, a woman is supposed to have sex only when she is in love, with only the one man who is her husband or at least her committed lover. A woman must keep her dignity, if not her virginity, so that she is not labeled "promiscuous" or, more punitively, "a slut." But modern sexual expectations call on her, once she is in bed with an approved mate, to turn into a passionate, uninhibited lover. With no independent "script" or directions on how a ladylike but passionate woman is supposed to act, many women follow the model that movies and custom create: They wait for the man of their dreams to show them what to do and what kind of lover to be.

Some scientists speculate that men learn to fantasize when they begin masturbating, which occurs earlier in life than women's masturbatory practice (Gagnon and Simon 1973). Furthermore, men have explicit masturbatory material, such as *Playboy* magazine, to guide their fantasies more so than women. Although women can use *Playgirl* magazine, erotic fiction, and specialty magazines, the more common form of "pornography" for women is romance novels. The consequence may be that boys and men have more experience with fantasizing. They may also have greater uniformity in their fantasies and be overly focused on the highly narrow vision of erotica created by men's magazines and pornographic books. Finally, men also have few models for being today's ideally macho yet sensitive lover. They therefore may continue to rely on old-fashioned seduction scenarios involving male leadership and aggression.

Recent erotic books (such as those edited by Susie Bright in the 1990s) may be liberating female fantasies from the traditional script. These may or may not be a reliable representation of female fantasies, but let us assume that they represent some women's fantasies. They suggest that women have the capacity to fantasize about torrid scenarios that have nothing to do with love and that can be as bizarre and orgasm centered as men's.

Men, on the other hand, may be more interested in fantasies centered on relationships and love than the original stereotype might suggest. A recent study of men's and women's response to romantic pornography and to more mechanical pornography found that both men and women found the romantic pornography more arousing (Quackenbush, Strassberg, and Turner 1995). Most everybody likes the combination of intimacy and sex, but social forces have given women greater permission to fantasize about intimate sex.

In a study done in the 1970s, the top fantasy for both men and women was "having sex with someone you love" (Hunt 1974). The second highest, "having sex with strangers," was appealing to twice as many men as women. This difference may not so much reflect possible fantasies or capacities for recreational sex as reflect the way the question was perceived. For example, women, much more than men, identify "stranger" with "danger," and not a sexy kind of danger. Women who might fancy a one-night stand must also intelligently evaluate the possibility that the man would be homicidal, brutal, or contemptuous and overpowering. If the fear and potential for violence that anonymous sex presents to women could be effectively removed, their fantasies might be different.

Initiation and Sexual Negotiation

Consistent with the pattern of more extensive male influence in relationships and higher expectations of male sexual intensity and desire, more men than women initiate sex. It follows that more women than men refuse sex. Can we conclude that men have a stronger sex drive than women? Or has tradition, based on the theory of men's powerful drives, assigned men the job of initiating sexual courtship and given women the prerogative to accept or reject?

TABLE 2.2

Sexual Initiation (in percentages)

Statement	Men	Women
Says more likely to initiate	51	12
Says more likely to refuse	16	48
Most common function of sex	Sexual release	Love

Source: Data from Blumstein and Schwartz (1983) and Brown and Auerback (1981).

As Table 2.2 indicates, survey respondents tend to see initiation as "men's work" and refusal as "women's work." Furthermore, Brown and Auerback (1981) found in their survey of 100 couples that women initiate sex for "love, intimacy, and holding," whereas men said they sought "sexual release." These are widely familiar expectations for how men and women should properly relate in heterosexual pairs.

This "norm" is so strong that women who step out of line and initiate sex "too much" often receive a nasty reaction. In the American Couples survey (Blumstein and Schwartz 1983), husbands reported negative feelings when wives showed more sexual initiative than they did. This finding is surprising for people who hold a strongly biological perspective on sexual desire. If initiation reflected only sexual appetite, it stands to reason that men would favor sex regardless of who initiates the opportunity. However, initiation is clearly also about power. Sex occurs according to men's agenda. If women initiated more, the sexual agenda might be quite different. The sexual experience, where power is skewed, is undoubtedly different from situations where power is shared. Thus, social construction, rather than biology, dictates the organization of sexual initiation and response. From a symbolic interactionist point of view, if men are the guardians of sexual frequency, they will try to initiate sex as an identity-confirming act. If women are guardians of intimacy, they will seek to have sex only when it constitutes a relationship-confirming act.

Differences in initiation also occur in gay and lesbian relationships, and they often have to do with power. Gay men, like heterosexual men, are comfortable with initiating. In fact, they are so comfortable in that role that they prefer not to relinquish it. When each partner of a gay couple was asked "who initiates sex?" in the American Couples study, both partners claimed the behavior. Initiation appears to be a measure of men's machismo and sexual competence.

However, initiation does not work the same magic for women. When lesbian couples were asked who initiates sex more often, both partners claimed that the other partner does most of the asking (Blumstein and Schwartz 1983). In other words, the role of initiation seems to be male regardless of whether the couple is heterosexual or homosexual. In fact, both lesbian and heterosexual women tend to see initiation as potentially too aggressive (Blumstein and Schwartz 1983). What exactly constitutes aggression? Definitions vary, but it may include behavior ranging from refusing to take no for an answer to asking for sex rather than allowing it to emerge consensually.

Women who are sexually assertive learn over time that assertiveness is not often welcomed, so most modify their behavior. This is particularly true among lesbians. Most lesbians have had the same sexual socialization as heterosexual women, but they also often live in a subculture that directly opposes male standards of beauty, conduct, and acceptability for women and masculine sexual styles such as assertiveness. Many books on lesbian couples cite severe arguments between partners when one or the other feels she is being "dominated" or aggressively controlled. This sensitivity exists within the sexual realm as well, with the outcome being fewer overall initiations and therefore less frequent sex.

If sexual assertiveness is seen as demeaning or inappropriate for women, it makes sense that even women with intense sexual appetites will modify them. Likewise, if sexual assertiveness is positive and rewarding for men, it makes sense that even men who do not have a big sexual appetite will try to live up to the current standards of masculinity and give at least an adequate gender performance. Initiating sex may not be any more "natural" for many men than it is for women, but the pressure to perform is different. Social conventions of gender mold individual behavior and wrap even unwilling men and women into the gender-appropriate sexual performance.

Orgasm and Stimulation

Although orgasm and ejaculation are not synonymous for men, they are nearly equivalent. Most men who get excited and have an erection will experience orgasm with continued stimulation. As anyone who has had an orgasm knows, orgasm is a powerful reinforcer; a man is likely to repeat the experience whenever an erection makes it possible. Some men have erectile difficulty and a much smaller number have trouble achieving orgasm, but most men have an orgasm fairly soon after any

FIGURE 2.7

Orgasms during Partnered Sex

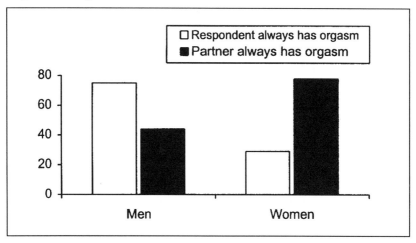

Source: Data from Laumann, Michael, and Gagnon (1994).

kind of stimulation, whether it is masturbation, intercourse, oral sex, or some other sex act.

Women often learn to have orgasms much later in life, and a minority have trouble ever becoming orgasmic. As Figure 2.7 illustrates, women are less likely than men to have an orgasm during sexual activity. (Notice, however, that more men report their partners having an orgasm during sex than women report having one.) Middle-class women are more likely than working-class women to have an orgasm during sex, probably because they have fewer environmental distractions and demands and more sex education (Sprecher and McKinney 1993). Sex therapists and advice books have sought to improve this situation. Feminist critics replaced the term "frigid"—used to describe women who had never had an orgasm during sex—with "preorgasmic." The new term reflects the belief that most women can be taught to have an orgasm, and books such as *For Yourself* (Barbach 1975) demonstrate how.

If orgasms constitute a central pleasure in life, it stands to reason that women would make it a priority to become orgasm experts the way men seem to be. So why are women inhibited in achieving orgasm? There are lots of reasons. First, women have less information about how to do it. Second, achieving orgasm takes practice, and women, taught to be modest and controlled, may be inhibited about taking the time to discover how their bodies work. A third influence is the social taboo against sexual pleasure—especially by and for oneself—that women experience more so than men. Remarkably, these social factors (and others) have the power to override the biological fact that orgasms feel just as good to women as they do to men. In fact, one study showed that men and women described the feeling of orgasm in almost exactly the same terms (Hatfield and Rapson 1996).

No name exists for men's orgasm problems, either because so few exist, because many men do not seek therapy, or even because men who can maintain an erection for a long time gain status for their endurance. The exception to this rule is *priapism,* a painful and dangerous condition in which a man cannot lose his erection because blood will not leave the engorged penis. This problem requires medical intervention.

At first glance, men's greater ease and frequency in reaching orgasm seems biological, what with penises being so easy to locate and handle. But we believe orgasms have a learned, social element. Perhaps the first place to look for social cues that influence orgasms is the different masturbatory patterns of boys and girls. Boys have much more experience masturbating to orgasm than girls. Gagnon and Simon, a creative pair of sociologists, wrote in *Sexual Conduct* (1973) that boys' ability to masturbate and their reinforcement for masturbating yield a rich, provocative, and even disturbing fantasy life. They hypothesize that one reason women masturbate less frequently than men is that women have a more minimal fantasy life. Of course, women's seemingly minimal fantasy life may be a consequence, not a cause, of less frequent masturbation. Furthermore, women's fantasy life is devitalized by internal constraints women develop early on to be sexual in socially approved ways, just as women's reports of fantasies may be more conservative due to external constraints. Men, too, desire to be sexual in socially approved ways, but their approved ways include a fuller expression of sexuality.

The social constraints women are subject to have an impact on ease of orgasm, because orgasm is at least partly a mental ability. Orgasms require focus. Both men and women experience inability to climax (Rosen and Rosen 1981) when tension, worry, distraction, or the accumulated distress of previous unsuccessful attempts overshadow the experience. But most women, unlike men, face the challenge of training their body to be excited and satisfied, because they tend to have fewer orgasmic experiences through masturbation and less sexual experimentation early in life.

Furthermore, the social script for heterosexual orgasm has convinced too many people that sex is good only if both partners achieve orgasms through intercourse. Some women who report no orgasm during sexual intercourse have never tried other methods, such as manual or oral stimulation. Or they may feel inhibited about touching themselves or being touched during lovemaking because they are worried, sometimes accurately, that it will insult their partner. Inability to climax solely through penile penetration is seen as either a rejection of the male partner or a commentary on his sexual competence. In this case, then, women's biological capacity for orgasm is overridden by social norms.

In fact, penetration may not be the easiest or the most efficient way for women to climax. The opening of the vagina is very sensitive, and the area around the cervix has a mass of nerve endings available for orgasmic stimulation. But most women climax more easily and intensely through direct clitoral stimulation. Certain sexual positions make it more likely that the clitoris will be touched during intercourse, but direct touching or oral stimulation may be kinder to a woman's most sensitive sexual organ. Still, when custom decrees that intercourse is the lone legitimate way to have an orgasm, people will bend themselves into pretzels to try to be sexually orthodox, even at the price of the very orgasm they are seeking. We could hypothesize that lesbians are more likely to be consistently orgasmic because the requirement of intercourse is not typically present (except when lovers use equipment like a strap-on dildo); touching is more likely to be perfected and appreciated as an important avenue for lovemaking (Blumstein and Schwartz 1983).

To add to heterosexual women's dilemma, men often do not know how to touch a woman effectively. She may not know how to tell him, or have the nerve to tell him, or she may even have tried to tell him and been rebuffed. For some partners, oral sex is a satisfying alternative, but for others, it is gross, embarrassing, or too intimate to even try. These difficulties keep many women either from finding a position during intercourse that helps them climax or from working out a sexual style that makes orgasm possible.

Women's reticence to seek effective sexual stimulation represents a distinct clash between the physical experience of sex and the social pressures that define and restrict sexual experience. A woman may consider requesting sexual acts that could stimulate her body more effectively to be sexually selfish or even unladylike. Some women avoid oral sex or other direct touching because it is so effective. These women may prefer a lower level of arousal rather than display themselves as out of control and therefore not "virtuous." Women may not recognize that social norms are structuring their negative response to oral sex or other alternatives to intercourse. Nevertheless, some women limit their sexual expectations accordingly and no longer try to be orgasmic all the time, or perhaps ever. This does not make sex undesirable, but it may make it somewhat less passionate or perhaps less reinforcing. Some women do not find an inability to climax frustrating, but others do, and it can diminish self-esteem, desire, or affection for a partner.

Numbers of Partners

Some research on sexual variety provides evidence that men, more than women, desire variety both in sexual acts and in partners (Blumstein and Schwartz 1983). In the NHSLS and General Social Survey (GSS) 1988-91 studies, around 56 percent of men reported five or more partners to date; slightly less than 30 percent of women reported this many (Laumann et al. 1994). When asked the ideal number of lifetime sexual partners, women report a lower average number than men do.

As Figure 2.8 illustrates, the gender differences in the middle range of the number of partners reported are not so high as the gender differences at the top end. Furthermore, when we look at only the youngest cohort surveyed in the NHSLS, people born between about 1964 and 1975, both women and men had more partners than older women did. Interestingly, in the youngest cohort more men than women had no sexual partners in the past year. This difference may in part be explained by women's increased sexual freedom, which gives them permission to have multiple partners as long as they don't have "too many." But it may also be a consequence of hypergamy—that is, younger women being courted by older men. Younger men don't have the same abundance of sexual opportunity early in life that women appear to have.

Laumann and colleagues (1994) addressed the problematic discrepancy in numbers of partners reported by men and women (see Figure 2.8). They provided seven hypothetical explanations of the gender inconsistency (p. 185), including the fact that about 8 million more adult women than adult men are in the population. In other words, heterosexual men have a larger set of potential partners to draw from than heterosexual women. Our view, however, is that women probably underreport somewhat because women are not rewarded for extensive sexual experience the way men are. By the same logic, men probably overreport. Nevertheless, women have the capacity to enjoy sexual experience to the same degree as men.

FIGURE 2.8

Number of Partners in Past 12 Months

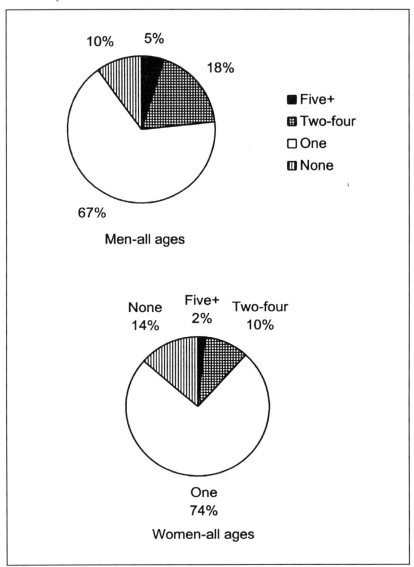

Sociobiologists hypothesize that men naturally desire variety in partners because it helps motivate them to have sex with many women and therefore be more likely to have many offspring. In addition, per-

FIGURE 2.8
Continued

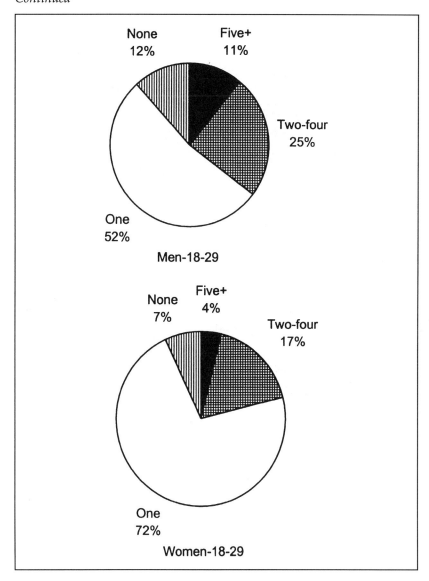

haps having a short romantic attention span helps men to detach from a woman they already had sex with, because she will not be available for reinsemination for at least nine months. A brief period of attachment allows men to turn their attention to impregnating other women.

This hypothesis is undermined, however, by the fact that sexual interest and attention wander or decline over time for all kinds of couples, even gay couples and others not interested in reproduction. Gay men have consistently reported higher rates of nonmonogamy than heterosexuals or lesbian pairs, particularly before AIDS made sexual adventurousness dangerous. We might conclude that men, unfettered by heterosexual convention or by women, are innately driven to more and more partners. However, emerging sexual trends among women show similar patterns. A young lesbian is much more likely than her lesbian counterpart of 20 years ago to seek sexual experimentation with more than one partner. Furthermore, the more liberal a heterosexual woman's attitudes are about sex, the more likely she is to seek and experience more than one lover. Differences in self-reports of sexual frequency may simply be influenced by social norms that encourage men to have many lovers and women to have few.

What psychological and social impact does number of partners have on men and women? Just as women have less experience with masturbation than men do, on average, women are likely to be less sexually experienced than men prior to marriage. Divorced women tend to have additional partners between marriages (as do men), but in general the gender difference maintains for both premarital and postmarital experience. A very small number of women have a large number of partners, but they do so in violation of both spoken and unspoken values regarding female sexual restraint, which is sometimes referred to as the sexual double standard. This double standard involves stronger punishments for women's sexual expression than for men's. Figure 2.8 suggests the sexual double standard: Men report having multiple partners more than women do.

From a sociobiological perspective, the double standard is a rule of nature. Men are driven to reproduce as often as possible; women are driven to protect and nurture the few offspring they have and offer their sexual exclusivity in exchange for male support and commitment. From a social constructionist point of view, the sexual double standard serves a different purpose: Men use it to obtain loyalty from women to assure access and establish paternity. In other words, this can be explained by the social norms that influence men's and women's response to questions about sexuality.

The sexual double standard still exists in most Western industrialized countries, even if it no longer requires wives to be virgins prior to marriage. The updated standard allows women to have sex within a nonmarital committed relationship, but having many partners is still often punished by disapproval or social isolation. A man with too many sexual conquests may be labeled a womanizer, if he is heterosexual, or a health risk, if homosexual. But women's sexuality is rewarded mostly in the context of sexual loyalty in relationships. A particularly liberated woman may intrigue sexually confident men, but fewer men seek to marry a "manizer" than a woman of more modest experience.

The urban and industrialized West is notably sexually liberal and tolerant when compared to the rest of the world. In other countries or even in conservative eras in the United States, a woman with a diverse sexual "past" is a woman with a dimmer marital future. This has been the story for women throughout most of history. Recall Hester Prynne, the main character in the nineteenth-century American novel by Nathaniel Hawthorne, *The Scarlet Letter*. Prynne was ostracized and marked with the scarlet letter "A" for her nonmarital, "adulterous" sexual activity. Or think of Blanche Dubois in the 1947 Tennessee Williams play *A Streetcar Named Desire*. Blanche's plans to marry (and thereby save herself from poverty) were foiled because her sexually permissive history in a small Louisiana town followed her to New Orleans and rendered her unmarriageable.

Such social sanctions are hardly the case today in the United States; nevertheless, no equivalent female term for "stud" exists; even seemingly complimentary phrases such as "femme fatale" have a more than slightly ominous tone. Films like *Fatal Attraction* (1987) are cautionary tales for men. In *Fatal Attraction*, a married man, played by Michael Douglas, has a one-night stand with a single woman, played by Glenn Close. The film turns into a horror story, with Close stalking Douglas and his family. You can look for the basic theme for yourself in other movies: A sexually loose, aggressive woman is an instrument of evil. When she is openly sexual, she has an ulterior, pathological motive and all too often a deadly agenda.

Remember, the majority of men and women remain in the middle of the overlapping distribution of sexuality. The majority of men look at media images of hypermasculinity and ready, indiscriminate sexuality—their models of manhood include Sylvester Stallone and Arnold Schwartzenegger—and they wonder who dreams these characters up. They feel no more affinity with those images, except perhaps as fantasy heroes, than women do the cartoonlike antics of the lead "bunnies" on TV's "Baywatch" (circa 1997).

Nonmonogamy

Although both men and women intend to "forsake all others" when they take their wedding vows, nonmonogamy does occur. Earlier studies indicated as many as a third to a half of married couples included an unfaithful partner, but the NHSLS estimates that only 15 percent of married people have had one nonmonogamous experience. Part of the low estimate of the NHSLS may be due to the fact that some of the interviews were conducted while the spouse was in the next room or nearby and might have overheard what the interview participant was saying about her or his nonmonogamous experiences.

Most studies indicate that men are more likely than women to report an outside sexual affair or one-night stand (less than 10 percent of women and about 25 percent of men; Laumann et al. 1994:214). Some analysts explain the difference as logical: Women are more satisfied by one relationship and more committed to having only one sexual partner, especially after marriage. Men are assumed to chafe under the sexual constraints of marriage even if they give in to them. Biologists and sociobiologists think these differences are perfectly compatible with different male and female reproductive strategies.

Social scientists hypothesize, however, that higher male nonmonogamy rates might be explained by the fact that women have fewer opportunities for sex outside marriage and higher costs, on average, than do husbands. Wives' schedules are fuller and more isolated with domestic work, child care, and, for the great majority of women, wage work. And women are more likely to be punished for nonmonogamy. Until the 1960s, a wife's infidelity (but not a husband's) was cause for justifiable homicide in the state of Texas (Finkelhor and Yllö 1985). It is still introduced in court as a mitigating circumstance when assault or homicide has occurred (see Chapter 4). A wife's infidelity is often more likely to undermine her chances in a custody battle than a husband's. Finally, women are likely to be more hesitant if they are economically dependent on their spouse: Although there is little direct evidence, when women are less economically dependent and in an egalitarian or "peer" marriage, they seem to be both more sexually frank within marriage and more similar to their men regarding nonmonogamy (Schwartz 1994).

Gendered nonmonogamy patterns persist in same-sex couples. Gay men in the 1970s and early 1980s rebelled against heterosexual models and asserted that they need not be monogamous even in a lifetime, committed relationship. On the other hand, like heterosexual women, most lesbians in couples believed in and enforced complete sexual fidelity. Today, AIDS has made gay male monogamy much more important, although gay men are still less monogamous than heterosexual men. As an alternative to risky kinds of nonmonogamy, gay men engage in nonmonogamous safe sex, including telephone sex, where men exchange fantasies but not bodily fluids, far more than lesbians or heterosexuals do. Similarly, gay male magazines have an enormous amount of erotic advertising and frankly erotic stories based on the assumption of instant sexual interest between men who encounter each another. Lesbian magazines, on the other hand, have traditionally focused on politics, including the politics of sexuality and relationships. Nonmonogamy may be addressed, but it is never assumed as part of relationships. Recently, however, just as there has been a rise in sex-positive lesbian bars and pornography, so lesbian magazines, such as *Girl Friends* or *On Our Backs,* have become more sexually explicit.

Consent and Coercion

One of the most frequently documented differences in male and female sexuality is the large gap between men's and women's standards for consensual sex. This is an area where the sexual continuum appears particularly polarized. About 1 percent of sexual assault cases involve women aggressors (Sprecher and McKinney 1993). By far the most dramatic number of sexual offenses against an unwilling partner are by men against women. The rates of rape (including acquaintance rape), incest, child molestation, and sexual harassment are an indictment of male sexuality (Koss et al. 1994). When these rates are examined in connection with nonsexual violence against women, including wife battering, the indictment of masculinity expands. The question is whether extremes in sexual aggression and violence are a product of fundamental, inborn gender difference or a result of polarizing social experiences. Discussion of this topic is highly politicized, and we will return to it in Chapter 5, which covers sexual politics.

The spillover across the boundary between sexuality and aggression is complex. Some observers agree with the essentialist view of male sexual domination: Men are naturally aggressive, and women are demure. Other observers look instead to the social context of sexual violence, such as the organization of young men into gangs, the greater likelihood that a young man will be called on to fight, and fathers' desire that their sons be athletic, physical, fearless and possess a host of other "boyish" qualities. Whether the tendency to be sexually violent is a biological and individual characteristic or a characteristic arising from social contexts and power dynamics has implications for choosing strategies to prevent, predict, and punish sexual violence.

An enormous amount of research has examined sexual violence, particularly since the early 1970s, when feminist scholars began to have some influence on selecting research topics for federal funding. A number of researchers conducted interesting studies about the attractiveness of violence to male research participants. In a study of U.S. and Canadian men, about 30 percent of men said that they were willing to intimidate, threaten, or physically coerce women into sex if they were sure they would not be caught (Briere and Malamuth 1983). At the same time, several studies showed that men often felt women "asked for it" and put themselves in situations that made male aggression inevitable (Malamuth 1984; Koss and Leonard 1984). Predictably, women did not think men systematically put themselves at risk for being raped, nor were rape perpetrator fantasies common to women.

As sexual violence research evolved, researchers began to study the prevalence of rape in the population, rather than studying official crime reports, prosecutions, or convictions, which tend to underestimate the problem. The rates are difficult to obtain, even in surveys where respondents' privacy is protected. In a study of college women (Koss et al. 1988), about 15 percent of women said they had been sexually assaulted. More than half these assaults were by men the women were dating. Other researchers have found rates of sexual coercion above 27 percent among college women (Miller and Marshall 1987). Some studies observe a prevalence of being victimized by a completed rape among adult women at around 20 percent (e.g., Burt 1979; Russell 1984; Wyatt 1992; as cited in Koss et al. 1994). Even if very conservative definitions of rape are used to exclude what some might call "unwanted sexual approaches," the evidence persistently indicates that a small but significant number of men practice sexual coercion.

Even rapes against men are mostly perpetrated by other men (Forman 1982). A few studies have investigated men who reported feeling pressured into sex by women, submitting to avoid appearing less than masculine, and these are typically cases in which women applied psychological, not physical, pressure (Struckman-Johnson 1988). Most information about sexual assault by men against men is anecdotal, because homosexual assaults are likely to go unreported. Occasionally, straight men will use sex as a way to subjugate other men in prison. The dominated man is meant to feel humiliated—and he does. A rape is not something he wants to make public. If he did, he would be violating another male requirement: being stoic and "taking it like a man."

Sexual aggression is also present between women. Interestingly, lesbians report instances of physically or mentally coercive sex more often than gay males do. In one study, 31 percent of lesbians and 12 percent of gay men reported forced sexual encounters (Waterman, Dawson, and Bologna 1989). Researchers tend to conclude that this difference has to do with what men or women define as aggressive rather than how much actual violence occurs among lesbians or gay men. Lesbian complaints are likely to include emotional abuse as well as physical abuse. Furthermore, lesbians are more likely to be sensitized to sexual coercion and more readily identify a range of behaviors as coercive, whereas gay men are more likely to see coercion as fair play. These gendered patterns of complaint provide insight into how much more women, compared to men, are likely to be alert to aggression. As women, lesbians may be more sensitive to power inequities than gay men, because women in general tend to have less power and therefore have more experience in recognizing and attempting to rectify differences in power.

The most chilling kind of coercive sex involves underage children. Again, a gender difference exists: Men are far more likely than women to see prepubescent boys or girls as sex objects. Although instances of female-perpetrated incest and child molestation occur, the offender is a man far more often (occasionally with a woman's compliance). In the United States, estimates of the prevalence of child sexual abuse range from 10 percent to 30 percent of all girls and from 2 percent to 9 percent of all boys (Finkelhor 1984).

The biological interpretation of the gender difference in child abuse requires belief that men, more than women, naturally have greater sexual desire and may have genetic propensities to molest. Social scientists have observed, however, that men are more likely to abuse children whom they did not take care of when the children were infants (Finkelhor 1984). The experience of caring for infants and small children seems to reduce the likelihood that men or women will subsequently view those children as sex objects. Symbolic interactions would explain that the caretaker status gets reinforced through the act of caring. Thus, we think that the fact that infant care is persistently relegated almost exclusively to women helps to account for the gender difference. The social organization of child care creates a location for women to connect with children more than for men.

Consequences for the child victims of sex abuse include adult depression, substance abuse, sexual problems, and a risk of being a victim or perpetrator of intimate violence as an adult. Furthermore, history of childhood sexual abuse can have consequences for adult sexuality, although those who have been sexually abused do not necessarily have sexual problems in adulthood (many victims do not). Because girls are more likely to be victims of child sexual abuse, adult women are more likely to carry the physical and emotional scars into their experience of adult sexuality. Thus, women more than men may have complex sexual inhibitions and ambivalent or negative feelings about sex because of early coerced sexual encounters with peers or manipulative older men. However, because men are expected to be invulnerable, boys molested in childhood also sometimes carry severe scars from the humiliation, shame, and secrecy.

Some scholars have hypothesized that the masculine propensity to rape is natural, part of the inborn male drive to dominate (e.g., Brownmiller, *Against Our Will: Men, Women and Rape,* 1981). Radical theorists, including antipornography activist Andrea Dworkin (*Woman Hating: A Radical Look at Sexuality,* 1991), have suggested that sexual penetration is always a form of rape, and thus rape is an extension of "normal" male sexuality. Some commentators argue that pornography is evidence of men's proclivity to reduce women to sexual objects. For example, law professor and activist Catherine MacKinnon (1987) states that pornography represents the theory, and rape in effect represents the practice of the misogynistic sexuality that animates men in patriarchal societies.

Despite ample evidence that men far more than women engage in aggressive sexual behavior, including rape, there are important distinctions. First, most men do not rape, including in our own society. Second, in some societies rape is very rare (such as Polynesia). Rape itself may be a feature of certain cultures, through the way one-on-one interactions are organized and through the social structure of power relations. Some argue that patriarchal societies, in which men maintain greater power and privilege than women, create an environment that supports rape. Indeed, a study of domestic violence indicates that U.S. states with more patriarchal laws (i.e., laws giving men more rights and more freedom than women) have higher rates of wife assault (Dutton 1988). In societies where men and women have the most vastly different statuses (legally not equal and sequestered from one another, or in other words, completely patriarchal), one would expect to find more rape. In fact, some cross-cultural evidence shows that rape is a consequence of sexual repression, especially in societies where women are held in contempt (see Hatfield and Rapson 1996). The more egalitarian and integrated the society, the less rape. The different rates of rape in different cultures and fluctuating rates of rape over time in the same culture suggest that society, not nature, influences men's proclivity to rape.

None of these hypotheses, however, diminishes the fact that women rarely rape. For starters, they are not physically designed to force sex. On the other hand, now that sexual harassment laws are being applied to men and women, it has become evident that women who have power sometimes pressure male co-workers or subordinates for sex (McCormick 1994). Many fewer women than men commit sexual harassment; however, there are also far fewer women than men bosses. Furthermore, the norms that cast men as sexual predators make it more likely that a man approached by a woman will be compliant; why would a man ever feel pressured into sex when he is supposed to be always ready for sex? Although female sexual aggression seems to be less lethal than males' (i.e., not nearly so likely to be linked to homicide or brutality), the ability to force someone to have sex may have less to do with whether one is male or female than with what socially is deemed a person's sexual prerogative. Such coercion can be devastating to men and women victims alike.

Sexual harassment, then, has to do with enforcing a man's desires in a manner that confirms traditional, gendered statuses. If women had inherited a legacy of sexual privilege, would their rates of sexual harassment equal men's? Alternatively, would men's rates of sexual harassment and other aggressions eventually equal women's? Until men and women experience similar opportunity to harass or victimize, the jury on the capacity to harass remains out. In this era, women continue to be the victims rather than the perpetrators of sexual harassment and sexual violence.

Conclusion

In this chapter we asked, is sex different for men and women? Empirically, the data suggest that on average, yes, it is. As we have observed, norms of behavior direct men and women toward different sexual behavior on the extremes of the continuum. We've also demonstrated that, above all, men and women want to have sex within relationships. That is, when it comes to intimacy, men and women are much more similar than they are different.

Historically, sexuality has changed enough so that we can document the plasticity of trends in gendered sexual differences. Recent data provide overlapping images of men's and women's sexuality. In the end, sexuality takes diverse forms—not merely male and female, heterosexual or homosexual. The configuration of these categories helps to sustain social and sexual control—the normative categories pull for conformity. But observations show sexual diversity, or a "continuum of sexuality." When we describe norms of sexual behavior, or a sexual script that people tend to follow, remember that social norms are simply the high point on a broadly distributed bell curve. Not only do different groups tend to overlap in the distribution of variables, including sexual variables, but as the wide spread of the bell curve suggests, there is great variety within groups.

How do the norms for men's and women's sexuality and the variety surrounding these norms influence people as they begin to be sexual? In the next chapter, we examine the historical and current trends and varieties of sexuality in noncommitted relationships.

CHAPTER 3

Uncommitted Sexual Relationships

In the movie *The Last Seduction* (1994), Wendy Kroy (played by Linda Fiorentino) flirts with a man in a small-town country bar in upstate New York. Wendy, who is on the run from her husband so that she can keep all the money they had stolen together in New York City, seduces a local and leads him to the parking lot, where she has intercourse with him up against a chain-link fence. The man is stupefied when she doesn't want a relationship with him. Later in the movie the man becomes her regular sex partner.

In *Thelma & Louise* (1991), Thelma (played by Geena Davis) flirts with a man on the dance floor at a local bar (much like the one in *The Last Seduction*) and leads him to the parking lot. After they kiss a while, the man demands sexual intercourse. When Thelma protests, he attempts to force himself on her. Thelma's friend Louise (played by Susan Sarandon) discovers the rape in progress in the parking lot and pulls a revolver on the man. When he insults Louise and moves toward her menacingly, she shoots him.

Both *Thelma & Louise* and *The Last Seduction* feature scenes of sex in a bar parking lot. Although both movies highlight sexual freedom outside of marriage (as well as, in the case of *Thelma & Louise*, some terrifying, violent consequences of sexual liberty gone awry), the scenes differ in their meaning because of the variation of a single, crucial factor: the gender of the pursuers and the pursued. In *Thelma & Louise*, a man is the sexual aggressor, and a woman is nearly forced to have intercourse with the man she was flirting with until her friend saves her. In *The Last Seduction*, a woman is the sexual aggressor.

In *Thelma & Louise*, a woman becomes temporarily victimized. Thelma flirts and dances close for the fun of it; the man views her familiarity as permission to have intercourse, but he is fatally mistaken.

71

In *The Last Seduction*, a man is baffled and humiliated by the fact that a woman wants to use him sexually but not emotionally. These painful results occur because, in this contemporary era of considerable sexual autonomy, people are confused about the rules for sexuality outside of marriage. Certainly, the norms that were in place as recently as the 1950s are no longer completely relevant.

In this chapter, we examine the persistent differences between men's and women's prerogatives and responses to sexuality without commitment. We review their origins and prevalence across cultures. Then we take a look at single sex under the microscope. The questions are: How does gender influence the experience of uncommitted sex? How does uncommitted sex influence the experience of gender? Who or what is doing the controlling? Who, if anyone, is exempt from control? And who benefits from this control? Above all, we wonder why and how sex persists in being gendered among people outside the protocols of marriage and other long-term committed relationships.

The Control of Sexuality: Over Time and Across Space

Most societies are not organized to help people have a good sex life. Sex drives are not extolled and encouraged by governments. But governments are certainly not disinterested parties. They are concerned with fertility rates, reproduction, marriage, and divorce. Nations benefit from predictable, orderly reproduction, so that they will have people to staff armies, to work in factories, and to raise the next generation to be similarly socially productive. Furthermore, the only ways most governments can afford to run a society are if parents assume the responsibility to raise children to become productive citizens and if families are organized to pass wealth from one generation to another. So it is not surprising that most societies make rules and regulations about sex that limit or even punish births outside of wedlock and prevent young people from marrying before they are capable of earning a living.

The control of sexuality takes many forms. Sweden and Saudi Arabia, for example, are remarkable contrasts in sexual control. Sweden, a sexually liberal country, has a long history of nonmarital sexuality, cohabitation, comprehensive sex education, and social services that assist parents with the costs of child rearing. Sweden also has a low birth rate and, like other Scandinavian countries, a very low teenage birth rate. In contrast, ultraconservative countries like Saudi Arabia and other religious fundamentalist nations believe that sex outside of marriage must be severely punished. A premarital sexual liaison constitutes a crime against family and state. It is a disruption in property relations and a crime against God.

Given the consequences some societies impose to keep people in line, one might conclude that premarital sex happens only in societies where the social sanctions for premarital births are minimal. Ironically, however, countries with more liberal views of sexuality tend to have lower birth rates (Jones et al. 1985). Despite their liberal sexual climate, these countries have relatively few unwanted pregnancies because of extensive, early public education regarding sex and contraception and a strong social welfare system. As we noted in Chapter 1, there is good reason to believe that education is more effective than coercion for limiting unwanted reproduction.

Whether liberal or conservative, governments have a strong influence over the way sex lives are conducted. But sex isn't determined solely by macrolevel institutions like governments. Individual desire—in all of the variety we described in Chapter 1—makes the sexual playing field more complex. Thus, even where severe sanctions are in place against nonmarital sexuality, the power of the flesh is awesome. Even in the most conservative societies, efforts to police sexuality rarely succeed completely. The tight controls may themselves carry the seeds of their own destruction. Strict rules over sexuality can fuel curiosity as well as fear. A scarce resource is a tempting one. Once young people have the ability to have sex, some of them will pursue their desires no matter what the personal cost.

Politicians and religious leaders know—even as they implore, threaten, lecture, and badger the unmarried to remain celibate until marriage—that they will not be completely successful. They know that people will find a way to have sex. In general, the more rigid the sexual code, the earlier young people are betrothed. Leaders would rather marry off their young than execute them for sexual transgressions or provide them with contraceptives. Conversely, where people generally marry later, teen pregnancy is lower (Jones et al. 1985). This outcome is explained mostly by contraception's availability rather than by national differences in the level of passion among the young.

Cultures do not differ solely in the way they punish people who violate the rules. Although nearly all societies seek to control the sexuality of unmarried women, they do so in different ways. In some countries, the concern for sexual control reaches obsessive proportions and uses the authority of religion. For example, many Arab and African

Islamic countries have a policy known as **purdah**: keeping women (unmarried and married) in isolation from men and strangers. Walk down a street in Northern African countries such as Morocco or Tunisia, and you will see the fine wooden bars or lattice work on windows that allow the person inside to look out but prevent the outsider from looking in. These bars are on the women's quarters in private homes. Outside, women walk around in long, dark drapes of cloth (known as **chador**) from their heads to their toes preventing others from seeing even the eyes. Women usually go out only in the company of their husband or mother-in-law. These practices reflect the nearly complete subordination of women in economic and other nonsexual domains. This subordination is justified by beliefs about sexuality. Women in such societies are too tempting, it is thought, to be exposed or empowered. Women are not merely controlled in sexual matters, they are defined by sexual matters.

The control of women and their sexuality usually corresponds with women's status, power, and civil rights in a given society. In strictly patriarchal countries, where women are second-class citizens, sexuality is tightly controlled. Furthermore, female sexuality is more guarded in societies where family name and reputation is a key to power. The behavior of one member of a family reflects badly on all, and wealth and land are transferred through family lines. Under such conditions, 100 percent "respectability" and 100 percent confidence of paternity is considered essential, and it leads to intense monitoring of women's sexual lives. Although such conservatism tends to be couched in terms of "natural" or God-given differences between men and women, biology doesn't drive the social system. If it did, the sexual rules for men and women would be the same in different times and places regardless of the social agenda of the government and the society.

Sociologist William Goode (1969) studied the extent to which the inheritability of property predicts the prevalence of love-based or arranged marriages in a society. He looked at many different societies and categorized them in terms of how many social patterns supported the familial transfer of wealth. Not surprisingly, his research supported the idea that love is the basis for pairing and marriage only where families have nothing at stake—no land, no prestige, no political power. When family wealth is influenced by marriage choices, love and sex are controlled by older generations, and women are subjected to higher levels of patriarchal surveillance. In general, modern, individualistic notions of sexual freedom and privacy are rare in religiously based societies, such as many Arab countries. Still, even in many Muslim Arab countries the strict restrictions on women's activities have been challenged.

Historical Change in the United States

The drive for sexual freedom in the United States started earlier than most people think. The sexual revolution is often associated with the late 1960s, but changes in premarital sexual attitudes and behaviors started in the seventeenth century in Europe and the United States. Historian Edward Shorter (1975) argues that as small European communities became less isolated, families exerted less control, as did local community, social sanctions, or actual laws. As urban centers flourished, people sought alternatives to the traditional ways of smaller, more rural communities. This period also saw a rise in individualism. With the age of Enlightenment and the rise of capitalism, people were encouraged to think in terms of their individual futures rather than family futures. Shorter believes the reduction in community control led more people to express their feelings and follow their hearts. During this period, women and men were encouraged to respond to sentiment. In eighteenth-century novels, literary critics observe, the same story recurs: A woman, if she is middle or upper class, is weakened by love, fainting at thoughts of the man she loves, or even a letter from him. A man (also with elevated social status) tends to be emboldened by love, even if boldness leads to tragic outcomes, such as losing a duel (Todd 1986).

Historically and today, the United States has been the most marriage-prone society in the Western world. Still, the United States has gone through almost every ideological position on sexuality outside of marriage since the precolonial era. Although the changes have not always been toward greater sexual autonomy, each generation has in general conceded a more liberal stance toward sexuality. Recall the community moralists, including the New England Puritans of the seventeenth and early eighteenth centuries, who might assign a woman a "scarlet letter" should she engage in nonmarital sexual relations. When the church lost authority toward the end of the eighteenth century, legal institutions continued to impose sanctions against sexual nonconformists (D'Emilio and Freedman 1988). Over time, however, the United States has backed away from most legal interventions that involve sex between consenting adults in deference to civil rights, especially the right to privacy. The notable exceptions, which we discuss below, are in cases of interracial or same-sex liaisons.

Despite a nearly worldwide preference for marriage as the proper institution for sex and the production of children, sanctions against nonmarital sexualities are not imposed equally. Furthermore, societies that outlaw nonmarital sexuality impose different penalties for men and women. In general, the punishments for female sexual transgressions are swifter, stronger, and more public than punishment for male (hetero)sexual transgression. For example, in the United States, a high school boy who impregnates a girl is rarely sanctioned and may not even have been identified. But girls who are pregnant and unmarried have been kept out of public institutions such as schools. This treatment may vary further depending on the race, class, and age of the girls involved. Upper-class, younger unmarried women who get pregnant may be pitied more than blamed, and their privacy may be respected more than the privacy of poorer women. Premarital pregnancy among the poor, particularly African Americans, may even be seen as unavoidable, but it is more shameful among middle-class African Americans. Religious families may still force an abrupt marriage.

Perhaps the sexual and romantic latitude of young people in the United States is a consequence of the less-well-defined class structure in this society than in Europe. In addition, less land or wealth has been passed on through generations in this country than in European and Middle Eastern countries, and therefore little is at stake if the lineage becomes unclear, except for the children of very rich families. Predictably, dating in the United States is more often controlled in the upper classes than in the lower classes. For example, upper-class families still have "coming out" or debutante parties when young women make their "formal entrance into society"—that is, into the society of upper-class men who are eligible for marriage. However, cohabitation has been rising among all classes in the United States since the late 1960s. Cohabitation originated in lower classes (Bumpass, Sweet, and Cherlin 1989) where property rights based on marriage are less relevant. Of course, children of the upper class cohabit these days, too, but parents resist it, especially if the cohabiting partner is the "wrong" person from the "wrong" class.

Despite the long history in this country of reducing control over who becomes emotionally and sexually attached, the exceptions are notable. As recently as 1967, states outlawed interracial marriage through **antimiscegenation** laws (literally, laws against mixing genes). Antimiscegenation laws, a legacy of slavery and racism, were instituted to prevent whites from marrying blacks and other racial minorities or even from "mixing" sexually.

The selective enforcement of antimiscegenation laws shows how sinister sexual laws tend to be: Countless white men raped black women at will during and after slavery. During the late nineteenth century, while white middle-class women were assigned the virtues of purity, chastity, and honor, white men consigned some black women to near sexual slavery. This crime was rarely punished. Only when a white man expressed love for a black woman would other men enforce the status quo by persecuting the white man. Love matches between whites and minorities were violently punished, especially when the romance was between a black man and a white woman. During slavery and through the first half of the twentieth century, a black man could be hanged for looking at a white woman in what was perceived as a lascivious or provocative way. Thousands of lynchings of black men in the early part of the twentieth century were caused by white racist sexual paranoia. Lynchings (or mob hangings) were rationalized as a defense of white women's sexual purity and chastity (D'Emilio and Freedman 1988). White paranoia was buttressed by a **sexual double standard**: sexual privilege for white men and sexual surveillance for men of color. Indeed, it was a combined racial and sexual double standard. In addition, white women were less available and more protected than black women, meaning white women were less vulnerable to sexual aggression.

The Shifting Double Standard

Even during racist sexual backlash in the South and other regions of the United States, the twentieth-century trajectory in the United States and western Europe has been a slow but sure (albeit fluctuating) liberalization of sexual norms and behavior. One important phase in the process was the formal dating ritual, an innovation in the 1920s that lasted through the 1950s. Dating teens obtained playful, independent experience with intimacy, often including kissing and touching but rarely including intercourse. Boys were initiators: They called girls for dates. But the couple negotiated plans and intimacy. By the last quarter of the twentieth century, however, formal dating rituals were tremendously eroded along with the concept of women's virginity before marriage.

Changing courtship patterns allow social scientists to observe the evolution of the gendered status of sexuality. Note the trends in Figure

FIGURE 3.1

Trends in U.S. Sexual Experience by Age Cohort

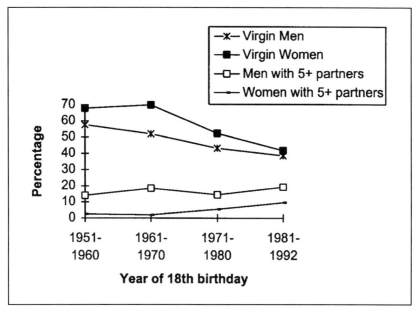

Source: Data from Laumánn, Michael, and Gagnon (1994).

3.1, which shows the percentage of men and women in different cohorts (generations) with either no sexual partners before the age of 18 or with five or more sexual partners before the age of 18 (the highest category of sexual experience in the National Health and Social Life Survey [NHSLS]; Laumann, Michael, and Gagnon 1994). Men and women born in the most recent years have nearly the same patterns of abstaining from sexual experience. Among those with high levels of sexual experience, however, the pattern is a little different. The youngest women were almost four times as sexually experienced at 18 as the oldest women in the chart. In contrast, the youngest men had similar sexual experiences as the oldest men in the chart. Although women's rate of change has been greater than men's rate of change, in the youngest cohort about twice as many men as women are in the most sexually experienced section (Laumann et al. 1994:328). Apparently, the double standard still exists even though it is diminishing.

In the middle years of the twentieth century—between the first wave of feminist activity aimed at women's suffrage and the second wave begun in the late 1960s—striking and sometimes pathetic stories of the sexual double standard were played out. For boys and young men to prove their virility, they were encouraged to test their potency as early into puberty as possible. Girls, on the other hand, were admonished to maintain virginity and "save it for marriage." Of course, this sexual double standard presented a dilemma because it constricted the pool of available partners for boys. One adaptation was that chaste girls would be labeled "good" and girls who followed masculine, rather than feminine, codes of sexuality were labeled "bad." Girls who experimented with sex were considered "loose" and "easy." Anne Roiphe, a feminist activist in the 1970s who came of age during the 1950s, explains the impossibility of women's positions: The men they were dating were simultaneously cast as sexual predators, whom they had to fight off, and as protectors, whom they needed for protection from other men (Friedan et al. 1996).

Sexual attitudes have been inconsistent with sexual behavior for much of the century. The famous Kinsey studies documented the increasingly sexually liberal behavior of people who went to work in the 1920s and 1930s. Kinsey, a zoologist by training, interviewed hundreds of men and women about their sexual experiences and practices. Kinsey's findings shocked much of the public in 1948, when his *Sexual Behavior in the Human Male* (Kinsey, Pomeroy, and Martin 1948) reported that 25 percent of boys had experienced sexual intercourse by age 14. In 1953, *Sexuality in the Human Female* (Kinsey et al. 1953) reported more sexual experience among women than anyone was letting on or wanted to hear. The "good girl," groused alarmists of the day, was becoming an endangered species. Even though most of the so-called experienced women had had only one premarital lover—usually the man they married—the convention of sex within marriage had been shown to be a rule on paper, not in practice. Kinsey's research—and the response to it—suggested that sexual behavior was more advanced than sexual attitudes in the early 1950s. Although Kinsey's report undoubtedly exaggerated or distorted some sexual practices and frequencies, many of his conclusions regarding sexual trends have since been confirmed by better designed studies.

The 1960s and the Sexual Revolution

The rate of sexual change slowed during the more conservative 1950s and into the 1960s. It wasn't until the last years of the 1960s that an undercurrent of sexual change became an explicit part of the cultural landscape. In the mid-1960s, oral contraceptives—known as the Pill—

became available. Although it was extremely difficult for unmarried women to obtain the Pill, younger generations' appetite for experimentation accelerated with its availability. The commentators on the 1960s labeled the ensuing changes the **sexual revolution.** The revolutionary manifesto challenged the idea that sex was respectable only in marriage and that sex was vastly different for men than for women.

During this era, feminists examined how sexual ideals, including virginity, were used to control women's sexual freedom. Feminists questioned a central tenet of the era: that marriage was good for women. Betty Friedan, who wrote about marriage (as experienced mostly by white middle-class women) in *The Feminine Mystique* (1963), described the "problem that has no name": which is simply the fact that American women are kept from gaining their full human capacities. She called for a halt to early marriage and the consignment of women to housewifery. During this era, age at first marriage began to increase, and the practice of cohabitation also began to rise. Feminists also challenged the notions that women need men to be sexually satisfied and that sexual experience is incompatible with a woman's marriageability or worthiness to a man.

Central to "women's liberation," as the feminist movement was first called, was the right for women to control their own bodies sexually and reproductively, both in and out of marriage. Women claimed the right to withhold (or give) sexual consent without fear of rape or stigma.

Reproductive rights became a central issue during this time. Women organized politically and in 1973 were responsible for creating the climate in which the Supreme Court would legalize abortion for the first time in the twentieth century, in the well-known *Roe v. Wade* decision. (Abortion was legal until the late nineteenth century, when the American Medical Association in conjunction with women activists concerned with protecting the purity of women helped make it illegal.) Nevertheless, the liberalization of abortion policy created a new arena of disappointment. Many women found themselves seeking abortion in isolation from the men who had been equally responsible in causing the pregnancy. Feminist books of the period, such as Marilyn French's *The Women's Room* (1977), are filled with recrimination and reanalysis of gender and power relations.

As feminism evolved, so did different perspectives on a feminist agenda. In particular, the concerns of women of color and lesbians were not always included in the mainstream feminist agenda. For example, when it was revealed that government-funded family-planning clinics were enforcing sterilization among young, poor women of color, mainstream, white feminists were slow to respond. Mainstream, white, middle-class feminism focused on access to abortion, but for poor women and women of color, the right of a woman to control her body also involved the right to reproduce. When conservatives tried to discredit the feminist movement by accusing feminists of being lesbians, heterosexual, mainstream feminists downplayed lesbian issues, leaders, and constituents (D'Emilio and Freedman 1988). Some feminist leaders sought to expel lesbians from feminist organizations. Gay and lesbian liberation movements fought back, and in the 1970s the National Organization of Women finally included lesbian rights in its list of goals.

In hindsight, the sexual revolution was obviously not completely revolutionary—especially for women. Many young women entered the period seeking sexual and personal freedom, only to discover that even men of the far left weren't particularly feminist. For example, at a conference of the Students for a Democratic Society in 1965, a feminist speaker was heckled with shouts of "She just needs a good screw." Women wanted sexual liberation to signify equality in relationships, but men often took it as an opening for sexual opportunism. Some men, who resented equality, used sexual liberation to be crude and to degrade women.

As much as people tried, men and women were not readily able to change entrenched attitudes toward sex and romance. Men continued to interpret women's behavior through the traditional seduction scripts they had learned as youths. Young adults in the 1960s and 1970s had been raised with traditional ideas about women's chastity and "respectability." Studies of the period showed that even among college students, the most liberal population at the time, people were sharply divided between egalitarianism and the sexual double standard that condoned nonmarital sexuality for men but abstinence for women (Reiss 1967). Such mismatched views created resentment and emotional pain for men and women. Sex in the 1970s was more ambiguous, attached fewer responsibilities, and generated less understanding and sympathy between the men and women participating. Although only a few may have actually participated in breaking sexual norms and using sex recreationally, everybody who was dating had to struggle with the atmosphere of hostility toward women and the confused expectations of that period.

The disappointments of the sexual revolution are not the complete picture, however. The sexual revolution was an era of discovery. Sex became more fun for more people than ever before. Feminists wrote treatises on how women's bodies worked, how to have orgasms, and how to masturbate. Women felt freer to masturbate and enjoy sex outside of marriage or even love. Some books on these topics had a worldwide impact. *The Hite Report: A Nationwide Study of Female Sexuality,* by Shere Hite (1976), and *My Secret Garden* by Nancy Friday (1973), failed as research but succeeded as consciousness-raising tools for men and women. Hite described hundreds of experiences and desires. Friday wrote a no-holds-barred account of women's diverse sexual fantasies. The detailed sexual stories signified that women could be just as sexual as men. The book explained how and when women wanted to be touched, made love to, or lusted after. Men and women gained information about what they were doing wrong sexually and what they were doing right.

The sexual revolution was different for men than for women, however. For men, the emergence and prominence of *Playboy* magazine and the "playboy image" provided a fantasy world, an opportunity to be perpetual adolescents looking for easy action. *Rabbit Run* (1960) by John Updike typifies the sexual license men were discovering. In *Rabbit Run,* a working-class man drops out of his family to discover libertine sex, leaving wife, children, and then his new lover behind as he focuses on his gratification and restlessness. In contrast, the sexual revolution for women was about sexual abandon, not Updike-style abandonment.

Reams of books followed, some of which are still in print today, that explored the possibilities of heterosexual and, for the first time for popular audiences, gay and lesbian sexuality. In short, the years between 1960 and the mid-1970s were a chaotic period in which sex was extolled, explained, and seemed to be done much more than ever in the past. But the politics of intimacy still gave men more power in relationships than women. And intimate relationships occurred in a context of economic imbalance: Men continued to hold more financial resources, more political clout, and more social freedom than women. These sustained imbalances made men and women increasingly angry with each other.

Nevertheless, by the end of the 1970s, attitudes regarding premarital sexuality had substantially changed. Virginity was no longer the badge of honor for women that it had been; loss of virginity before marriage became expected rather than mourned. During the 1980s, rates of nonvirginity among unmarried women began to equal those of unmarried men (Sexuality Information and Education Council of the United States

[SIECUS] 1995). Age at first intercourse has steadily decreased for both men and women. Men and women have different perceptions of sexual encounters, but their agendas for sex outside of marriage have become increasingly similar. Today, at least in Western countries, sex in the context of affection is considered legitimate for both men and women in all but the most conservative of subcultures (Laumann et al. 1994).

Trends in sexual change vary by race and by class, however, although the trends are moving in the same direction. For example, between 1971 and 1976 the percentage change in the number of 18-year-old women who had had nonmarital intercourse was 17 percent among both African American and white women. But the rates in 1971 were higher for African American women than white women. Whereas the rate for whites moved from 39 percent to 56 percent, for African American women the rate moved from 62 percent to 79 percent (Modell 1989:306). The divergence has been explained by some (e.g., Guttentag and Secord 1983) as related to **sex ratios.** A sex ratio is the proportion of men to women in a given population. If the population is half male, half female, then the sex ratio is one. If the ratio becomes greater than one or declines to less than one, so the theory goes, the way men and women interact economically as well as romantically will change. (In Chapter 4, on sex and marriage, we will return to this concept.) The proportion of eligible white men to white women has remained much more stable than the proportion of eligible black men to black women over the past several decades. Thus, although changes in sexuality have generally been in the same direction for whites and blacks, the base rates of sexual experience have been different, reflecting the different sociological reality that whites and blacks tend to experience.

Regarding class and cohabitation, the trends have been similar among all subgroups, although the experience has been different. When nonmarital cohabitation began to increase in the 1970s, most people considered it a trend that emerged from college campuses, among middle-class and upper-class youth. Instead, the trend began in lower and working classes and diffused up the class ladder (Bumpass et al. 1989).

Since the 1960s, individuals have increasingly claimed the right to make choices about their sexuality. The expansion of individualism and personal autonomy in the sexual realm accompanied Vietnam War protests and abortion rights protests as well. Many observers have written that the shift to personal autonomy from tradition, obligation, and respect for one's parents was the most critical change in human relations to have happened during this period (e.g., as reported in Reiss 1980:188).

Although the sexual revolution is the main story of our recent past, it is not the only story. U.S. society was not uniform in the shift toward personal choice. This transition was resisted by conservative religious communities, Christian colleges, and church groups. In these environments, personal autonomy is subsumed by obligation to God, religious hierarchy, family, and country. Such conservative movements as the Campus Crusade for Christ exhort young adults to defer sex until after marriage; some listen. Organized religion in the 1990s has again become very strong (Stark 1996). Today, about 16 percent of men and 20 percent of women still remain virgins until marriage (Laumann et al. 1994:503).

The Sexual Climate in the 1970s and 1980s

The story of the 1970s and 1980s is primarily a change in the sexual control of women. Somewhat less well examined, however, is the lack of commensurate change in men's sexuality. The changes for women are the consequence of three major social forces: technological, demographic, and sociological. However, these forces were hampered by overt efforts to stall the convergence of men's and women's sexual patterns.

The **technological** variable is birth control. Those born since 1962 might have trouble imagining how much their sexual behavior is influenced by easy access to birth control outside of parental or medical supervision. Birth control—through condoms, withdrawal, abortion, or folk remedies—has been around for centuries. However, the fact that women could take charge of birth control with much greater reliability, especially with the Pill and the IUD (an intrauterine contraceptive device that is inserted for long periods of time), altered their sexual behavior. Both methods of birth control allow sexual intercourse with no special preparation. Women using the Pill or an IUD are "ever ready" and almost always safe from pregnancy. Safety from pregnancy and sexual spontaneity removed many traditional anxieties that had inhibited sex before the 1960s. The Pill was a green light for sex until the recognition of AIDS in the mid-1980s.

But birth control became women's work and changed women's experience of sex much more than men's experience. The shift from condoms used by men to birth control that required female agency and responsibility altered both women's approach to sex and men's attitudes toward women as sexual partners. Women have always had to be concerned about birth control, but the Pill multiplied that responsibility. Women have always borne the burden of unwanted pregnancy, but in previous eras, the men involved in an unwanted pregnancy sometimes took some responsibility. In the era of high-tech birth control, men were liberated from even their tenuous tie to unwanted pregnancy or contraception.

How did this technological change influence sex? Women, like men, were at greater liberty to have sex outside of commitment, but only men were free from any responsibility. This had the effect of conferring additional power on men in sexual relationships, because they could feel less responsibility for unintended pregnancies. Furthermore, the fact that women held more responsibility for birth control and reproductive consequences of sexuality made it easy for the reproductive rights and politics to be cast primarily as a women's issue rather than a human issue.

The second force that changed the sexual world was **demographics.** The huge cohort of people born during the baby boom (between 1945 and 1962), especially those in the vanguard, grew up in a benign economic climate, with enormous opportunity. Many of these children were the recipients of their parents' good fortune in the best economic climate the United States had ever experienced. These first baby boomers (now in their 40s and early 50s) experimented more with sex. The double standard was still very familiar, but it had lost its potency. One reason was that baby boomers had so many partners to choose from. The very size of their cohort helped baby boom women and men feel they need not hurry; they had no need to get married. Fewer people were living in small towns, and when they went to college—in greater numbers than ever before—it was like kids let loose in a candy shop!

College also had an impact. Not only were more young people in college in absolute terms, but the likelihood that someone would attend college increased, especially for women. The longer people stayed in college and out of the marriage pool, the longer the temptation to have nonmarital sex. So just by staying in college for two or four years, young people were much more likely than before to lose their virginity. Furthermore, more women obtained advanced degrees, and they were likely to use these degrees in the workplace before settling down to have a family. Interestingly, the more education a woman had, the later she was likely to marry, but the reverse has been true for men. Thus, women of this era were adding on new roles: intellectual, professional, financial. Men, on the other hand, had little incentive to add to their repertoire the domestic obligations traditionally fulfilled by women, and in general, they didn't.

In another break with tradition, few of these young people inherited family farms or family businesses, which were losing their dominant place in the economy. Some middle- and upper-middle-class youth rejected the "safe" course of traditional jobs like accounting and engineering that they felt their parents had wrongly chosen to the detriment of "personal growth" and freedom. With neither the advantage nor burden of family economic obligations, young people started to enjoy life. As the 1970s ran into the 1980s, a growing proportion of young men and women in their 20s stayed unmarried and delayed childbearing. Those who did marry during this turbulent time were caught between traditionalism, the new promise of self-determination, and feminist critiques of marriage.

These young people, who criticized old values of loyalty and traditionalism and duty, were predictably hard on their own relationships. Although the divorce rate in the United States had been increasing steadily since the late nineteenth century, the divorce rate took a sharp upward turn in this period (Cherlin 1992). Between 1960 and 1980, the divorce rate increased by about 250 percent. Two-thirds of all young people were married by age 24 in 1960, but that percentage was reversed by the 1980s: two-thirds of 24-year-olds were single, never married, or already divorced (Cherlin 1992).

As the baby boomers aged, the marriage market became more troublesome. Women tend to partner with men several years older, but the pre-boom generation had fewer men for baby boom women to choose from, and the pre-boom men had married earlier than those in the following generation. Baby boom women who delayed marriage in favor of education and work or whose first marriage didn't work out came back into the marriage market and found it rather sparse. Although the problems of the marriage market were vastly overestimated by the media in the 1980s, demographic realities still constrained women's dating options. Some women felt cheated and misled. They wanted experimentation, a career, and the freedom to leave a bad marriage and not lose out on finding a life companion eventually.

By the mid-1980s, these demographic facts, along with increasing awareness of AIDS, rendered sex a bit less recreational than it had been in the 1970s. The sexual climate was shifting again. The conservative influence of the 1980s, a tighter job market, and a more dangerous disease environment created an atmosphere of caution, even if it didn't reverse sexual trends. The baby boom generation started getting older, settling down, producing children, and drifting toward greater conservatism. Furthermore, women who had attended college acquired progressive feminist ideas, but many women and men who had not gone to college or embraced progressive ideas tended to hold on to more traditional sexual attitudes. Although progressive political ideas were prominent in the 1960s and 1970s, this movement planted the seeds of a backlash among people who were not sexually or otherwise liberated. And although some sectors of the baby boomers remained politically liberal, younger generations reaching adulthood in the 1980s and 1990s appear to be more conservative.

The third influence on women's changing sexuality has been the **sociological**, cultural context. The growing women's movement located men and women in an uneasy emotional engagement with one another. Men were unsure of where feminism and the sexual revolution were taking them. Some were angry at being attacked and labeled oppressors; some were enthusiastic supporters of women. Still others retreated, confused by the changes happening around them but not to them (Messner 1997). Just when sexuality seemed to be heading in a more liberated direction, it became imbued with intimate politics (or power struggles). Feminist issues like pay equity, abortion, divorce, and equality in the household packed a personal punch. The questions were hard to answer: What constitutes equality in the home? Who has the right to abortion? Should marriage be modified, rejected, or not changed at all? Should women be treated as sexually vulnerable or as equal sexual players, no holds barred? Should men take more responsibility for sexual encounters?

Heated rhetoric flew back and forth. Feminists divided regarding the costs and benefits of sexual liberty as it had been defined through cultural trends. By the 1980s, many men and women were living with the consequences of the positions they had taken earlier. Some were thrilled with the new personal latitude that the women's movement had given both men and women. Others had regrets.

Thus, three social forces—dramatic shifts in birth control technology, the demographics of the baby boom generation, and the cultural diffusion and diversification of feminism—ushered in a novel sexual era, with the promise of gender equality and a corresponding reduction of the double standard in sexuality. But the promise has not been completely fulfilled. Gender persists in being a principal organizing feature of sexuality today. Technological, demographic, and sociological changes ushered in as the baby boom generation came of age changed women more than men. Furthermore, the use of sex and sexuality as a mechanism for social control had not died; it may have been limping a bit, but it had not died.

Frontlash and Backlash in the 1990s and Beyond

By the end of the 1970s, liberal trends in sexual behavior had turned into norms that were solidified in television situation comedies, movies, advertising, and social arrangements like the coeducational dormitories on many college campuses. The "wanton" sexual behavior that became widespread in some groups by the 1980s sent shock waves through the public, just as Kinsey's reports had shocked the public in the 1950s. A conservative, moralistic backlash began to grow. It condemned premarital sex, abortion, gay rights, and women's rights, and it promoted socially conservative themes that have persisted. The rallying cry was around "traditional family values," which enshrined sexual conservatism and traditional gender expectations in the family. In the media, the sexual revolutionaries of the 1960s and 1970s were replaced by a group of resentful citizens who had been relatively silent throughout the preceding era.

The family values movements linked urban decay and violence to the sexual emancipation of women; early sexual experience for men and women; and new family forms such as single-parent families, stepfamilies, same-sex partners, and heterosexual cohabitors (Coltrane 1997). In fact, the family values movements blamed practically all social ills on changing "morality," not on economics or politics.

Americans who had lived under more conservative norms—and who had not been at the center of the sexual revolution—were discombobulated and, at times, disgusted, by the new, increasingly acceptable forms of adult social arrangements. They assumed that traditional norms had characterized the majority of U.S. households during the baby boom era of the 1950s. Ironically, however, the stay-at-home mom and breadwinning dad touted by family values activists have never predominated in the United States, as Coontz explains in *The Way We Never Were: American Families and the Nostalgia Trap* (1992). By the late 1980s, fewer than 10 percent of all U.S. households were "nuclear family" households: stay-at-home mom, employed dad, and a couple of kids.

A particular focus of alarm for family values activists was the spread of abortion services after the 1973 *Roe v. Wade* decision, which legalized abortion during the first and second trimesters of pregnancy. This emphatically feminist and civil libertarian Supreme Court decision infuriated conservatives. It did not matter to them that abortion services were used mostly by married women or that unmarried teens who bore their children rather than abort were highly likely to raise them in poverty. The consequences of enduring an unwanted pregnancy were less important than the fact that traditional morality had been observed. Teenage motherhood was unfortunate, but "immoral youth" deserved to suffer the consequences of their behavior. The child was somehow lost in these righteous pronouncements. For those moralists who considered the child's welfare, the answer was for young unmarried women to give their children up for adoption. The emotional cost to the mother was regrettable but an insignificant cost compared to the terrible implications of premarital sex and abortion from the family values perspective.

The family values movement had a core flaw. The movement sought to sustain tradition and promote gendered sexual behavior. However, it extolled a traditional family form that was becoming rarer and rarer, out of economic necessity as much as feminist progress.

During the 1980s, many people expressed anger about abortion, divorce, premarital sex, and not incidentally, women's defiant rejection of their historical classification as the upholders of purity, family, and motherhood. Despite their lobbying and impassioned rhetoric, however, the sexual habits of Americans continued to become increasingly diverse and permissive. A majority in the United States did not support "family values"; their own lives, or their children's, had changed too much. Individualism, a foundational, constitutional principle in the United States, had deep and strong roots and was hard to trim back or cut down. People may have given lip service to traditional values, but the majority of people followed their hearts, not their ancestors' examples or their church's traditional morality. In fact, parents, churches, schools, and laws had to change to deal with the ways people now mate and marry.

Homosexuality and Bisexuality

It isn't just the sex lives of heterosexuals that are controlled and influenced by culture. Homosexuals and bisexuals are equally, if differently, subject to gendered forms of sexual control and are subject to conduct codes regarding sexuality. Gay men and lesbians have at least avoided the contraception dilemma, unless they are also having sex with the opposite sex. But a major realm of control for gay men and lesbians involves access to marriage. Gays and lesbians are still not allowed to marry and are always considered "singles" by the state, even when couples are in a long-term committed relationship. Marriage, from the perspective of the state, requires a gender difference. (Same-sex marriage will be discussed in Chapter 5.)

Nevertheless, social attitudes toward same-sex relationships have progressed quite a bit. The relationships were tabooed until 30 or so years ago, but same-sex relationships have now become much more visible. They have also, therefore, become more controversial.

Most gay activists date the beginning of the gay political push for recognition and equal rights to the 1969 riot at Stonewall Inn in Greenwich Village. Gay bars, where both uncoupled and coupled gay men (and sometimes lesbians) could meet, were subjected to periodic police raids in the late 1960s. In general, the men would be arrested, humiliated, exposed as gay (and therefore put in danger of losing their jobs), and then let go, only to worry about when the next arbitrary raid might occur. But when the police raided the Stonewall Inn in 1969, customers resisted, and a full-fledged riot erupted. This was the start of an aggressive civil rights movement that changed the way many gay men and lesbians lived their lives. The slow movement of gays and lesbians into mainstream culture since the late 1960s has meant another very clear challenge to traditional gender norms and traditional romantic sexual scripts (D'Emilio and Freedman 1988).

Today, there is less harassment of homosexuals (though such harassment still occurs, and in some geographic areas appears to be increasing), especially in urban communities, and a much wider variety of places that gay people can use for courtship, dating, and sex. However, being a single homosexual is much more difficult than being a single heterosexual. First, adolescents are exposed only to heterosexual social opportunities, especially in traditional organizations like schools, sports, and churches. Heterosexual youth experience public pairing, organized dances, and activities in open groups of unpaired but eligible opposite-sex partners. This process socializes youth into gendered heterosexual norms: Boys can do this, girls can do that. When dating begins, heterosexual youth have many people to confide in, compare notes with, and learn from.

None of this social support is available to gay and lesbian youth, unless they are fortunate enough to be in an environment where a gay culture is visible and where they can be "out" enough (and supported by their parents enough) to be able to participate in it. Moreover, most individuals assume they are heterosexual, just as people tend to think others are heterosexual until otherwise informed. The young person who has disconfirming evidence, such as attraction to a same-sex person or lack of attraction to the other sex, may be confused and resist a homosexual attraction. It may take years of self-examination to embrace an identity that tends to be stigmatized. As a result, many young gay people reach adulthood having dated little or having had only furtive sexual encounters in anonymous places rather than an orderly and approved dating life. Some may marry, hoping that making a commitment or having children will "straighten" them out. Years later, however, these marriages might break up, with much heartbreak all around. Some of these men first enter the gay dating market in their 30s, 40s, or even 50s—unformed in their tastes and in gay social skills.

Homosexual women may have even less same-sex experimentation than men, because our culture discourages women from sexual experimentation. Thus, although lesbianism tends to be less stigmatized than male homosexuality, it is also less sexualized. A woman can have deep emotions for another woman and not recognize sexual attraction for quite a while—perhaps forever. Female friendship is affectionate and physical, which normalizes desires to hug and kiss one another. It is often hard to know who is flirting and who is merely showing deep heterosexual friendship. Lesbians often tell tales of signals misread and friendships gone awry, as a woman who loves women misreads the actions of a woman who merely likes women. Of course, sometimes both women love women, and a love affair begins. Often, however, lesbians have to wait until they get to a big city or a safe environment for lesbians to meet (such as a YWCA lesbian resource center) before they learn about their sexual tastes and desires.

Today, many lesbians and gay men learn more about homosexuality than homosexuals in previous generations, thanks to the books, magazines, and journals that now help connect gay people to a gay community. But even so, being young, single, and gay is a challenge. Some people find each other in high school, become lovers, come out right away, and have parents who support their choices. But this is hardly typical. Even understanding parents are unlikely to support gay dating in the early teen years. More likely, people will try to talk young homosexuals out of their attraction, label it as a passing fad or fancy, or even send them into psychotherapy. Due to such alienation, suicide is more common among gay than straight teens.

This lack of support is particularly true for people who are attracted to both men and women. There is a strong presumption in society that people who are not heterosexual are gay. In fact, such an essentialist assumption is a mirror image to dichotomous ideas about gender. There is little social support for a bisexual, even though quite a few people say that they are, or have been, seriously attracted to both men and women.

Recently, the popular media have "discovered" bisexuality. Kinsey's scale (see Chapter 2) has resurfaced, and the concept has become hotly debated. The Kinsey scale suggests a continuum of sexual attractions. Although bisexuals are defined by some degree of attraction, fantasy, or experience with both sexes, rarely is there the same intensity with both.

The "authenticity" of bisexuality is a position that the majority of the population wishes to deny. Heterosexuals deny it because they are afraid it gives people license to experiment and perhaps fall in love with the same sex—and thereby forsake family life and social approval. Homosexuals tend to deny it because they believe it allows men and women a way of escaping gay identity; a bisexual could always forsake a gay partner and flee to the more comfortable heterosexual world. There is also apprehension that bisexuality might function as a "higher status," thereby undermining gay and lesbian solidarity and political clout. Above all, bisexuality threatens essentialist beliefs in a fixed and unchanging sexuality that is defined by your own gender and the gender of the ones you love.

A *Newsweek* magazine (Leland 1996) cover story on young bisexuals emphasized their rejection of any essentialist positions, whether hetero-sexual or homosexual. The *Newsweek* story noted that a number of young people were aggravating schools and families by denying that they had to limit their romantic interest to one gender. Although no research has confirmed that casual homosexual experimentation is increasing in the young, stories in the popular media indicate greater acceptance among many younger groups for individuals having lovers who are men and women.

When bisexuality is practiced, it truly complicates the dating and sexual scene. It brings up fear of contagion in this day of AIDS, and it intensifies insecurities manufactured by the dating experience. The fear of being dumped for someone else is supplemented by the apprehen-sion that one will be the lesser attraction because she or he is the "lesser" sex. A colleague recounted his experience:

> I fell in love with her in the most complete, hopeless way. We were
> graduate students together; we were pals, colleagues, lovers. She was

the most charismatic person. I knew she had had gay experiences. She never misled me, but I always believed, down deep, that I was too attractive to pass up and to be totally honest, that the heterosexual pull would be greater. But it wasn't. Even while we were living together, she fell in love with one of her professors and moved in with her. They are still together ... I don't think I will love anyone again like I loved her. ... I feel misled by her—and myself.

Bisexuality has been studied less than straight and gay sexualities, and it has much to reveal about gender and sexuality.

Sex Practices Among the Uncommitted

There is a direct relationship between sexual climate and sexual practices. But there isn't a one-to-one correspondence between what people think they are supposed to do and what they end up doing in private. As liberating as passion can be, men and women are remarkably influenced by cultural norms of sexuality. Even the way people remember and report what they have done is influenced by what they think they are supposed to do. In this section, we examine the sexual experiences that single people report.

The Lost Art of Petting

Petting is a 1950s and early 1960s word. It used to be the center of young romance, although intercourse eventually occurred more often than myth suggests. Today, petting is sometimes called "making out," and it involves kissing, touching, feeling, rubbing, and groping.

One of the more remarkable changes from past sexual courtship rituals is that these days people proceed quickly from first kiss to first intercourse. Before the sexual revolution of the 1960s and 1970s—and still among some groups—people talked about getting to "first base" (kissing) before they had a "home run" (intercourse). Sexual permission escalated slowly. People who are in their 50s today rhapsodize about the deliberate pace, as does this woman:

Oh, it was delicious. I remember the thrill of letting his arm hang over my shoulder and slightly, ever so slightly, touch my breast. That went on for weeks. And then I let him touch me "above the waist"—over my sweater of course. Weeks went by, and then I let him touch me under the sweater. That was the big step for months. After a long time, he put his hand up my skirt, and we fought over that for a while until I thought it was OK. It took me the longest time to touch him—either over or under his clothes. We did this for two years before we attempted intercourse—and that was our big graduation present to each other—literally. We did it on the senior prom weekend.[1]

These days, things go faster. Petting is now foreplay. Touching and stimulation occur, but the expectation is that partners are preparing for intercourse. With first intercourse happening at ever-younger ages, there doesn't seem to be time for a sustained period of petting—unless it is happening at ever younger ages, but that is unlikely. Unlike earlier decades, sexual desire is now more genitally focused. In earlier decades, women had been cast as the "gatekeepers," saying "no, no, no" to intercourse. But the elimination of the need to say no made intercourse the main focus of much sexual interaction for women and men alike. This seems to be more of a male vision of sexuality than a female vision, however. Women often say that they love prolonged petting and touching, but men tell of becoming enormously frustrated. Although increasing rates of masturbation among women have diversified women's imaginations, the intercourse-focused version of sex seems to have triumphed. Modern sex therapy has fueled this change by generating sexual norms that glorify erection, penetration, and orgasm.

Women may miss prolonged touching and foreplay, but it is quite possible that men, too, prefer more integrated sexuality that involves sensual, sustained touching, as well as intercourse. However, it remains nonnormative for men to express such leisurely sexual tastes. The gendered sexual scripts that were so powerful before the sexual revolution have a tenacious hold. But old scripts will be cleared away gradually, and individual tastes will emerge and give us a thorough understanding of what constitutes satisfactory and rewarding sexuality for men and women, whether straight, gay, or bisexual.

Heterosexual norms of intercourse-focused sexuality are also the inheritance of gay men and lesbians, but they are often obliged to find personally authentic and rewarding sexuality. Alternatives to intercourse, like slowing down the escalation of sexual acts, may be occurring among gays and lesbians more than heterosexuals. For instance, gay men who are interested in sexual variety but chastened by the danger of contracting HIV have searched for turn-ons that avoid penetration or exchange of bodily fluids. This was required because anal intercourse is likely to transmit the virus (if infected). Public health campaigns emphasizing safer sex have been very successful (although not perfect). Large numbers of gay men have figured out how to sustain arousal and achieve satisfaction through nonpenetrative sex. Petting, sexy talk, and other old-fashioned methods of sexual intimacy have come back into vogue out of necessity.

For lesbians, intercourse has never been the focus. Like heterosexual women, lesbians have always enjoyed petting. However, lesbians have had greater freedom from male definitions of sex. Thus, they have never had the imperative to proceed quickly to intercourse. Most of what constitutes foreplay in heterosexual relationships is the core of lesbian lovemaking. Although penetration occurs—with fingers, a vibrator, a dildo, or some similar object for stimulating the vagina—it is not the "main event."

First Intercourse

Men still receive more admiration for sexual expertise than women, so it stands to reason that boys start having sex earlier than girls and tend to be happier about their first experiences. The NHSLS (Laumann et al. 1994) reveals that for people who are currently cohabiting, the age of first intercourse is around 16; for married people, it is around 17 for men and 18 for women. Other studies, including those done in the 1980s (e.g., Zelnick and Shah 1983), have come up with the age of 15.5 for first intercourse for men and slightly older than that for women. Most people have sex with one or two partners, at most, before marriage. Increasingly, however, the number of partners is rising, and younger women and men are becoming more similar in this area.

First intercourse is not an unproblematic, carefree event. Several studies (Call, Sprecher, and Schwartz 1995; Laumann et al. 1994) demonstrate that people have mixed emotions about sexual initiation. These emotions are organized in part around gender; in other words, men and women have different reactions to the same act. Hollywood images of sex—sexual outlaws like Madonna, femmes fatales like Sharon Stone—are still just far-away fantasy to most women. Such images may be more appealing to men, although in truth many men would be intimidated. Still, most young women feel less comfortable with their bodies than young men do, and young women feel less adequate as a sexual or romantic partner and suffer from lower self-esteem than a person needs for ego-taxing first sexual experiences.

Figure 3.2, based on NHSLS data, shows male and female evaluations of the circumstances of their sexual initiation. A diverse group of men and women were asked whether they would characterize their first sexual experience as something they desired, did not desire, or were forced to do.

FIGURE 3.2

Evaluating First Sexual Experiences

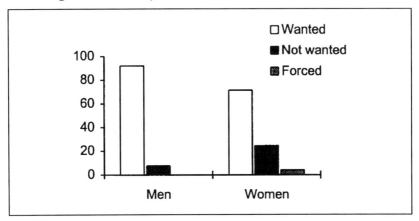

Source: Data from Laumann, Michael, and Gagnon (1994).

Although the majority wanted their first experience, a quarter of the women did not want intercourse their first time, three times the number of men who did not want it. A small number of women had a terrible, forced experience, and they outnumbered men who forced by about 20 to 1. Keep in mind, however, that men's first experience may not be as ideal as the 92 percent figure suggests, nor the unwanted or forced category so small. Men are expected to enjoy intercourse no matter how disappointing or strange the experience may be. Ambivalence about sex is not normative for men. Only in some qualitative research, where men share stories about first intercourse, do they sometimes reveal that they felt trapped into a sexual situation that was not to their design or liking (as reported, e.g., in Hatfield and Rapson 1993).

Some argue that women also experience forced sex more often than the statistics reveal and that even more women did not want their first experience. Some women, the logic goes, are in denial and not really facing up to the fact that they were forced. Many young women are so accustomed to capitulating to men's desires in both sexual and non-sexual settings that it may not occur to them that their compromises are not voluntary. These commentators may be right, although it is important not to assume that women are typically sexual victims (they aren't) or that men are typically sexual aggressors (they aren't). Of course, accounts of first experiences, given retrospectively, are re-creations of what happened, not firsthand observations. As with other sexual self-reports, they are hard to interpret.

In *Going All the Way* (1996), journalist Sharon Thompson presents interviews with a diverse sample of teenage girls across the United States. She shows how young women in high school sometimes trade sex when they are promised love in exchange, only to find that the love doesn't follow and that the sex is something they didn't really want. The young women who were interviewed repeated statements like "I really didn't want to, but it was easier just to please him than to keep saying no" or "I figured it was going to be with someone and while I really didn't want it to be him, he convinced me that I had led him on and that I better do the right thing." Thompson shows that mostly better-educated, older, more privileged youth have the opportunity to negotiate sexual and romantic experiences on their own terms, and they have more pleasing, egalitarian outcomes. Many young girls make sad statements of capitulation. Only the fortunate find their sexual initiation to be the epitome of love and erotic sensibility, expressed by this college senior:

> We were totally in love. We wanted this to be the best experience of our lives. We were at his apartment and we had done everything right. We had talked about it, planned for it, saw this as the highest expression of our joint future. He was very caring, very slow with me. I felt empowered, beautiful. It was a great night.[2]

Why isn't first intercourse that way for most women (or men)? The answer resides in the culture of sexual ambivalence that we live in and in the unsure relations between men and women. But even the majority of women who say they wanted to have intercourse have less glowing reports of the event than men do. Ignorance and fear make many men and women less than sensitive lovers, particularly starting out. The approval that men obtain by simply "scoring," however, makes less than virtuoso performances more rewarding for men than for women. Also, perhaps with the number of people having sex who really don't care deeply about each other, participants aren't particularly dedicated to ensuring that it is a happy experience for both partners. It may also be true that because men still tend to be the initiators in dating and sex, women are more likely to be approached by men they don't really want to have sex with at the time. The experience is bound to be more pleasant for those who control the choice of partner and the timing of the event.

FIGURE 3.3

Reasons for First Intercourse

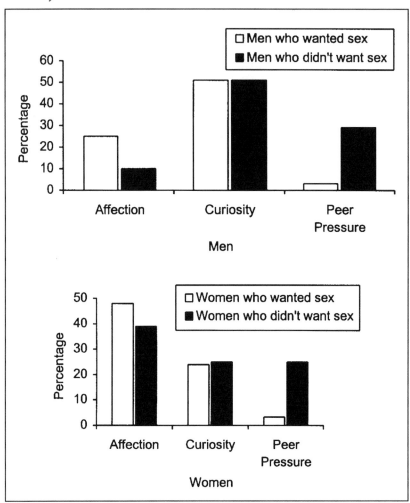

Source: Data from Laumann, Michael, and Gagnon (1994).

Many of these feelings may have to do with the presence or absence of affection in the relationship. The NHSLS data show that almost half the women who wanted intercourse had sex out of affection for their partner but that only a quarter of the men did, as indicated in Figure 3.3. Of those who didn't want sex, only 10 percent of the men and 39 percent of the women were motivated by affection. Perhaps women are more likely than men to rationalize doing something that they didn't clearly want "for love." Perhaps men are more ikely than women to admit less than romantic motivations. At any rate, men and women don't appear to always be on the same page when it comes to deciding to have sex.

Gendered responses in the NHSLS are reversed when it comes to sexual curiosity: Men were curious, women less so. When you examine the affection row and the curiosity row in Figure 3.3, notice that a good number of women who had sex out of affection must have had sex with a guy who did it for the sake of curiosity. Even for men who didn't really want sex, curiosity and feeling "ready for it" were big reasons to do it. Note that 25 percent of the women who didn't want to have sex went forward with it anyway on account of curiosity. But ultimately they apparently didn't feel good about their decision; otherwise, they would have responded that they did want sex.

About a quarter of both men and women surveyed in the NHSLS cited peer pressure as another reason they had first intercourse when they didn't want it. Today, young men and women assume they will not be virgins for very long. Some start to feel virginity is a burdensome status they would just as soon eliminate and seek out whoever is available to have sex.

Despite the emphasis on pleasure that has characterized the modern sexual revolution, only a small number of NHSLS respondents said that their first experience was based mainly on pleasure. The men gave that answer more often than women (12.2 percent vs. 2.8 percent, respectively).

What emerges from these self-reports is that young people are aroused and interested in sex but that men's and women's motivations diverge. Fewer men than women state that they were in love with their first partner. Fewer women than men have their first experience to just see what it is like. But regardless of the gender differences, most young men and women are similarly affected by their introduction to intercourse. They want it, but it is difficult for them. Equal numbers of young men and women are pushed ahead by peers before they feel good about sharing sex as their own choice.

Frequency and Sex Partners

Despite all the images of hip never-married 20-somethings running around bedding everything in sight, divorced people have more sex partners than young singles, and married and cohabiting people have sex most often (Laumann et al. 1994). This fact makes sense when you think about it. Married people have access; single people, unless cohabiting, have to put out a lot of effort to find a sex partner. Even if they are dating someone seriously, their lives aren't as synchronized as when people are living together. Married people are also more likely to be on the same sexual program; dating couples may not yet have worked out when and under what conditions sex will take place.

The gender differences in sexual frequency among the never married are larger than among the divorced. Single men have sex more frequently than single women but divorced men and women have sex at nearly the same rate. The difference in the gender gap between the two groups suggests that experience and age reduce women's inhibitions regarding nonmarital sex. Women who are sexually experienced may modify their earlier, more traditional vision of how committed a relationship should be before sex is part of the picture. They may want sex for sex's sake now that they are deprived of something they were free to enjoy in marriage. Sex is like anything else: If you get used to it, you might miss it and therefore seek it less ambivalently than never-married people do. Conversely, a marriage gone wrong usually means a deteriorated sex life. Sometimes divorced people are in a hurry to rectify an emotionally painful period. They want some love—or even what might pass for love—soon after (or before) the breakup to reassure themselves that they are still desirable. For example, in a 1995 unpublished letter to Glamour magazine columnist P. Schwartz, a person wrote,

> Our sex life was awful. He never made love to me and the few times he did it was completely unsatisfying. I stayed married because of the children but as soon as I could get divorced I did . . . the first thing I wanted to do was be touched again by someone who didn't make me cringe. I needed to feel like a desirable woman again. I slept around a lot, just to know I was sexually alive. When I finally found my present husband I wasn't so desperate anymore and I could appreciate him for what he was—a great guy and a great lover.

Although the effects are difficult to quantify, dating itself takes a toll, and people modify their sexual strategies the longer they are on the dating market. Men who run around like panting animals may go through a series of disappointing relationships and modify their readiness to jump into bed. Women who were "looking for love in all the wrong places" often decide they would rather be celibate than disappointed. Access becomes less important than self-respect and emotional balance. As one woman in her late 30s explained, "Most of the time I would rather stay at home with a good book. I would rather be truly alone with myself than feeling alone in the middle of sex."[3] A colleague, frustrated by women who wanted more commitment than he did, said,

> I don't want to be with someone just for fun anymore because it's never just for fun. I went out with this woman, and she was really all over me for sex. I'm human, I liked it. But I just kind of liked her and told her it wasn't going to go anywhere. To be honest I also told her that I was quite attracted to her. But I did say I was not available in any significant way. She said no problem and we had a great night. Then she called night and day for the next week, accusing me of leading her on. It just isn't worth it.

Disappointments from casual relationships and the potential for misunderstanding both make single sexuality less intense than the media portrays it (and than many adolescents wish it to be). As Figure 3.4 indicates, half the single population reports having sex only a few times a year or less (Laumann et al. 1994). For both single men and single women, they are not enthralled in sexual freedom.

The picture is somewhat different for college-aged people, 18 to 24 years old, who are less likely to be encumbered by work or children and have many more partners to choose from. Figure 3.5 indicates that more than 50 percent of the youngest group were having sex at least a few times a month. (Note that as sexual frequency increases, the rates for men and women converge.) The younger group may be more open about sex. They are in prime dating years and have a lot of sex in their relationships. Frequency of sex among the young might be explained as a consequence of greater hormonal activity. But as we demonstrated in Chapter 1, hormonal activity can be a response to the environment, and youth live in an environment where sex and romance are high priorities. These data, although not perfect, suggest that less sex is going on than the media suggest but that the young are definitely doing sex more than older people.

The rates of sexual activity also shift once we limit our observations to relationships with some level of commitment and affection. There is a "honeymoon" period in both married and nonmarried relationships. The starstruck couple has eyes only for each other and has significantly more sex than the two will have after the newness of the relationship has worn off. However, even committed couples tend not to have sex on a daily basis. Risman et al. (1981) found that only 12 percent of the cohabiting, college-aged couples from the Boston Dating Couples study

FIGURE 3.4

Sexual Frequency Among Singles

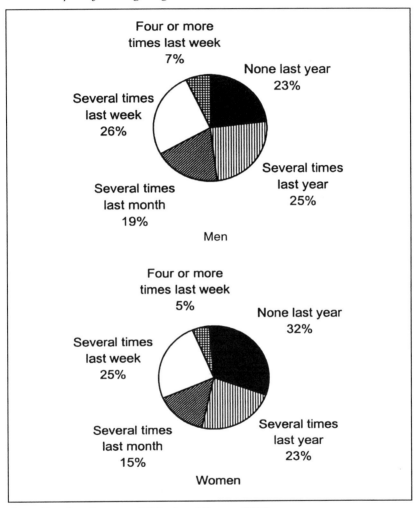

Source: Data from Laumann, Michael, and Gagnon (1994).

had sex six times a week or more. A dating couples study by Simpson and Gangestad (1991) found that the couples had sex slightly less than twice a week. And Peplau, Rubin, and Hill (1977) did an imaginative study comparing couples who engaged in sex very early in the relationship with couples who delayed. The couples who had sex during the first month of the relationship had a median frequency of four or five

FIGURE 3.5

Sexual Frequency for Single 20-Somethings

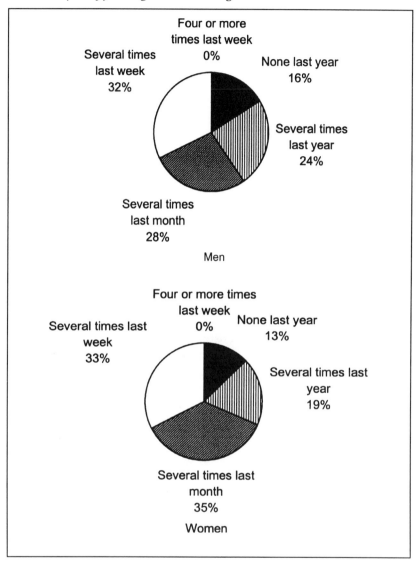

Men

Women

Source: Data from Laumann, Michael, and Gagnon (1994).

times a week; the couples who waited longer had less sex—approximately two to three times a week at the beginning of the sexual part of the relationship.

Is the experience similar for gays and lesbians? Although AIDS has changed the sexual climate for gay men, they still retain a taste for sexual variety. The AIDS epidemic has caused most to resist meeting places (like "the baths") for anonymous sex based on attraction and nothing else. Indeed, few baths even exist anymore. But the notion of sex as a form of play has persisted. Gay men find ways—like telephone sex or mutual masturbation—to have sex with a variety of partners. Lesbians, like heterosexual women, primarily prefer sex in a context of love. However, lesbians, like gay men and cohabitors, are subject to more frequent breakups than married people, and so they accrue more partners over time. These patterns vary considerably by age. Just as younger generations of heterosexual women engage in more casual sex, so casual sex is more common among younger lesbians now than among older lesbians or lesbians in earlier times.

Sexual Etiquette in the 1990s

Older rules for sex outside of marriage may have faded, but social control of sexual activity hasn't disappeared. A new term—sexual etiquette—has emerged in connection with the new dating landscape. People are relatively free to have sex whenever and however partners agree to do so. But traditional constraints on sexuality have given way to new constraints, which are especially concerned with sexual health and the reproductive consequences of sexual involvement.

Heterosexual Etiquette: Contraception, Safe Sex, and Abortion

Here's a challenge for an updated "Ms. Manners": In a dating couple, who raises the sexually transmitted disease (STD) issue or the birth control issue? In what detail and at what point in the relationship should they learn each other's views on abortion? Some people solve these problems by ignoring them as long as possible. At best, most people act erratically. For example, only about half of all single people use some kind of prophylactic the first time they have sex together (Holmes et al. 1990). Over time, they are inconsistent, either because they really want to escape the feeling of a condom or because they think they have assessed the risk of contracting an STD. As affection grows, partners rationalize that neither could be diseased, but of course, they don't know for sure.

A few heterosexual couples go down to the health department together (or to their doctor), get HIV tests to make sure they are virus free, and then proceed to use nonbarrier methods of contraception that do not affect spontaneity or enjoyment. One woman told us that she had convinced her boyfriend to go with her to receive an AIDS test. They were white, bohemian urbanites in their 20s, and both had had about a dozen lovers in the past and no same-sex experiences. Their plan was to clear any doubt about their sexual health so that they could stop using condoms during sex. The plan was sensible and, in a contemporary sense, romantic. It was a sign of the couple's commitment to each other. After their tests came back negative, the woman said, "I guess this means we won't be seeing other people." But the man had a different idea. "I can't promise that," he said. "I'm not planning on having sex with anyone else, but if I do, I can promise that I will use a condom." To her, his response was not sufficiently "safe." What seemed like a sexual issue had become a relationship issue: She was expecting fidelity, he couldn't promise. And progressive as this couple had been, they were simply in a new version of that hackneyed romantic script: She wants commitment, and he wants freedom.

Even though this couple couldn't quite agree to the same rules of safe sex, they were doing better than most couples. Most heterosexuals, knowing their statistical risk is low, just assume that they will not be unlucky. Tragically, some have been wrong. Transmission rates for HIV in the United States have increased more among younger heterosexuals than other groups in recent years.

Dating homosexuals know that the odds of infection are terrible. The estimate of HIV incidence in the population of homosexuals has been variously estimated, depending on the city, from 25 percent to 80 percent (Holmes et al. 1990). Gay public health campaigns have reinforced behavior change, and social action groups have worked together to promote safer sexual behaviors for their constituents. Because gay men had rarely used condoms (except as a lark) before the AIDS crisis, the campaign had to create a new habit rather than simply encourage a familiar one. Helped by the desperation of the situation, advertising eroticized condoms, showing sexy pictures of men using them and reciting slogans to reinforce the message that safe is sexy. Lesbians became part of the movement, partly as an act of solidarity. Also, most lesbians have had sexual activity with men (50 percent have had intercourse with a man), and more than heterosexual women, their male sexual partners might be bisexual or primarily homosexual.

No STD before AIDS has fostered this kind of behavior modification program. When herpes began to make the rounds in heterosexual circles in the 1970s and 1980s, there was an enormous amount of media attention and public outcry; *Time* magazine made it a cover story. Herpes, like HIV, is a virus that is permanent and recurring, is extremely painful for some (though nonsymptomatic for many), and is potentially lethal to an infant delivered vaginally during an initial outbreak of the virus. Still, the publicity and fear about herpes did not create a revolution of safer sexual behavior.

The difference in responses to herpes and HIV were due largely to social forces. When herpes broke out, the Pill was still popular. Men had stopped bringing condoms. Couples got used to the feeling of skin against skin. Men were reluctant to use condoms, even resistant to using them, even though they and their partners were at risk of contracting the herpes virus and having it forever. Nothing less than the threat of death—HIV infection—convinced many men and women to start using condoms again. But even the possibility of a lethal sexual experience hasn't convinced everyone to use condoms. A majority of college students whom Gray and Saracino (1991) studied said they tried to guess whether a new partner was likely to have HIV rather than insist on using a condom.

Immediate pleasure is a more powerful motivator for many people than future consequences. And the depth of that power is breathtaking. Customers will pay a prostitute more money not to use a condom than to use one (Lever 1994b). And people will lie about their HIV status or other disease status when they feel desperate for sex. Cochran and Mays (1990) interviewed over 400 sexually active college students in southern California and found that 20 percent of men and 4 percent of women said they would lie, if necessary, about the results of an HIV test. They would also subvert other attempts at assessing risk: 47 percent of the men and 42 percent of the women would purposely underestimate the number of previous sexual partners if asked.

Similar carelessness attends decisions about contraception. One of us has been in a women's group for over 20 years. The women meet every few months to talk about their lives, loves, careers, relationships, and marriages. At a meeting during the late 1980s, three of the single, 30-something women were talking about the first date each of them had had in a long time. The first thing the rest of the women in the group asked was, "Did you use contraception?" The three women looked downward and each one truthfully answered no. Stunned that they each had taken that risk, the group asked them why not. Each one said the man had refused. The men preferred no sex at all to sex with a condom. Each woman wanted to have sex so much that she decided to go ahead "just this one time."

The women in this group had encountered another interesting fact about contraception: For heterosexuals, who suggests using it, when it is suggested, and how each person feels about using it is gendered and difficult. Most sex education has been directed toward single women and girls, on the assumption that they are more articulate about relationships than men and that they have more at stake. Young women, the logic goes, are gatekeepers of sexuality, and somehow it is up to them to protect themselves and their partner. Lever (1995) points out, however, that although young women may be good about talking about relationships and be uniquely at risk for pregnancy, the power dynamics between adolescents make it less likely for a woman to prevail over a man. Young women still find it difficult to assert their rights as much as necessary, and too many are persuaded to do what their guy wants.

When sex involves heterosexual intercourse, the potential reproductive consequence is a woman's burden. The pregnancy is in her body. For women, part of the cost and danger of single sex is the possibility of having to carry a baby to term, with all the life changes and stigma that go along with such a decision. Abortion is another option, and although the majority of abortion services are sought by married women, single women and their partners use it as a back-up method to contraceptive failures. Before *Roe v. Wade* (1973), women pursuing abortion faced a scary proposition. Doctors who did abortions often ran a shady business and charged high fees. Entrepreneurs who did abortions without medical experience could make fatal mistakes, such as puncturing the uterus or causing infection.

The loosening of sexual mores preceded the 1973 *Roe* decision, as did the rising trend in nonmarital pregnancies. However, when abortion became legal and safe, many more women chose to end unwanted pregnancies, which reduced the number of nonmarital births. As Figure 3.6 illustrates, for teen women the abortion rate offset the birth rate up until 1990.

As any reader of newspapers knows, abortion is still very much disputed, in part, because it is a critical aspect of single (and married) women's ability to cope with sexual "slip-ups" (i.e., unintended conception) without changing their lives dramatically. Particularly in the absence of adequate social services, single motherhood in the United States can be an isolating, impoverishing experience. Opponents of the

FIGURE 3.6

Teenage Fertility Events, Rates for Women Ages 15-19, 1972-1990

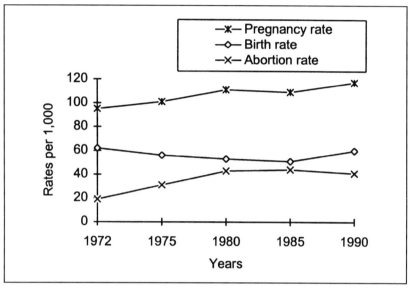

Source: Data from Luker (1996).

right to abortion have noted that the "fail-safe" of abortion makes women feel less afraid of an unintended pregnancy and therefore less cautious. Indeed, abortion rates in the United States are much higher than in western European countries, where access to abortion is similar but child and maternal services and financial support are greater. European women and men typically receive more and better sex education than their U.S. counterparts, and their overall birth rate is lower than the U.S. birth rate. Thus, the lower abortion rate may be due to more effective and consistent contraption usage. However, their abortion rate may also be lower because the social safety net in most European countries also means a woman need not fear personal and economic disaster if she has a child.

Legal abortion may also influence men to be less concerned about conception. They know they have a fall-back position against unintended fatherhood. Although some groups of adolescent men and women want to have a baby to prove their adulthood or to fulfill a need to love something "all their own," many anticipate how much having a baby will disadvantage their lives and affect their plans. Young men were held accountable for out-of-wedlock pregnancies before the mid-nineteenth century but were under less scrutiny for the next 100 years or so because of a double standard that held women to be the guilty party. However, now boys and men are increasingly being held account-able for supporting their children, because of the extraordinary expense to the government of taking care of these children (Lerman and Ooms 1993). Whether or not state legislatures are pro-choice, they are increas-ingly pro-paternal responsibility.

Miscommunication and Sexual Privilege

The sexual revolution's legacy is the expansion of sexual variety and autonomy for singles. But the sexual revolution also left a legacy of miscommunication, misunderstanding, and abuse in the form of sexual harassment, date rape, and rape. In Chapter 2, we talked about gen-dered patterns of coerced sex. Here we return to these patterns to examine their impact on singles. (We will return to the subject again in Chapter 5 on sexual politics.) We believe, however, that these problems are not a consequence of the sexual revolution but that they came to light because of the freedom to talk about sexual problems that the sexual revolution initiated.

We opened this chapter with two scenes of "sexual conquest." The parking lot scene from *Thelma & Louise* we defined as a rape in progress; the parking lot scene from *The Last Seduction* we defined as unusually aggressive sex. The sexual revolution made it possible for these scenes to be frankly portrayed in mainstream movies. Note also that these provocative portrayals illustrate how sexual misunderstanding and coercion can be confounded. In *Thelma & Louise*, the aggressive guy thought Thelma's flirtation was tantamount to sexual permission. In *The Last Seduction*, the reticent guy was too fearful of humiliation to back down from an anonymous sexual encounter.

Sexual Coercion

Some sexual interactions are not about misunderstanding or sub-tlety. They are about coercion, terror, shame, and self-doubt. Sexual coercion can occur within marriage or to married people by people other than their partners. But for singles it is a particular problem, be-cause in dating situations men and women can have very different agendas. Social scripts can still set up some women to be victims rather than lovers and some men to be predators rather than suitors. We won't talk here about men with mental instability or homicidal or serial rapists and sexual sadists. We are instead concerned with attacks by "ordinary" men in pursuit of sexual satisfaction on a date or at a party, as was the case in *Thelma & Louise.*

Women more than men have shifted their behavior and standards in response to the sexual revolution. Thus, in *Thelma & Louise*, Thelma is emblematic of the change. She has broken away from her controlling husband and feels she can flirt with a fellow in a bar without fear of reprisal. But the guy is more traditional, and he reads her flirtation as "sluttish" sexual teasing—to him, this is license to dominate her and demand sex. Thelma's good time evaporates as she realizes he is about to rape her brutally. Louise saves her by shooting and killing the man when he refuses to take Louise's threats to shoot seriously. He cannot imagine Louise will do it. Such mismatched consciousness generates a homicide. In other circumstances, it might just generate hurt and angry feelings.

Research supports this fictional account. The more traditional a man's attitudes about women's roles, the more likely he is to feel that any sexual interest that a woman shows entitles a man to proceed to intercourse. Some research has indicated that when the woman asks the man out (contrary to tradition) or when the man pays for the date (especially when it is expensive), intercourse without the woman's consent—in other words, rape—is seen as more justifiable (Muehlen-hard 1988; Muehlenhard, Friedman, and Thomas 1985). A woman who is sexually alluring is believed to be "leading a man on" (Muehlenhard and McNaughton 1988). The script for a man involves conquering such a woman to assert his masculinity. If the woman rebuffs his advances, she diminishes him and assaults his manhood. For most people, this whole scenario seems ridiculous. Who would want to have sex with someone who doesn't want it?

But men, who were less the focus of change than women during the sexual revolution, are more likely to be influenced by old-fashioned macho ideology. Some men still seek bragging rights about their con-quests or bond with other men by talking degradingly about women. In the process, they become more willing to perpetrate sexual violence.

Sometimes sexual violence is even a rite of passage, a ritual a young boy goes through to show he is one of the guys. In *Makes Me Wanna Holler* (1995), journalist Nathan McCall describes the practice of seduc-ing unsuspecting, trusting women for "trains" in which a group of men sequentially rape a woman. In one episode, some guys have abducted a teenager from the neighborhood:

> I learned that the girl was Vanessa, a black beauty whose family had recently moved into our neighborhood, less than two blocks from where I lived. She seemed like a nice girl. When I first noticed her walking to and from school I had wanted to check her out. Now it was too late. She was about to have a train run on her. No way she could be somebody's straight-up girl after going through a train. (P. 45)

The author writes this scene out of regret and guilt, but at the time his peer group was far too powerful to resist. He thinks about saving Vanessa but then decides "I couldn't do that. It was too late. This was our first train together as a group. All the fellas were there and everybody was anxious to show everybody else how cool and worldly he was" (p. 47).

Sometimes men have no idea, even when they find themselves in court as defendants, that coercive sex violates not only the law but also ethical standards of conduct. In studies of sexual aggression and force, many men, including college men, indicate that they feel entitled to press on even when a woman doesn't consent. A large number of cases (Sprecher and McKinney 1993) show between 8 percent and 25 percent of men admitting to forcing intercourse. Even more, 30-50 percent, say they had used several kinds of verbal manipulation to force a woman to comply. Again, group peer pressure aggravates and incites the participants.

A number of rape charges are brought every year against actions following incidents within fraternity houses. In the early 1990s, for example, a rape charge was successfully brought against some members of a fraternity at the University of Washington in Seattle. Some fraternity men found a thoroughly intoxicated women and took turns raping her. The men believed it was her fault for getting so drunk. When they were charged with rape, they were mystified and outraged. Remarkably, even after the trial, these men still held on to their good-girl/bad-girl ideas, which give women who like to party fewer rights than women who abstain. A survey of sorority women revealed that 13 percent had been in a situation that could be classified as rape; 60 percent of those rape incidents had occurred at a fraternity house or with a fraternity member. Ninety-six percent of the incidents involved alcohol (Copenhaver and Grauerholtz 1991). A study that compared fraternity men with nonaffiliated men found that the frat men reported more abusive sexual behaviors (like using drugs and alcohol to gain sexual access) and that they had more friends who supported the idea that it was reasonable to push sexual intercourse even when the woman was unwilling (Boeringer, Shehan, and Akers 1991).

What seems to happen in fraternities occurs in other homosocial (i.e., same-sex) environments, such as the military, where numerous cases of sexual harassment and sexual assaults have been publicized in the mid-1990s. A very aggressive vision of male sexuality, untainted by restraint or moral judgment, becomes the standard of masculinity. Considering women as opportunities rather than people is encouraged. The vision of "bad" or "easy" women and the notion that men have the right to treat them as masturbatory aids or tools for male bonding help promote a standard of male sexuality that, among those who embrace it, leads to a much higher likelihood of sexual coercion and rape.

Sexual Confusion

Certainly, rates of date rape and other kinds of sexual violence are disturbing. And it is easy, and for our view, reasonable, to condemn sexually aggressive men's attitudes. But the matter is complicated. Research has demonstrated that men and women sincerely misread each other's cues. This research argues that some of what is framed as coercion is coercion, but that sometimes it is more of a case of miscommunication.

Some studies examine whether miscommunication occurs because of ambiguous cues that might vary depending on gender. For example, in a laboratory study where friendly staff members interacted with both men and women participants, Abbey (1982) found that men were more likely than women to code a woman's friendliness as seductive or even promiscuous. Men who observed another man interact with a woman were more likely than women to code the man as sexually attracted to the woman. Other studies indicate that more men than women tend to code interpersonal warmth and attention as sexual. Women tend to be unaware that their actions are being labeled as flirtatious or sexual.

Here's the inevitable complication: Although women may in general intend to be seductive less often than men think, sometimes women are trying to be seductive. And women who intend to be seductive are not necessarily seeking intercourse. In fact, both men and women have been found to use indirect rather than straightforward approaches to show and compel sexual interest (Sprecher and McKinney 1993); being indirect is essential to seduction. Some of the strategies women used in a study of college students (Perper and Weis 1987) were seductive dressing, creating a sexual or romantic mood, using sexy or romantic talk, cuddling close, and touching.

It is rarely difficult to differentiate flirtation from sexual consent. However, there are shades of meaning in between flirting and consent that may be difficult to define. Women often have a firm idea of what they mean by their acts, and they expect the person they are with to "get it." But men, who in U.S. culture are expected to be continuously sexually interested and ready, are unsure of how forward to be. What constitutes permission? What is offensive? Men are often more afraid of failing the first qualification (being ready and interested) than the second (being offensive or out of bounds). They may also hold on to some older definitions of what entitles them to sex, and cry, "But she was leading me on!" In the *Thelma & Louise* scenario, indeed Thelma was flirting. But from Thelma's perspective as well as Louise's, the flirtation ended when Thelma said no. For men like the character in the movie, a woman's saying no does not negate the prior positive signals. Some men are baffled when their initial attempts at seduction are rebuffed; they are mystified when a woman is angry with them for overly sexualizing a situation. It is possible to accept that there are situations where a partner may be slow to comprehend that another person is saying no; this is a case of miscommunication. But being slow on the uptake is quite different from willfully ignoring or distorting the communication between adults, as occurred in *Thelma & Louise*.

Some research indicates that men with traditional beliefs, who feel they have been led on, may push very hard for intercourse. If they believe that at some point a woman is no longer entitled to say no, they will rationalize that they can have sex without her consent. If she prosecutes for rape, a court may agree with her point of view, but often it does not. Social scripts are just too strong: Louise took her understanding of courtroom biases into account when she used a gun to stop Thelma's aggressor. Because of her own prior experience, Louise anticipated a judge and jury blaming Thelma for her flirtatious behavior, instead of holding Thelma's attacker accountable for proceeding after a refusal.

Men complain that it is difficult to know what consent consists of these days. A lot of men claim to believe women say no as "token resistance" on their way to saying yes. In two studies (Muehlenhard and Hollabaugh 1988; Muehlenhard and McCoy 1991), young women were asked if they had ever said no to the guy they were with even though they had every intention to eventually have sex with him that evening.

A surprisingly large number, 50 percent in the first study, 37 percent in the second, said they had. The most common reason given by the women in the first study was that they did not want to seem promiscuous. On the other hand, in a cross-cultural study of sexual consent (Sprecher et al. 1992) researchers found that 44 percent of the American women in the study had said yes even though they really did not want to have sex. How should we interpret this ambivalence?

Some have attempted to replace ambiguity about what constitutes consent with clear rules that any kind of no should be taken at face value. Men should assume it really means no. One attempt to clarify rights and privileges was organized by the students at Antioch College in 1992. The students sought to eliminate the gray area between consent and rape in evolving sexual situations. The path they chose was to specify that each and every sexual escalation had to receive verbal permission. Otherwise, a rape was in progress. If a woman was being kissed and her partner wanted to touch her breast, the partner would have to ask, "May I touch your breast?" Theoretically, these permissions were reciprocal. Women who wanted to touch a man would also have to ask explicit verbal permission. However, the script is clearly written with the idea of vulnerable women and more sexually aggressive men in mind.

Here's the dilemma with a plan like Antioch's: It doesn't respond to sex as it tends to be practiced and enjoyed. The how, who, where, when, and why of sex are determined through social processes that begin long before people commence sexual activity; nevertheless, there is a certain happy aspect to sexual momentum that seems unfairly constrained by the Antioch rules. They imagine partners in sexual interactions to be cooler, more conscious, more in control, and more aware than most sexually aroused people. More to the point, the Antioch rules put the onus on the person who seeks to move ahead more quickly, who is often the guy.

Although we have argued that the sexual revolution helped advance women's sexual consciousness more than men's, we are wary of establishing rules that cast all men as sexual predators and all women as victims. There are three problems. One is the assumption that men are always more mature than their partners (they aren't) and that they really know when they are proceeding without heartfelt permission (they don't). Another problem is the assumption that people don't give mixed signals (they do). And finally, such rules assume that female sexuality is so passive and unconscious that women can't be held accountable for their acts (of course they can). Simply put, the Antioch perspective on sexuality is patronizing to women.

Perhaps the most regrettable aspect of the Antioch rules is that they undermine one of the key tenets of the sexual revolution: Sex is pleasurable. True, the sexual revolution's hedonistic vision may have failed to anticipate some undesirable consequences of liberalized sexual norms. Nevertheless, the Antioch rules are a far cry from the sexual ideology of the 1960s and 1970s, which moved college students to fight for adult sexual privileges and had, as its foundation, a vision of sexual equality for men and women.

Sexual autonomy and accountability are issues that will continue to be controversial; we can't resolve the conflicts here. But be wary of solutions that inadvertently reinforce notions of gender difference. An example of a sexual harassment case will help illustrate this point: In North Carolina, a six-year-old boy, at the invitation of a classmate, kissed her on the cheek while they were at school. The story made national headlines in the fall of 1996 when the school responded by suspending the boy from school for sexual harassment. In this draconian application of sexual harassment rules, innocent child's play was treated as if an adult were victimizing another adult. From our point of view, the punishment sends the opposite message: The boys are powerful enough, by virtue of being boys, to invite such trouble, and girls are weak enough, by virtue of being girls, to be destroyed by such trouble. Thus, the lesson glorified the notion of sexualized gender difference even among children who are presexual (in the adult meaning of the word) rather than minimizing conceptions of gender difference.

Women's Response to Sexual Aggression

Many women have become politically and personally astute about the dangers in dating relationships. Still, women have a tendency to blame themselves when miscommunication occurs and to wonder if, indeed, they have behaved in a way that invited or permitted sexual aggression. In particular, if a woman consents because of verbal manipulation rather than brute force, she tends to believe that she is at fault. In addition, studies have shown that women, especially more traditional or conservative women, have some of the same beliefs about rape that men do. If a woman "led him on," if she was sexually tantalizing but then declined to go further, or if she was known for her previous sexual experiences, even other women are likely to judge her as being as much at fault as the man who pushed the issue.

Nevertheless, since the sexual revolution, sex has been held to the standard of mutuality. Sex is supposed to take place between people who want to have this experience together. If women do not want the sexual experience, how can they be talked into it? This is a complicated question to answer, and the answer varies situation by situation. Perhaps a better question is, why should they be talked into it? This question takes into account the fact that sexual coercion arises from power differences on and off the sexual playing field.

The obvious power difference, which we have already referred to time and again, is the one between women and men. However, the gendered power differences that influence sexual interaction are often confounded with the ambivalence people have about sex and their lack of communication skills for talking about it. In a culture that fires a U.S. surgeon general for talking in public about masturbation, it should come as no surprise that many people are frazzled and defensive in sexual situations. Their goal, far from love or pleasure, may be getting through the experience without humiliating themselves. They may be particularly unhappy in sexual situations when they are just beginning to date and lack sexual self-confidence, or just reentering the dating market after being in a long relationship. They may especially lose their composure when the person they are with is of a different class, ethnicity, country, or culture. Words and cues that are well understood by one group may be completely missed by another.

Sexual pressure and abuse of power is not confined to male-over-female manipulation or force. A case that made national news recently involved a married woman high school teacher who was having an affair with a male student at school. When she was found out, a national debate began over whether this was harassment, or whether the boy had just "gotten lucky." Would people have felt the same way if this incident had involved a male teacher and a 15-year-old girl? Was this boy unlucky or lucky? Damaged or educated? Undoubtedly, men under pressure to have sex can feel victimized and regretful. The parking lot sex scene from *The Last Seduction* illustrates this point further. Wendy was pushing her companion beyond his sexual limits. He was less at ease having a quickie against a chain-link fence with a stranger than she was, but it was his "manly" duty to rise to the occasion. As the movie progresses, however, it is clear that he is being victimized by her sexual aggression. His persistence in the relationship hinges on the importance for him, as a man, to be prepared to meet any sexual challenge and to overcome discomfort. (Notably, Wendy turns out to be a psychopathic killer; indeed, such sexually aggressive women characters tend to be villains in the movies.)

These pressures are not present in all societies. But in the United States, we have a volatile mix of opportunity, mixed signals, uneasy and often angry relations between the sexes, and changing gender scripts that leave men and women unsure about how to present themselves and how to interpret one another's intentions. Thus, sex between two single people has multiple meanings and expectations. It often needs much more translation than it receives. Sex can be hazardous to both men and women unless mutual respect and communication become the norm rather than the exception.

The Future of Single Sex

Some of the misunderstandings and conflicts between men and women have increased the possibility of legal intervention and other institutional constraints on individual sexuality. There is a battle among feminists, for example, about whether some forms of sexuality, such as casual sex or pornography, are a common good or a common threat. For some women, sexuality is still part of women's liberation. For others, sexual freedom is just another word for oppression, and the politics of sexuality are a politics of containment. Joining the fray, conservative religious movements have commented on the fallout of uncommitted sexuality—premarital pregnancy, broken hearts, rape suits, paternity cases—and offered single people a vision of a simpler, more protected time. They preach for a return to nonmarital celibacy and a renewed commitment to having sex only within the relative safety of wedlock.

The fear of AIDS; the delicacy of trying to have safer, protected sex; the emotional difficulties of negotiating condoms; and the renewed stigmatization and poverty of single mothers have created a new anti-single sex platform that feels right to at least some young people. This antisex group hasn't influenced sexual trends at this point. In fact, more and more people are engaging in nonmarital sex, and the age of sexual initiation is getting younger. Still, nostalgia for easier-to-negotiate male-female relations threatens to send us back in time rather than forward, and images of sexual gender differences that are simplified into visions of "men from Mars and women from Venus" fuel the media.

It is not clear what people want in the single sex world. On the one hand, most singles and divorced people want the ability to have a complete sex life without marriage. On the other hand, old definitions of what makes someone worth respecting aren't fading, and these old scripts cause problems for women whose suitors may not be comfortable with a more frank sexuality. But both women and men sometimes prefer to be freely sexual and sometimes prefer to be involved sexually with one person whom they love and are committed to. Whether recreational sex is fun or dangerous depends not only on whether you are talking to men or women but also on how well people know their preferences, and how well they understand their partner's preferences for commitment or recreation. Finally, single sex is not just a prelude to early marriage, nor is it the rush of sexual activities between marriages or commitment. Increasingly, singlehood, with varying degrees of sexual activity, is a way of life, and one that we expect to become more common and more diverse as time marches on. Singlehood as a life choice (rather than a transitional status) eliminates the "gender-polarizing" influence of marriage and committed heterosexual relationships, and the presence of it in our culture also serves to accelerate the reduction of gender differences in sexuality and in other parts of life for those who prefer singlehood and even for those who prefer life in pairs.

Conclusion

We began this discussion of uncommitted sex by asking why sexual freedom and sexual control continue to be influenced by gender. We have explored some of the tools of influence: the state, racial control, even biological essentialist beliefs that women are primarily vessels of reproduction. Media images alternately stigmatize and glorify sexuality. Families are a strong influence both through child-rearing practices and through the political use of family as a synonym for traditional sexual mores. Why the gendered organization and experience of sexuality should persist, however, remains elusive. Social institutions, some more concrete than others, anchor this structure. And no institution anchors the gendered experience of sexuality more than the time-honored institution of marriage, to which we now turn.

Notes

1. This quotation is from unpublished transcripts from focus group conversations conducted in 1995-96.

2. This quotation is from a 1993 sociology class undergraduate essay.

3. This quotation is from unpublished transcripts from focus group conversations conducted in 1995-96.

CHAPTER 4

Sex and Marriage

Why Do People Marry?

In the 1959 movie *Pillow Talk,* starring Rock Hudson and Doris Day, Hudson's buddy, played by Tony Randall, explains why he is eager to marry for the third time.

Tony Randall: Brad, as a friend I only hope one day you find a girl like this. You ought to quit all this chasing around and get married.

Rock Hudson: Why?

Randall: Why? You're not getting any younger, fellow. Oh sure, it's fun, it's exciting dancing, nightclubbing with a different doll every night, but there comes a time when a man wants to give up that kind of life.

Hudson: Why?

Randall: Because he wants to create a stable, lasting relationship with one person. Brad, believe me. There is nothing so wonderful, so fulfilling as coming home to the same woman every night.

Hudson: Why?

Randall: Because that's what it means to be adult: a wife, a family, a house. A mature man wants those responsibilities.

Hudson: Why?

Randall: Well, if you want to, you can find tricky arguments against anything. I've got to get out of here. What have you got against marriage, anyway?

Hudson: Jonathan, before a man is married he's like a tree in the forest. He stands there independent, an entity unto himself and then he's chopped down, his branches are cut off, he's stripped of his bark and he's thrown in the river with the rest of the logs. And this tree is taken to the mill and when it comes out, it's no longer a tree. It's a vanity table, a breakfast nook, a baby crib, and the newspaper that lines the family garbage can.

Randall: No. If this girl [his fiancée] weren't extra special then maybe I'd agree with you. But with Jan, you look forward to having your branches cut off.

This scene caricatures the social meanings of marriage, but the caricature nonetheless is revealing: Marriage transforms a relationship into something tame, like a breakfast nook, rather than something wild, like a tree in the forest. It also suggests different statuses within marriage for men and for women. Men submit to monogamy, and the quality of the woman is the incentive for submission. Finally, this caricature associates marriage with the acquisition of property. Marriage triggers such consumer events as the purchase of a home, a car, and all sorts of other big-ticket items. With all the social weight and obligation of marriage, the notion of marriage as a passionate, sexual union may seem like an afterthought.

In this chapter, we examine some cultural scripts and social structures that influence sexuality in marriage, we observe the ways marriage supports the sexual double standard, and we report on sexual practices within marriage and other committed relationships. At the end of the chapter, we consider a threat to the institution of marriage: The U.S. culture has become highly sexualized, but it has eroticized youth and autonomy more than commitment. Thus, we provide some ideas about the conditions under which culture can be sexualized—or **sex positive**—and at the same time marriage and commitment can thrive as a part of a sex-positive culture.

The Social Context of Marriage

Three out of every four adults in the United States are married or have been married at some point (Tucker and Mitchell-Kernan 1995). Nine out of 10 will marry before they die. Although rates of marriage have declined in recent decades, the United States continues to be the most marriage- (and divorce-) prone society in the world.

Today, marriage takes on a variety of forms—dual career, long distance, traditional (i.e., husband as breadwinner, wife as homemaker), nontraditional, sexually open, sexually dead, utilitarian—each with a social meaning and a private meaning. Marriage promotes trust,

FIGURE 4.1

Sexual Frequency in Marriage by Length of Marriage

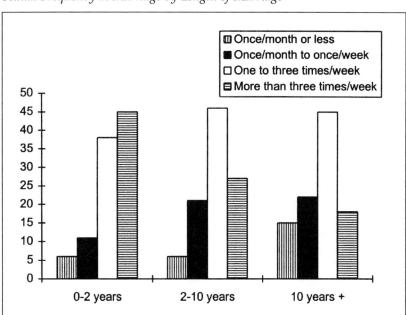

Source: Data from Blumstein and Schwartz (1983).

predictability, reliability, commitment, and sexual exclusivity for partners. Especially since the 1950s, when marriage was idealized and the study of sex was nascent, marriage has increasingly been expected to fulfill its participants emotionally, socially, and sexually, like never before in the past.

The issue in this chapter is whether sexual interest can be sustained in marriage. Research suggests that most married people are satisfied with their sex life together. Figure 4.1 displays patterns of sexual frequency by length of marriage. Despite the decline in frequency over time, 65 percent of couples still have sex more than once a week after 10 years of marriage. Despite living in a hypersexualized culture, people appear to easily satisfy their sexual needs within committed relationships.

Do they remain together because marriage offers greater opportunities for sex than the single life does? Or do couples' needs and expectations decline as the marriage wears on? There is some truth to both ideas. Marriage is in fact "sexier" than dating relationships: Married people

FIGURE 4.2

Marriage Status and Average Sexual Frequency per Month

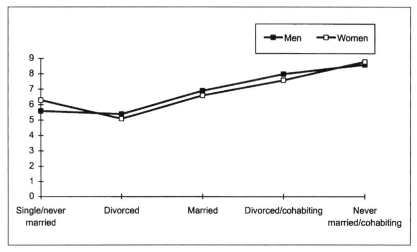

Source: Data from Laumann, Michael, and Gagnon (1994).

and long-term cohabitors have sex more frequently than singles, mostly because they have access to a partner every night. But marriage and sex within a marriage can also become boring and inconvenient as partners age and become more familiar and as life events occur (especially the introduction of children). In truth, the actual experience of marriage usually diverges from both the romantic expectation of constant eroticism and the pessimistic expectation of death of passion. Figure 4.2 describes patterns of sexual frequency by relationship type. Note that married and cohabiting couples have more sex than singles or divorced people. It is interesting to observe that commitment, in the form of cohabitation, improves sexual frequency; however, moving on to marriage apparently reduces the frequency of sex. Furthermore, never-married women report more sex than never-married men. This is consistent with our interpretation that marriage tends to amplify and even produce gender differences such that men gain an advantage by being married.

Gender, Ethnicity, and Sexual Orientation

Whatever the impact of marriage on adults' intimate lives, most people want to pair up. They will lust after the same person for quite a while and find their sexual interests bolstered by abiding affection or love. They cannot emotionally countenance the thought of being un-paired or unmarried for their whole life. Nevertheless, one need simply review magazines at the grocery store check-out line to see that our culture emphasizes women's desire to marry and men's desire to stay single. But despite the image of the reluctant groom, men marry volun-tarily and eagerly. Most men who divorce will eventually (sometimes quickly) remarry. However popular marriage bashing may be in bars and locker rooms, the truth is that most men want to be married more than women do. Indeed, across all races and ethnic groups, men desire marriage and remarriage more than women (Tucker and Mitchell-Kernan 1995:157).

Marriage as the Enactment of Gender Difference

Men like to be married because they benefit a great deal. They gain in terms of quality of life, mental health, and professional opportunities considerably more than women who marry. Although the flow of resources between partners is complicated, overall the flow of social, material (except financial), and sexual resources is from wife to hus-band. In other words, men gain more out of being married than women do, especially among whites. Of course, this flow of resources is not foremost in the minds or hearts of the matrimonial pair. At this level, people interact based on cultural and individual contingencies.

Yet marriage has a social function, reinforcing norms and conven-tions. Marriage constitutes a relationship between a woman and a man that is not simply different in degree; there is no natural progression to relationships that culminates in a socially, religiously, and legally sanc-tioned institution. No, marriage is a relationship different in kind. It is a social convention that, more than any other convention, relies on gender difference. The 1996 Defense of Marriage Act even legislates gender difference by endorsing states' rights to ignore marriages con-stituted in other states when those marriages are same-sex rather than cross-sex.

Even when individuals seek to experience marriage as something other than a social institution, the rest of the world still insists on responding to married people in the conventional manner. For example, outsiders assume that married people have promised sexual fidelity to each other and that those who are married are not available for liaisons with other people. Another example is the difficulty encountered by wives who keep their family name; they must go out of their way to inform people that they do not wish to be known by their husband's name. The few husbands who take the family name of a wife must make an even greater effort to inform others of this choice, because it is so nonnormative.

Social norms for gender difference in marriage have awesome power. A married couple may begin as equal partners, but the marriage sets in motion a wife's duties to household and kids and a husband's duties to earning money for the family. Even when both partners work to earn money (as in over half of all current marriages), more often than not the marriage tends to become polarized by gender (Schwartz 1994). Thus, the majority of couples who consider themselves egalitarian are actually "near peers." They end up falling into gendered patterns of domestic, economic, and emotional labor even when they don't intend to. The fact that most men earn more than most women is what typically tilts the division of responsibilities. In fact, the norm of the man being the provider is so strong that even if the woman has money from her family or earns more than her husband, the man will still be granted the perks of the provider status. Some consider it emasculating for the man to do the housework or for the woman to decide such matters as whether or not they'll get a new car.

This same set of assumptions sustains the caretaker, "mommy" status. Women carry a greater burden of domestic labor than men do, even when they are working full-time and even when they are earning more than their partners (Brines 1994). The world, from hospitals to schools, assumes that mom is the primary parent. Through everyday interactions, the traditional roles of men and women are reinforced. Suburban folklore provides accounts of a father who goes to parent-teacher conferences and gets ignored in favor of the mother. Another image is of the dad who gets extra attention for volunteering time for, say, the fund-raising bake sale, just for showing up. Although these are anecdotes, the message is familiar: Caretaking for children is women's work. The same kind of enactments occur regarding men's work and men's socially sanctioned roles. Almost every cross-sex couple has experienced a common reinforcement of the male provider role. After a meal out, even if she gives her credit card to the waiter, the card is likely to be returned to any man over age 12 at the table. Interaction after interaction works to keep a couple in traditional gender roles. These everyday interactions are reinforced by the social structure that tends to sustain marriage as a gendered institution. Despite the feminist critique of marriage in the 1970s and changes in women's status in society (especially their growing representation in the workforce), women and men experience marriage differently. For example, men continue to be expected to initiate sex more often than women do. Although women have gained rights to sexual initiation, they walk a fine line. In couples where wives initiate sex more than their husbands do, the husband's marital satisfaction tends to decrease (Blumstein and Schwartz 1983).

Heterosexual cohabitation is similar to marriage, in that it tends to be a monogamous relationship of more than trivial duration and is usually founded on love and the hope for a continued future. Cohabitors and married people differ, however, in terms of economic dependence and the likelihood that children are present. Although heterosexual cohabitors often drift into polarized positions economically and domestically, the division of labor is even more divided for heterosexual marrieds. Half of married couples are dual-earners, but income and household data demonstrate that husbands end up the primary breadwinner and, when children are present, wives the primary parent, in charge of the home. These stark differences are less present in cohabiting relationships (Blumstein and Schwartz 1983).

Race and the Significance of Marriage

The differences in the degree to which men and women in different ethnic groups desire marriage reveal powerful social influences. For example, Latino men desire marriage more than other men, but Latina women are also more favorably disposed toward marriage than other women. African American women are less likely than other women to express an interest in marriage. White men are the least likely to express interest in marriage or remarriage (although they are still more interested than white women) perhaps because white men on average have greater opportunities in life than men of other racial groups even without the advantage of having a wife (Tucker and Mitchell-Kernan 1995).

Differences in who actually gets married within different ethnic groups demonstrate that marriage is more of a social than a private institution. Prior to the 1960s, whites and African Americans had similar profiles in terms of age of marriage and proportion married at any given time. Since then, however, the flight from marriage has been much greater among African Americans than whites. Blacks get married later in life, marriages are shorter in duration, divorce is more frequent, and remarriage is less likely than it is for whites. The explanation has much to do with gender: By tradition, marriage dictates the man be more dominant than the woman in the economic sphere. However, African

Americans, more so than whites, have a smaller gender difference in terms of income. Put another way, black male employment is positively related to marriage rates. Therefore, high rates of unemployment depress the likelihood that black men will marry (Tucker and Mitchell-Kernan 1995:93). Black men, like white men, earn more than women of either race, but for blacks, the gender difference is smaller. The size of the gender difference is crucial for understanding heterosexual marriage, which tends to be structured around wives' dependency on husbands. In the absence of alternative styles of marriage (such as peer marriage, which we discuss at the end of this chapter), minimal gender differences tend to minimize interest in heterosexual marriage.

Do ethnic differences in marriage influence marital sex? This is a difficult question to answer definitively, but we think so. For example, in the American Couples survey, black heterosexual pairs, which constituted less than 9 percent of the sample, had a smaller gender difference in patterns of sexual initiation and refusal (Blumstein and Schwartz 1983). Where social power is shared more equitably, so sexual entitlement may also be more similar. Furthermore, Chapter 2 presented data showing that masturbation rates, duration of sexual episodes, and rates and patterns of giving and receiving oral sex vary with race and ethnicity, and differences in sexual patterns are not limited to these categories.

Ethnic differences appear to be caused partly by economics but also by culture and social class. For example, black women tend to be less eager to marry than women of other racial groups, perhaps because they receive fewer economic benefits. However, more than economic independence is involved. Once economics change the balance of power, there may also be changes in the way men and women interact. Men may feel that women who are not economically dependent on them will not be "good wives" in the traditional sense. Black women are more independent on average than other women and therefore less likely to be as suppliant as traditional men might prefer. It is also true that lower income is associated with a higher divorce and separation rate. Moreover, African Americans often feel, because of the history of institutionalized racism in the United States, that legal bureaucracies do not operate on their behalf and tend to be less invested in ratifying their personal or family lives. For them, marriage becomes a more personal event, and therefore African Americans are more likely to cohabit rather than to marry legally—especially among the poor.

Cultural themes can even overcome class differences. In Latino families, for example, Catholicism is an important cultural influence. Because many Latinos are Catholic, the church's rules about sex and relationships are followed more closely among lower-income Latinos than among lower-income whites or African Americans. Few other racial groups have this kind of religious homogeneity. Thus, we would expect to find sexual commonalities among Latinos of all social classes—like lower masturbation rates—and we do. The extent to which these sexual practices are changing among Latinos is a good measure of **acculturation,** or the adoption of mainstream "American" trends and the rejection of traditional religious teaching.

Another example of acculturation is the increasing tendency of ethnic groups to intermarry rather than marry only one another. Chinese-Japanese marriages—unheard of in great numbers until very recently—expose two highly homogeneous groups to new values and new behaviors. Increasingly, Asian Americans are marrying the person they fall in love with rather than their parents' choice of spouse. That is part of being Americanized. Interracial and interethnic relationships, as well as relationships involving biracial individuals (i.e., Latino and African American) are only beginning to be studied, as the practice becomes increasingly common. In a study of heterosexual, biracial undergraduates, Twine (1996) observed that whom one pairs with was almost explicitly linked with individuals' ethnic identity. The study of such pairs promises to provide useful observations about the connection between the social structure and individuals' romantic and sexual imagination.

Same-Sex Commitment

With no legal institution of marriage available to them, homosexuals can feel less societal pressure—or at least, less family pressure—to move in together, restrict sexual access to others, and make emotional commitments. Nonetheless, the urge to bond with another person is strong, and it seems that a majority of homosexuals do so. Lesbians and gay men, like heterosexuals, are socialized into the two-by-two world, and their requirements for bonding come from early socialization and a social structure that relies on pair bonding. A pair of studies reported by Janet Lever (1994a, 1995) in a national gay and lesbian lifestyle magazine, the *Advocate,* indicated that more than 92 percent of homosexual men and women favor being in a couple. The *Advocate* survey was not a random sample, but the information that gays and lesbians prefer couplehood has been observed repeatedly.

The interest in commitment among gay men is a recent phenomenon related to the threat of AIDS and the aging of the baby boom population. Although gay men are currently more interested in commitment than they were in the 1980s, commitment doesn't necessarily include sexual exclusivity, as it tends to for heterosexuals and lesbians.

Even though lesbians value commitment and sexual exclusivity, they have a higher than expected break-up rate (Blumstein and Schwartz 1983). Perhaps lesbians develop strong emotional relationships with women outside the relationship that turn quickly to sexual attraction and even extrarelationship sex. Because sex and love are ideologically united, "cheating" is more likely to prompt a breakup of the original relationship and formation of another.

As proponents of same-sex marriage point out, no institutional framework exists to help keep homosexual relationships intact. Without the institution of marriage, the idea of lifetime commitment, 'til death (or complicated legal extrication) do you part, is less likely. But the idea of marriage has great appeal. Almost three-quarters of the lesbians and 85 percent of gay men would legally marry if allowed to do so (Lever 1994a, 1995). Some lesbians and gay men have put the right to marry at the top of their political action and advocacy agenda. (See discussion of same-sex marriage in Chapter 5.)

The Importance of Sex in Marriage

Just as Noah lined up the animals two by two, human beings tend to pair and then weather the storms that come along. Unlike Noah's animals, however, humans today are not solely focused on the procreative bond that is at the center of sociobiological explanations of sexuality. In fact, it seems that sexual expectations have escalated to the point that a marriage is often considered a failure if it does not foster sustained sexual interest and pleasure. In many centuries past and in many countries today, sexual boredom would not be an important consideration in gauging a marriage, but today sex is often considered a central element of happiness. Not only do people think that they deserve great and frequent sex, but if they do not have it, they may question the strength of the rest of the relationship.

Some evidence suggests that the sexual expectations of women and men are not the same, however. In the American Couples study, women who reported that they had a mediocre or bad sex life might still rate their marriage as very good, depending on the extent to which domestic labor was shared and on other aspects of intimacy. Men were much more likely to rate their marriage as flawed if they considered their sex life poor.

For both sexes, particularly in younger couples, the expectation of an extremely good, if not spectacular, sex life has become a common part of committed relationships. Even couples who recognize that sexual frequency typically declines over time may struggle with this reality. "Not us," they say. Truly, a certain amount of romanticism is crucial to creating marital bonds. Despite the well-publicized rates of divorce—one out of every two marriages will end in divorce—people keep marching into the institution with the blithe optimism that the likelihood of divorce is for someone else, not them. Pairs have faith that their passionate spark will not dim.

Part of the definition of couplehood in the United States and in most of the West is having sex together. Sex is seen as the validation of the relationship, proof of the couple's compatibility. One of our grandmothers liked to say that sex is the least important part of a marriage, but if the couple's sex life isn't right, nothing else is. That is, sex is a barometer for the rest of the relationship; a mundane sex life equals a mundane love. This is a common belief. Leonore Tiefer (1995), psychologist and therapist, notes that the sex therapy industry has advanced the notion that sexual disappointments augur poorly for the relationship, even though "marriage counselors and therapists say that sexual dissatisfaction is often a consequence of marital troubles rather than a cause" (p. 14). Nevertheless, happily married couples can and do experience sexual problems.

The expectation of a stellar sex life and the fear of being mediocre have made twentieth-century couples very interested in sex studies, sex books, sex movies—you name it. Everyone wants to know how they measure up. People wonder what normal sexual behavior is, how often others "do it," and every other detail. The science of sex has given us a general picture of sexual behavior among married couples. But the fetish for counting undermines our understanding of the details. It also overemphasizes certain sexual activities, especially intercourse and orgasm, rather than alternatives like prolonged touching for sexual pleasure.

In reality, as a relationship goes on, and especially as partners age, sex can become a much less important part of life. As Figure 4.1 shows, after 10 years, 15 percent of respondents in the American Couples survey were having sex once a month or less. For a few, sex may even become nonexistent. Part of this decline can be explained by individual and socially constructed difference, including gender difference. Part can be attributed to the relationship itself. And part of the attenuation in sexual activity is a function of habituation, fatigue, or absorption in work, child raising, or everyday issues and worries.

Remarkably, the "culture of couplehood" may help to sustain the rates of intercourse in a marriage. That is, with marriage comes the expectation that you have to "work at it." As powerful as the dictum to "work at a relationship" is, the notion of work and the experience of sexual pleasure are rarely compatible. Nevertheless, marrieds may have some kind of "normal" sexual frequency because it is part of the definition of being married: "It's Friday night. We have to do it, like it or not!" Early in a couple's romantic career, sex is about seduction, attraction, and excitement. But within marriage it is often a "duty" and, on rare occasions, an epiphany of commitment and closeness.

Traditionally, however, duty has been the impetus for sustained sexual involvement within married pairs. Catholic tradition, for example, obligates couples to have sex, primarily or even solely for reproduction. This is "God's will." In Protestant tradition, marital sex is often viewed as a "wifely duty." In Jewish rabbinical law, however, sex is viewed as the "husband's duty." Sex is a mitzvah—a good deed—from God, and sex on the Sabbath is a double mitzvah. Thus, sex turns out not to be a private matter at all but a matter between the couple and their god.

In legal tradition, husbands and wives have been entitled to file for divorce on the basis of "sexual abandonment." Sex has seemed to be so much of an entitlement that, until recent years (Finkelhor and Yllö 1985), a husband who forced his wife to have sex with him could not be prosecuted for rape. In some countries, this is still the case. Even in the United States, spousal rape is still a hard charge to make stick, unless the couple is legally separated or physical damage can be proved.

Heterosexual and homosexual cohabitors experience patterns of sexual erosion (as well as the growth of intimacy) that are similar to—although not the same as—patterns within marriage. Cohabitors experience declines in sexual frequency over time. However, married couples start out with lower levels of sexual frequency than cohabitors do. Married couples are also far more likely to have offspring, who facilitate the decline in sexual satisfaction (from exhaustion, diminution of time together, conflict). The presence of kids also tends to generate or extend the gender gap. But the presence of children also increases the likelihood that pairs will remain together (Morgan, Lye, and Condran 1988).

In general, society is geared to support married couples and to treat other couples as more ephemeral. The very act of treating couples as permanent helps instill in couples a sense of commitment despite any disappointments in sex and other areas. With a less formal commitment and a relationship based on satisfaction more than obligation, heterosexual and homosexual cohabitors are less likely to tolerate a tremendous decline in sexual frequency.

To summarize, people in long-term committed relationships—whether marriage or cohabitation—have higher rates of sexual frequency than people in shorter-term relationships or no relationship at all. But married couples have more sexual opportunity and stability. Cohabitors, whether heterosexual or homosexual, have greater sexual frequency but more fragility.

Commitment and Passion

Does the perception that marriage suffocates passion have anything to do with the gendered quality of marriage? Recall the image presented in Chapter 2: Men consider sex a sport, and women consider it an outcome of intimacy, an interlude to "playing house."

The idea that sex is tamed by commitment and that women turn from lovers into mothers and wives is a fear before marriage and for some men, an angry complaint after marriage. Men's magazines eroticize the stranger or lover, not the wife. Movies generally use the live-in partner—cohabitor or wife—as the foil for the exciting outside relationship. If a marriage is identified as vibrant and sexy at the start of the movie, it is usually endangered soon: a kidnapping, murder, or some other threat allows moviegoers to root for the husband and wife to stay together. Love stories are about searchers, beginnings, affairs, all as-yet-uncommitted lovers. Commitment and sexiness don't go together in men's magazines or other popular media.

Meanwhile, women's magazines supplement their stories of love affairs and physical chemistry with articles about how to keep your man, how to have great sex "with the one you love," how to make love grow, how to keep your marriage sexually exciting, and so on. Romance novels always put sex in the context of eventual love and marriage: For the most part, free and unattached sexuality is not a female fantasy.

These are the stereotypes about gender differences in committed sex. To determine their validity, we can look at data regarding sexual frequency, patterns of initiation and refusal for sexual activity, and patterns within same-sex pairs.

Sexual Frequency

There is an old saying that if a couple puts a penny in a jar for every time they have sex in the first year of marriage and then takes a penny out of the jar for every time they have sex the rest of the marriage, the pair will never empty out the jar. Surveys suggest that during the first year couples have a lot of sex—an average of about three times per week. Some impassioned spouses have sex every minute they can get their hands on each other. But frequency declines definitely and impressively after the early years, and every year thereafter sex gets a little scarcer, as Figure 4.1 indicates.

Although the decline in sexual activity is associated with aging, novelty has a similar impact. The sex lives of 50- and 60-year-old newlyweds resemble younger couples' sex lives more than long-married couples their same age. And older newlyweds, like their younger counterparts, soon follow the course set for all marriages (Blumstein and Schwartz 1983).

Three things are worth discussing here: the decline in frequency, the maintenance of a sex life over the long haul, and sustained emotional commitment and marital stability among some abstinent couples.

Sexual decline is generally understood as the consequence of habituation. All evidence about sexuality indicates that passion is fueled by novelty, uncertainty, achievement of someone's love, and desire. Marriage itself mitigates uncertainty and the need for achievement of someone's love. Thus, marriage itself reduces some of the prime motivations for sexual arousal. Women, trained to have a taste for commitment, may rely less on erotic motivations and somewhat more on relationship satisfaction. But just like men, women can become bored by predictability.

Even women who find commitment sexy ultimately get distracted by the demands of daily life. Couples evolve into partners rather than lovers. Another factor is declines in marital satisfaction from time to time. The dictates of everyday life—especially those related to the care of children—diminish marital satisfaction and sexual behavior. Couples may enjoy sex as much as or even more than they did earlier in their relationship, but they just don't desire each other as often. If a marriage is highly conflicted, sex may diminish so much that eventually the couple no longer even try to have sex together. Finally, one of the partners may simply be less interested in sex than the other partner. In any case, the result is less sex in the relationship.

Even when couples enjoy sex, they tend to enjoy it less often as time goes on. In some cases, sex disappears but the marriage remains together. One man who was interviewed for an article on parenting was in a 23-year marriage, in which there had been no sex for the past 10 years. When asked why he, a successful lawyer and an extremely handsome man of 45, would stay in a marriage like this, he said,

> It's not so hard to understand. I have three amazing children who are my whole life, and who I would never leave. I have been very financially successful, and I have no desire to lose all that for myself or my children because of a messy divorce. I have a few meaningless affairs every so often when I start feeling too sorry for myself. And that makes things bearable. If I could have a good marriage with a reasonable sex life, I would do that. But I don't, and this isn't the worst of all compromises.[1]

The belief is that when you contract marriage, "You've made your bed, so you lie in it—even if you don't lay in it!"

In most marriages, however, sex becomes less frequent but not less pleasant. As long as couples still have sex, as long as sex is not a disaster when it happens, couples feel they are meeting the signature requirement of marriage: that sex happens. When sex is so spare or absent, or when it is unpleasant or hostile, it becomes a vulnerability in the couple's life and may start to undermine the marriage.

These patterns apply to heterosexual cohabitors as well. Figure 4.3 indicates sexual frequency by length of relationship. Sexual frequency declines over time. However, sex is more frequent among long-term cohabitors than among long-term married couples (refer back to Figure 4.1).

Initiation and Refusal

As we discussed in Chapter 2, initiation and refusal are deeply gendered sexual customs that affect sexual frequency. Because leadership and dominance are considered masculine, men are required to take charge in various ways. One of the simpler ways of showing masculinity, as it is stereotypically defined, is to be the director of a couple's sex life.

FIGURE 4.3

Sexual Frequency for Heterosexual Cohabitators

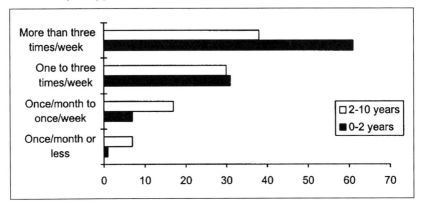

Source: Data from Blumstein and Schwartz (1983).

It is also true that one of the elements of arousal is desire. For many men, their own desire tends to be a sexual cue; for many women, their partner's desire tends to be the cue. If men always initiate, they are responding to their own internal signals of desire but are then less often the recipients of lust. When women are mostly the recipients of desire, they must wait for cues from their partners to commence satisfying their own sexual appetites. Women learn to experience their partners' desire as erotic.

Despite the strong social pressures on men to initiate sex, studies have shown that men want women to initiate more—just not too much. Men want to be wanted, but they don't want to give up the thrill of being the sexually dominant partner. Some data show that men like a woman to initiate often but that when she starts to initiate more than he does, satisfaction decreases (Blumstein and Schwartz 1983). Women have been given leeway to be sexual, but it is unclear how sexual they can be before reprisal. Desire still is supposed to begin with the male. Of course, some images in the popular media present a woman seducing a man—recall the bar parking lot scene from *The Last Seduction*, which was described at the beginning of Chapter 3. Many people find these stories sexually stimulating. But just like the guy in *The Last Seduction*, many men are uncomfortable, even humiliated, by female initiation. The statistics still tell a traditional story. Men do more of the initiating than women in all age groups.

The same traditions persist when it comes to refusal. No longer are wives expected to have headaches and be forgiven for their lesser interest in sex. On the other hand, refusal is still a woman's tool for controlling or responding to her partner. Similarly, men are not supposed to refuse, even if they are in long-term, perhaps boring, sexual relationships. The politics of modern sexuality profess to give men as much right as women to refuse sex, but in fact women sometimes feel extremely rejected when their spouses respond to advances with "I'm too tired." Women see their own right to say "I'm tired" as quite a different thing. The stereotype of men's greater sexual appetite is still alive and well. A man's refusal is seen as going against his natural instincts, whereas a woman's sexual refusal tends to be interpreted as a reflection of her natural, lesser desire. We never see a man refuse his wife or lover in the movies unless he is angry at her, drunk, dead tired, or having an affair with someone else.

The traditional imagery of initiation and refusal recurs implicitly and explicitly in the process of sex education. Men and boys are instructed to resist their own desire. Women and girls are advised to resist the other person's desire so that they can protect themselves. These stereotypes make it difficult for men and women to experience the full range of sexual expression. The exceptions to this rule, like the heroine in Spike Lee's film *She's Gotta Have It* (1987), are so rare in this culture that the mere introduction of a lusty, demanding, unapologetic, independent female sexual initiator becomes a cultural event, and her character, not just the movie, is discussed in magazines, in newspapers, and on talk shows.

Same-Sex Pairs

According to the men-as-initiators custom, gay men should have the most sex and lesbians the least, and there is some truth to that. However, other issues complicate it. Figure 4.4 shows patterns of sexual frequency among homosexuals. As with other groups, frequency declines over time. But these statistics show that frequency is not dependent on gender. If women's socialization to have less sex were a factor, lesbians would have a pronounced change in sexual frequency. Gay men would not. But they do; 33 percent of gay men in relationships enduring more than 10 years have sex once a month or less. Gay couples and heterosexual cohabitors start out with higher sexual frequency than lesbian pairs, but over time, all relationship types move toward reduced sexual activity.

FIGURE 4.4

Sexual Frequency among Gay and Lesbian Pairs

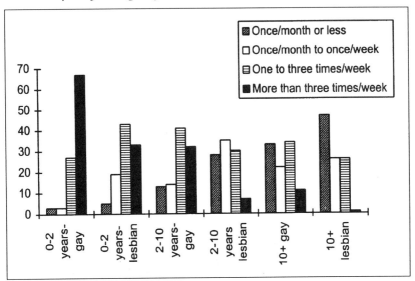

Source: Data from Blumstein and Schwartz (1983).

Differences between gays and lesbians in sexual frequency have several ramifications. For instance, men in our culture—straight and gay—are tantalized with visions of sexual variety. Rock Hudson's incredulity at Tony Randall's pitch for marriage in the scene from *Pillow Talk* that opened this chapter is based on the understanding that men would always prefer a variety of romantic options to one romantic, and domestic, option. In various polls, straight and gay men tend to rate the desire for variety higher than do women. This creates a special challenge for long-term gay relationships.

If variety spikes desire among men and desire is required for initiation, gay men in committed relationships may decrease initiation. Without the marital sexual obligation, gay male couples must find new ways to cultivate sexual connection. Many do, with sex toys, videos, or outside partners. But others allow sexual frequency in a long-term relationship to slide.

The cultural expectation that men are more sexually predatory is costly to gay men. Whereas women are perceived to temper men's desire, men who love men theoretically have little to stop them from sexual extremes. Sex research reveals that gay men do in fact have much higher sexual frequency and seek greater variety than other sexual pairs. However, society's expectation for all men also shapes homophobic views. Gay men are seen as dangerous sexual predators or as hedonists who can't be trusted, especially with children. In reality, a prodigious sexual appetite has nothing to do with desiring children or observing other sexual norms like choosing socially acceptable partners.

Lesbians, like straight women, share the custom of initiating less than men do and refusing more. With lesbians, however, if each woman expects to be approached and both wait for the other woman to initiate, inevitably sexual frequency slows down. Likewise, if both women feel comfortable saying no, less sex is likely.

Additionally, many lesbians are sensitive about sex as a source of power. Power issues are a common theme for lesbian pairs, who tend to be more politically aware and wary of manipulation. Because many lesbians are in a position to be able to reject the hierarchical nature of heterosexual relationships, they are sensitized to any replication of those patterns in their own homes. A sexually intense partner, especially one who likes sex for its own sake, may be seen as aggressive and unfeeling. Sexual gratification is not seen as a right so much as an outgrowth of a good relationship (on a good day in that relationship). "Pushing it" can be seen as a power trip or, even worse, as coercion or rape. (Obviously, the mechanics of coercion depart from heterosexual rape; the American Couples study used any genital contact as the definition of lesbian sex, whether consensual or coercive.) In couples for whom sexual aggression is a sensitive issue, sexual initiative can be complicated.

The cultural expectation for lesbians to be loving and relationship focused further complicates life. Some lesbians, especially younger women, don't fit the mold and don't want to be seen as nonsexual or passive. Women who want to date, delay commitment, and follow their career can often be seen, from other quarters of the lesbian world, as struggling with a damaged psyche rather than as exercising the same rights to sexual independence and curiosity that men are free to express. A sexually adventurous lesbian may be tagged as predatory and some-how less womanly if she steps out of her gender's sexual script. Even a movie that defies that sexual image, such as *Bound*, a 1996 thriller in which a sexually aggressive, beautiful "butch" lesbian successfully pursues a woman who is being "kept" by a [male] mobster, still is essentially a love story. In it, the two women quickly become totally committed. This was a "mainstream" movie, not a lesbian movie for a primarily lesbian audience. Nevertheless, it was clearly designed to be attractive to lesbian sensibilities.

Everyday Influences on Committed Sex

In predicting sexual frequency, gendered social scripts are perhaps more important than gendered sexual scripts. Everyday life and family events may have greater effect on a couple's sex life than anything else. After all, the sex must occur in the context of the ongoing, daily lives, with demands, burdens, and triumphs that influence how pairs feel when they are in the bedroom.

All couples have external pressures that reduce sexual desire. They have everyday issues that create the biggest barrier there is to sexual frequency: anger and resentment. A preponderance of marital therapy research (i.e., Gottman 1994; Jacobson and Christensen 1996), which focuses strictly on troubled marriages, supports this assertion and explains it in terms of a **demand/withdraw cycle** in communication. A demand/withdraw cycle is a polarizing process whereby a partner's demands for greater intimacy leads to the other partner's withdrawing and retreating. The order can also be reversed: It is as often a withdraw/demand cycle.

This pattern tends to be gendered: Women are demanders, men are withdrawers. But don't confuse this imagery with some sort of essentialist vision of "men are from Mars and women are from Venus." In a significant proportion of troubled relationships, women are withdrawers and men are demanders. Furthermore, research on communication patterns among healthy couples, both heterosexual and homosexual, demonstrates that demand and withdraw patterns in communication are less associated with gender and more clearly associated with power. The more powerful partner has the privilege of being withdrawn (Kollock, Blumstein, and Schwartz 1985).

Interestingly, the demand/withdraw pattern in communication tends to be the inverse of the sexual one, where men tend to be demanders and women withdrawers. This pattern makes sense. The person with more power is more entitled, including more sexually entitled. But sex may not be particularly appealing to the person who has less power, who withdraws sexually. The other person, if offended by the sexual refusal, may retaliate by withdrawing emotionally. The less powerful partner then responds by becoming more demanding emotionally. However, to the extent that withdrawing from sex is related to power, women's power of refusal defines them as having only sexual power.

Among highly conflicted couples, sex becomes rare or nonexistent. Sometimes high-conflict couples are turned on by the regrets, apologies, and recommitment the couple has to go through to stay together. But for the most part, conflict depletes the sexual agenda rather than stokes it. Even in good relationships, sexual frequency gradually decreases. But sex usually doesn't disappear.

Emotional Complications for Heterosexuals

The demand/withdraw cycle in marital relationships can be exacerbated by the arrival of a first child and consolidated by subsequent children. There is substantial evidence that children depress both desire and sexual behavior (Call, Sprecher, and Schwartz 1995). One reason is that babies increase anxiety levels. But they don't produce the pleasant anxiety that lovers feel trying to impress and possess each other. No, this is the anxiety of paying bills, doing more in the same amount of time, and managing the baby schedule so it doesn't undermine work commitments.

Babies are also exhausting, and fatigue is a staunch enemy of sexual desire. People have only so much energy, and a baby who doesn't sleep through the night for a year or more creates a greater desire for sleep than for sex on the part of overwhelmed parents. Especially when children are infants, sleep deprivation falls more heavily on a mother than on a father because of the demands of breast-feeding and the social expectations of mother-focused child rearing.

A woman may love her husband as much as or more than she did before the baby came, but her energy is focused on this new human being. A woman who isn't emotionally engrossed in her infant is treated with suspicion. Reprisals come in the details of everyday interaction, but custody battles are also illustrative. For example, in 1995 a white, single mother in her early 20s was denied custody of her infant because she was a full-time student at the University of Michigan. The baby's dad was also a white, full-time student, but his mother agreed to stay home with the baby, so the dad won out over the mom—at least until the father's mother died in 1996 ("Parents End Battle" 1996).

Husbands, though often understanding about a baby's needs, may feel dislocated, lonely, pushed away, or even pushed out. Unless they are highly involved in their child's life (despite being discouraged by norms of work and family leave), they may be angry about the severe constraints on the affection and sexual relationship they were accustomed to with their spouse. Some marriages run aground in this period, and marital satisfaction typically declines with the entrance of children into the couple's lives.

Same-Sex Burdens

Same-sex pairs share most of the burdens of everyday life that influence heterosexuals, but there are also impediments unique to homosexuals. Lesbians, for example, are often under more economic pressure than other kinds of couples because two women more rarely have incomes that protect them from financial crises (Klawitter and Flatt n.d.). Of course, women who are single parents, whether heterosexual or lesbian, are even more vulnerable to financial problems.

Gay men and lesbians, because they are more discriminated against than heterosexual couples, may constantly be placed in situations that stress them (Patterson 1995). Both gay and lesbian couples are more often rejected by their partner's parents and perhaps by their own than other kinds of couples. Families sometimes blame their child's lover for his or her homosexuality. Or they will continue to treat their gay family member well but be awkward or unaccommodating toward their family member's partner. They may refuse to cooperate in major ways, perhaps by blocking child custody rights for a gay partner when the family member dies. But they may also raise barriers in pettier ways, as when they exclude a gay partner from a family photograph. Heterosexual in-laws and long-term partners may be included without a second thought. Even such seemingly small matters can lead to resentment between partners or to a cutoff from one's family (and from any of the emotional and material resources that families provide) or both.

Issues of whether to stay "closeted" or be "out" to the world become relationship pitfalls when the two partners disagree about how to handle them (Patterson and Schwartz 1994). This dilemma is heightened by the cost of being in or out. A gay man in a mainstream career may seek to remain closeted or discreet about his relationship, but his partner may feel strongly that being out is a political statement. Being closeted or out has economic and political consequences that can make these conflicts very intense.

FIGURE 4.5

Sexual Frequency per Month by Age (for Marrieds)

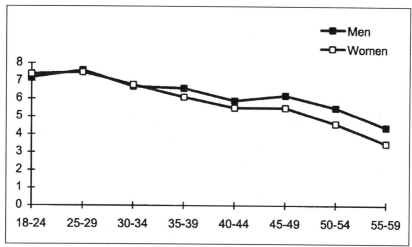

Source: Data from Laumann, Michael, and Gagnon (1994).

The Special Problems of Older Partners

Age may biologically depress desire, but it doesn't extinguish it. The issue of age and sexuality is sure to grow in the next two decades as the population of elderly persons rises, from 32 million in 1991 to an estimated 51 million by the year 2020 (Masters, Johnson, and Kolodny 1995). Increasingly, elderly people will be those who came of age during or after the sexual revolution, and they are less likely to go gently into their later years.

Figure 4.5 demonstrates the decline in sexual frequency by age. After age 60, frequency tends to level off to several times a month either until sexual disability becomes a factor or until a person reaches his or her 70s or 80s (Masters et al. 1995). Many people in their 70s and 80s still report sexual activity and enjoyment. The single biggest enemy of sex for older people is health. But if health is held constant, the desire for at least some sex continues.

With aging and the mellowing of a long-term partnership, sex lives still have the potential to improve. The security of a marriage or a long-term commitment emboldens some partners to ask for exactly what they need and allows them to work out a mutually satisfying sexual style. Paradoxically, the consistency that tends to reduce sexual frequency also provides the conditions for sexual satisfaction through intimate negotiation.

Social Trends in Improving Committed Sex

Sexual improvement and sexual knowledge do not come naturally for pairs. Although sexual desire may emerge from a complex mixture of biology and social experience, sex is something people learn how to do. Consider the old joke "How do you get to Carnegie Hall?" Answer: "Practice, practice, practice!" The punch line certainly applies to improving sex between committed partners. Still, couples can be as incapable with each other after 10 years of practice as they were in their first sexual encounter, because sexual partners don't typically arrive in bed with an instruction manual, and giving one's partner directions can feel embarrassing or awkward. After many years, though, a couple may feel particularly stymied if much time has passed with no change or improvement. The sexual dilemma can be distressing:

> Imagine how you would feel if playing gin rummy, and playing it well, were considered a major component of happiness and a major sign of maturity, but no one told you how to play, you never saw anyone else play, and everything you ever read implied that normal and healthy people just somehow "know" how to play and really enjoy playing the very first time they try! It is a very strange situation. (Tiefer 1995:11-12)

Anybody can have sex. But good sex takes practice and communication. The matter of learning how to do sex is made complicated, however, by today's intense media climate. There is informal sexual instruction in almost every program on TV, advertisements tell the public how to dress erotically, and movies show seduction scenes and graphic sexual moves.

Sometimes the examples highlight sexual disappointments. For example, a 1995 episode from the television show "Seinfeld" focused on oral sex. The character Elaine was dating a sexy saxophone player but was troubled that he never gave her oral sex. Later on, after she had figured out how to introduce the subject, she and her partner were excited to go test the new sexual activity. The punch line of this story was that after an episode of cunnilingus, his mouth was tired and he couldn't play the sax that night. Everyone watching understood the joke: When they had finally gotten around to oral sex, it had been an exhausting exercise that left Elaine's boyfriend's mouth numb. It was their first time having oral sex, and the pair needed more practice and more instruction.

Sexual instruction is available through seminars, videos, books, and standard textbooks. For long-term couples, much of the content deals with habituation, boredom, or lifestyle obstacles to good sex. The focus on the need for extra stimulation seems to intensify each year. For example, *The Multi-Orgasmic Man* (Chia and Arava 1996), which reintroduces tantric sex, suggests new ways to be a great lover. (The joke among marrieds, of course, is that multiorgasmic means more than once a month.) This particular book publicizes ancient techniques for controlling ejaculation while enabling orgasm. Probably the most popular of such books, and perhaps more mainstream, were the beautifully illustrated *Joy of Sex* (Comfort 1972) and *More Joy* (Comfort 1974), which introduce couples to the idea of multiple positions under the idea of "gourmet sex"—something couples can "cook up" collaboratively and thus be happier with each other.

Social commentary on sexual issues not only illuminates problems, it may also create them. Almost every decade shows an increase in a certain kind of sexual dysfunction that disappears or vastly decreases as a new problem emerges to take its place.

Social Trends of the 1960s

When Masters and Johnson published *Human Sexual Response* in the 1960s, few people read it but almost everyone talked about it. The book gave many people permission to identify and address sexual problems in their relationships. A new specialty, sex therapy, based on Masters and Johnson's observations, advertised help to repair sexual difficulties. Thus, long-term couples who had given up on sexual happiness now had names for the problems they were having and had a place to go for help.

Masters and Johnson's research provided the beneficial knowledge that there was no hierarchy of orgasms for women, with some types better than others. The father of psychoanalysis, Sigmund Freud, along with his followers, had declared that clitoral orgasms (rather than vaginal orgasms) were "immature" because they weren't stimulated by intercourse. From this early psychoanalytic perspective, intercourse constituted the pinnacle of sexual expression. This remained the psychological party line until Masters and Johnson's research disclosed that vaginal and clitoral orgasms are physiologically identical. This finding gave women greater permission to seek a variety of routes other than intercourse for achieving orgasm.

The change in perspective had symbolic as well as physical importance for women. Women who were married or living with someone and earning an income in the newly opened up workforce could also see themselves as full partners in the bedroom. As independent sexual beings, they could now pursue orgasms whether or not they were having sexual intercourse. Before Masters and Johnson destroyed the idea of the superiority of vaginal orgasms, women felt guilty that they had "inferior" orgasms during masturbation or were somehow damaged goods if they couldn't be orgasmic during intercourse. Masters and Johnson told women that some orgasms might feel better than others (e.g., if a person hadn't had an orgasm for a long time and was extremely turned on or if she was being touched more expertly than usual), that their intensity has nothing to do with whether they are produced by a penis rather than some other kind of stimulation. In fact, the pendulum of scientific opinion swung the other way. Once women were freer sexual agents, sharing personal sexual histories more freely and comparing experiences, many found that a large number of other women were more easily and more intensely orgasmic through oral sex or touching.

Masters and Johnson's groundbreaking research, which made fewer presumptions about how sex works than the Freudians had, depended on a new consciousness about how sex had been defined by men. In turn, these new authoritative "scientific" findings were required to give women the confidence to listen to their own bodies rather than try to fit Freud's vision of "good" and "bad" orgasms. Married women could now demand sex on their own terms, much the same way they were requiring more equity in the marketplace. Nevertheless, Masters and Johnson were hardly the last word on sexual functioning. As we noted in Chapter 1, the sample of men and women in their study were not particularly representative of the population.

When the first Masters and Johnson book appeared, the most common presenting complaint to sex therapists was vaginismus or dyspareunia for women and erectile failure for men. **Dyspareunia** is a generic term used for painful intercourse. It may have been extraordinarily common at the time because so many people were ignorant about making sure a woman was aroused before the entry of the penis or even a finger into the vagina. Insufficient natural or commercial lubricant could make penetration painful and lead to **vaginismus,** an involuntary clenching of the vaginal muscles that could make entry of the penis impossible or painfully difficult.

Erectile failure includes everything from total impotence (inability to get an erection) to situational erectile failure or inability to become hard enough for intercourse. Situational impotence is quite common— probably even more common than we can guess, because men with this problem may solve it privately and never seek a clinical assessment. But the "uncovering" of this fairly common problem was big news in the 1960s, and many men were encouraged to seek treatment and did. In fact, so many people sought treatment that many articles were written musing over the possibility that erectile failure was a direct response to the women's movement and the usurping of traditional male roles and privileges. For people who believed that ready and willing sexual desire is a natural part of masculinity, even situational erectile failure was considered a disruption of the laws of nature. It was a handy "crisis" for people who objected to the women's movement. Whatever the actual rate of sexual problems, it may have been emphasized for political purposes. One clue: Although situational impotence still exists, the media rarely mention it.

Trends of the 1970s

In the 1970s, discussion became centered on simultaneous orgasms and multiple orgasms. As the sexual revolution extolled new sexual frontiers, many couples began to feel that simultaneous orgasm was the height of sexual competence and intimacy. After all, a couple who had been together for a while ought to be able to "come" at the same time, went the thinking. This trend was in direct response to all the discoveries about what women could do and the pressure for couples to make sex the cosmic center of their lives. In the early days of the women's movement, women were touted as sexual athletes who were entitled to all the pleasure their bodies could provide, and men's performance was measured by the ability to provide all that pleasure.

Couples sought sex therapy to learn more control and better timing. But learning to produce simultaneous orgasm was so hard (and the effort made so many people feel frustrated) that ultimately there was a backlash. A number of writers began to say that simultaneous orgasm was more trouble than it was worth (e.g., Barbach 1975).

However, the mounting pressure to be multiorgasmic, particularly for women, was tenacious. Men were told that it was now their responsibility to be more accomplished lovers, but there were few measures of how well they were doing. Giving your partner multiple rather than single orgasms was the most measurable evidence of excellence yet, and so it became the new sexual standard for couples. Producing more than one paltry orgasm gave bragging rights.

This sexual expectation eventually died down but did not entirely go away. Competitive or anxious men still use this handy yardstick to prove their sexual prowess. However, such a standard is tough to meet even for partners who know each other well, although it also places a great deal of pressure on single and dating men and women.

Trends of the 1980s

The 1980s, the beginning of the AIDS epidemic, was a much more somber sexual age. Single heterosexuals and gay men were not the only ones who began to worry about what their sexual past might do to them. The fun and games encouraged in the 1960s and 1970s stopped with a rather sudden dull thud. Baby boomers, the largest part of the population, started settling down, marrying, and forsaking their single life and, for some, their wild and experimental pasts. It was perhaps inevitable that settling down was going to be difficult in a culture that had given them a free hand, in a culture that still touted sex from every billboard and every entertainment.

The complaint of the decade was called **inhibited sexual desire.** The problem was that one or both members of the couple simply did not want to have sex with each other enough—or ever. Of course, one could only determine what was enough by making a comparison to a norm in the culture. Sometimes inhibited sexual desire turned out to be a relationship problem; desire in general was not damaged, just desire for each other. Other times, the couple, although unperturbed in everyday life, worried that they were abnormal because so little sex was going on. Therapists dedicated to the idea that everyone ought to need and want sex were only too happy to help ratify a new sexual dysfunction and try to treat it. The diagnosis of inhibited sexual desire shifted the popular fetish for counting sexual events to a fetish for pathologizing sexual events (or nonevents).

Trends in the 1990s

In the 1990s, the sexual current again shifted. The United States has always been schizophrenic about sex, giving license and then being punitive about it. But the 1990s accelerated this tendency. As the AIDS crisis increased in ferocity, particularly among gay men, the inability of some people (both straight and gay) to curtail their sex lives in the face of overwhelming evidence of terrible danger created a new sexual therapeutic specialty. This has been the age of **sexual addiction.** People who could not control their sexual contacts or modify them in their own best interests were called "sex addicts." Programs were created that paralleled other addiction services, including various 12-step approaches similar to those used in drug and alcohol addiction treatment. How many people were actually compulsive sexually and how many were, like overeaters, mired in dangerous and self-destructive practices but not psychiatrically classifiable is not clear. But again, the moment in history influenced the definition of sexual pathology and sexual health.

When concerns about levels of sexual activity are raised in therapy, more women wish to be on the celibacy end of the continuum than men. As we have mentioned, women are more likely to get engrossed in their children and put the rest of their lives and sex on a back burner. More men than women turn to sex counseling with the complaint that their partner doesn't want them anymore; more women than men complain that their partner isn't "considerate" and presses them for more sex than they want. In fact, many lesbian couples seek sex counseling when one partner wants more sex than the other. Not uncommonly, the partner who wants less sex wants very little sex or no sex at all.

This gender difference follows from the fact that more men than women are socialized to be adventurers. Women still need more permission than men to open themselves up to an intense sexual life. For example, the research from the 1970s on "swingers" (couples who go to commercial sex clubs or advertise for couples to have sex with them) indicates that mostly the husbands convince their wives to try these experiments. Men were also more ready to quit the experiment than their wives were (Bartell 1971). It seems that once women got over the stigma of sexual liberality and nonmarital sex, they were as enthusiastic and perhaps even more adventurous than their husbands. We think this pattern holds true in the 1990s, too, although swinging is hardly as common these days.

The taste for adventure or for celibacy comes from how one was brought up and the experience a person has had up to the time of commitment to a long-term relationship. Women's legitimacy as people has traditionally been tied to their sexual purity and restraint, but that stereotype is increasingly untrue for them. As women's location in the social structure shifts, for example, as they obtain more power and influence in the marketplace, they can be more autonomous sexually.

Just as social conservatives have feared, growing levels of premarital sex, longer periods of sexual experience before marriage, and liberalization of female sexuality have affected the behavior of heterosexual and homosexual women. These trends are bound to shift the gendered reactions to sex in long-term relationships as well.

The Problem of Outside Temptations

One of the problems that many long-term partners fear, even if it never happens to them, is **nonmonogamy.** We are talking about sexual liaisons outside a committed relationship, which may be a single episode, a long-term affair, or a number of affairs. Most people refer to such affairs as cheating or infidelity because they believe they are a transgression of marriage vows. In fact, most studies on attitudes toward nonmonogamy show that more than 85 percent of both men and women disapprove of it (e.g., Laumann, Michael, and Gagnon 1994). Affairs are a threat to marriage and, because marriage is a powerful institution that tends to preserve and expand gendered differences, a threat to gendered expectations for sexual and other experience.

With such high disapproval ratings, we might guess that infidelity never happens. Some of the studies suggest that there is indeed a low rate of nonmonogamy. In the National Health and Social Life Survey (NHSLS; Laumann et al. 1994), 79 percent of men and 89 percent of women said they had been monogamous all of their marriage. However, nonrandom samples have reported lower rates of monogamy, and higher rates of nonmonogamy—anywhere from 25 percent to 30 percent (i.e., Hunt 1974; Blumstein and Schwartz 1983) to 50 percent plus surveys reported in popular magazines like *Playboy* and *Redbook.*

It is hard to know the truth. The methodologies used in some of the random sample surveys like the NHSLS may depress the actual numbers. Respondents had to pass their questionnaires back into the hands of the interviewers and thus may have been worried about anonymity. Also, some individuals may not want to talk about their affairs, because they don't want to admit it to themselves, much less to some impersonal questionnaire or interviewer. Furthermore, people have varying definitions of what constitutes an affair. One national politician has said that he preferred to have only oral sex with women other than his wife so that it "wouldn't count" as an affair. Still, there is evidence that monogamy is the case in the majority of marriages and that nonmonogamy may be more feared than real.

FIGURE 4.6

Lifetime Rates of Nonmonogamy among Married People

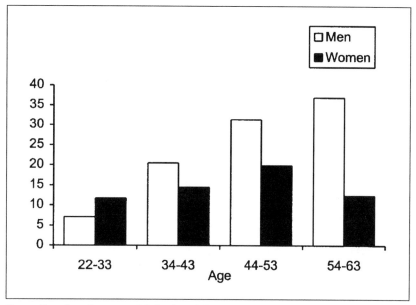

Source: Data from Laumann, Michael, and Gagnon (1994).

Some groups may be more at risk for nonmonogamy than others. In fact, research data about rates of extramarital affairs may not be as informative about how much nonmonogamy occurs as they are about the relative likelihood of different groups engaging in it. The NHSLS shows that rates of affairs are higher among people in the lowest educational category (did not complete high school) and in the highest educational category (completed a graduate degree). The most conservative group were college graduates. Urban dwellers and people of low professed religiosity were more likely to have affairs than others, and very poor people were more likely to have affairs than richer people. The NHSLS found that cohabitors had many more affairs than married people, perhaps because of their lesser level of commitment and more frequent exposure to opportunities (Laumann et al. 1994). Similarly, people who have multiple marriages are more likely to have an affair than those who remain in a first marriage.

Looking at two simple variables, age and gender, suggests some ways that the sexual double standard may have changed—or from another view, how it may not have changed much at all. Figure 4.6

shows the percentage of men and women who have been non-monogamous by age group.

Note that in the youngest age group, more women have been nonmonogamous than men and that women's rates increase less than men's throughout middle age, and then decrease in the oldest age grouping. These statistics suggest a trend: Over time, women have gained license to be nonmonogamous (and to admit it in a survey interview), although only the youngest women are more nonmonogamous than men in their age group.

You may also notice that as men age, their rates of nonmonogamy increase. Men in the oldest age group in the survey—ages 54-63—have had affairs at three times the rate of women. Of course this discrepancy is partly due to generation: men who were raised in the 1940s and 1950s have more "gendered" permission for extramarital sex. But the difference is also due to the way sexual attraction is gendered. In a crude sense, younger women have a higher "market value" than older women. Their power in a committed relationship and their allure to alternative mates make them more likely to have an affair. Alternatively, men's "market value" increases as they age, in general. This is a common explanation for **hypergamy**—younger women marrying slightly older men.

Homosexual couples are more vulnerable to affairs. Gay men have a high likelihood for extrarelationship sex, calculated as high as 95 percent. Lesbians are also more likely to practice nonmonogamy than heterosexual couples, with an estimated 38 percent for pairs together for 2 to 10 years having engaged in affairs (Blumstein and Schwartz 1983). For people who fit one of these higher-risk profiles, it may seem like everyone they know has had an outside relationship. But, in fact, those who have been nonmonogamous represent only a minority of the American population.

These general statistics are unimportant, however, for a person who discovers that a partner has betrayed the understanding about fidelity at the center of their relationship, or for a person contemplating an extramarital affair despite his or her committed relationship. Quite a few gay men and a substantial number of lesbians have a stated or tacit agreement that outside sex is possible under discreet and limited circumstances, but the vast majority of married and cohabiting heterosexuals do not. Ask most heterosexual married couples why they are monogamous, and they tend to find the question odd. The reply often is to the effect of, "Why get married, if you don't want to be monogamous?" Or, "a marriage is built on exclusivity and trust." Quite a few people would quote scripture and Bible and say that adultery is a sin. End of story (Lawson 1988). In other words, marriage is fundamentally a social institution: Affairs generate chaos. And yet, some people do go outside the relationship for sex and intimacy.

Why Do People Have Outside Sexual Relationships?

Whole books are devoted to the question of why people have affairs. How could someone betray a partner? As Frank Pittman (1989), a family therapist and "infidelity expert," notes, affairs are rarely about sex.

In many cultures and across time, a wife's infidelity has been much more harshly punished than a husband's. As a biological view of sexuality proposes, men's nonmonogamy has been considered a natural way to advance their genetic material; women's nonmonogamy undermines men's genetic investment in offspring. As a social constructionist view of sexuality proposes, women's nonmonogamy is punished as a way to control women's sexuality and fertility.

Looking the other way when men have affairs, however, has become less common in recent decades. During the presidency of John F. Kennedy in the early 1960s, journalists discreetly ignored his many extramarital liaisons. Thirty years later—after the sexual revolution, the divorce revolution, and the crises of herpes and AIDS—a public figure's infidelities are seized on with gusto by the media. During his campaign for election in 1992, President Bill Clinton was hounded by stories of his affairs, and he continued to be threatened with sexual harassment suits throughout his two terms. Public interest in the adventures of England's Prince Charles and Princess Diana was obsessive—and rewarded with details of their most private conversations, acts, and betrayals. This shift seems to have less to do with changing morality than with changing permission to talk about sex. The rumors of President Clinton's and other public figures' illicit sexual escapades is grist for the public mill of prurient sexual tales. And marital infidelity is considered an easy "example" of bad character.

Of course, infidelity is not so simple to explain. This is a difficult phenomenon to account for, but seven major reasons, culled from Lawson (1988), Pittman (1989), Jacobson and Christensen (1996), Glass and Wright (1992), and Blumstein and Schwartz (1983), merit attention.

1. *Emotional incompatibility.* Sometimes a marriage turns sour, but it still remains intact. Partners grow apart, they might not even like each other anymore. But they love their children or their place in the community, or they don't want to suffer the economic losses that divorce would

entail. They barely communicate anymore. If they still make love, they usually do so infrequently and more for an outlet than as an expression of intimacy. People in this category may have an extended affair or one-night stand occasionally just to regain a remnant of passion or affection in their life, even though they have no intention of breaking up their family or marriage. However, some marital therapists think such an affair can also be a way to generate a "crisis" to get out of an incompatible marriage (i.e., Jacobson and Christensen 1996).

2. *Boredom.* Some couples look at the person they are married to and wonder, "Is this all there is?" They miss experiencing passion or being seen again for the first time and appreciated anew. Even though sexual frequency usually declines in the course of committed relationships, sexual imagination may remain lively. People who seek affairs because their sex life has become so predictable and unexciting often cite the need for "an adventure." Or they cite the need to experience some sexual act or a rendezvous that will bring romance and excitement back into their life—or into their life for the first time. In these cases, the motive for nonmonogamy may be purely recreational. The person may or may not feel guilt about such an adventure, but in many cases, it has nothing to do with the marriage. These cases have more to do with identity and how the person feels about the need to be daring and to create a new self.

3. *Sexual incompatibility.* Some couples care greatly for each other but have ceased to desire each other. For instance, one woman wrote to Ann Landers complaining of having had sex with her husband for over 40 years just to please him. She was now tired of it and felt she shouldn't have to have sex with him anymore. She asked Ann Landers if there was some safe place men could go and exercise their desires and leave unwilling wives alone. On the other hand, a disability may make sex physically dangerous or painful. The nondisabled partner might discreetly see others to satisfy sexual desires the spouse cannot, or no longer wishes, to accommodate. In these cases, looking for sex outside the marriage has little to do with how loving the partners feel toward each other.

4. *Anger.* For many people, the act of nonmonogamy is a way of punishing the partner for emotional slights (Lawson 1988). People who feel unloved or neglected rationalize that they have the right to seek solace

elsewhere. Anger makes extramarital sex more likely in two ways: It makes making love to your partner difficult, thereby fueling a sense of deprivation; it also makes having sex outside the relationship seem like a good way to get even, especially when a direct approach is seen as impossible or ineffective. Partners who feel like they don't have the power to change things (and these might more often be women, because overall more women than men have less power in their relationship) do things in private as a secret, but satisfying, retaliation. Anger also reduces the guilt or shame of infidelity: "He treats me like dirt. I don't owe him anything."

5. *Flattery* (power/beauty). Sometimes nothing is wrong with the marriage. Instead, the attentions of an attractive or successful person are just too flattering to resist. The attentions of a worthy suitor may be especially tempting for someone whose self-esteem is low, especially if the spouse doesn't treat the person as attractive or exciting. The temptation is magnified if the suitor is someone the person could not have dreamed would have wanted her or him. But people who are in good relationships and who have good self-esteem can still sometimes end up having a fling or even a full-blown affair if tempted by an especially attractive person.

6. *A way out.* Some affairs are begun so that they can be found out and break up the relationship. A husband comes home with lipstick on his collar; he says he's someplace that he's not and knows his wife will check; or the girlfriend picks up the phone at the hotel. Many such stupid mistakes are meant to happen. Engineering a situation that will make the spouse angry is an indirect way to back out of a marriage, but it isn't rare. People who employ it can't quite make up their minds to leave or can't face talking to their partners. It is easier to allow themselves to be "discovered." Occasionally, they use this method to see if their partner still loves them, if the other person will want to save the relationship, but more often they use it to bring things to the boiling point.

7. *Love.* Sometimes affairs are based on "true love." Probably the most common circumstance is that two people who have been thrown together a lot start out as friends and then progress to much more. Two co-workers who have been on the same team for years, learning respect each other and like each other and trust each other, may fall in love (Glass and Wright 1992). Affairs between collea

occur when the primary relationship is satisfactory as well as when things aren't going so well at home. Or neighbors or people in the same friendship circle may learn to depend on and care for each other. Occasionally, "love at first sight" prompts an affair. Those affairs more rarely turn into the kind of relationship that lasts a lifetime. But some people who suddenly fall in love believe that they have met their "soul mate." No matter what the affair does to their home life, family, or marriage, they feel they cannot afford to let this new person go. One might guess that love would most often be the basis for an affair for women, for whom love is so important; paradoxically, some research suggests that love might be a more important motive for men's affairs. Although women are expected to have sex only when they are in love, and women's reports of sex and romance often are consistent with this social rule, men appear more likely to be "true" romantics than women (Rubin 1976) and more willing to throw away everything for love. Women are often less economically and socially independent than men and cannot disregard the financial and social upheaval such a love affair represents. They might fall in love but decide they cannot leave.

Is Nonmonogamy Gendered?

When it comes to extramarital affairs, the double standard flour-ishes. Men and women realize different benefits and costs for sex outside the relationship. Some men's freedom to be sexually aggressive and recreational guarantees that, at least in the heterosexual world, they would have more extramarital sex than women. Remember that the concept of adultery has historically applied only to women. Only in modern times, in some countries, has it been defined as a male trespass.

Women, on the other hand, have rarely had the standing to complain about their partner's behavior. Men's sexual acts outside the marriage may be considered deplorable, but they have never been seen, until quite recently and in only a few Western countries, as a great trespass. Even today in Western society some people wink at what they consider the built-in ual appetite but scowl and become punitive when extramarital sex. U.S. law no longer allows men to us wives with impunity. However, a wife's tres-abusive or murderous husband's sentence. In civil versions of the O. J. Simpson murder trials, the murder victim, Nicole Simpson, as a "party und and who therefore would have had many rs. The idea was not only an alternative explanation for her murder but also a way to make her a less sympathetic character. This is a pretty typical strategy. In a 1995 case in Texas, the judge gave a lighter-than-expected sentence to a man who killed his wife after catching her with another man. The case gained notoriety when the judge said he was sorry to have to give this guy any jail time at all.

Women are less likely to have sex outside the marriage, but the reasons are unromantic. First, they are simply more economically insecure than men. They fear losing economic support for their children and therefore have more conservative attitudes about sexuality. Second, women tend to be raised with a concern for "reputation," which influences their appeal to men. Third, most women have been trained to be champions of family values, and their sexuality has been geared to that responsibility. Finally, women tend to be more vulnerable to sexually transmitted disease than heterosexual men are. "Free spirits," women who are able to think of sex in recreational terms and who are financially capable of absorbing any fallout from their behavior are rare, particularly among the married.

Both women and men still have powerfully strong feelings against nonmonogamy, which are linked in part to the family values movement. Women are somewhat more likely than men to be critics of nonmonogamy, although the majority of both men and women condemn it. Women, however, are more vulnerable to the economic vicissitudes that follow divorce, and so are their dependent children. Men, with less to lose, are more often supportive of their own, or other men's, peccadilloes. This is an excellent example of how complicated a gendered perspective on sexuality can be. Although repressive sexual norms tend to control women's sexuality more than men's, this control is cast as a benefit to family stability, which in turn, tends to be in the interest of women who are more likely to be caretakers of any children. Whether or not concern for marital fidelity in fact helps to stabilize families is an as yet unanswered, empirical question. Concern for fidelity, however, is certainly treated as a benefit to families. Thus, on the one hand, concern for marital fidelity tends to benefit women, who are less likely to have affairs and more likely to suffer economically if a marriage breaks up. On the other hand, such conservatism casts women as the stakeholders of virtue, fidelity, and family values, and this undermines a pro-feminist, sex-positive attitude that promotes women's independence and autonomy. We will return to this dilemma and men's a women's different agendas regarding sexuality when we look at politics in Chapter 5.

The Problem of Sustained Desire in a Divorce-Prone Society

Seattle novelist Tom Robbins begins *Still Life with Woodpecker* (1980) with a monologue about the Last-Quarter-of-the-Twentieth-Century Blues. "There is only one serious question. And that is: *Who knows how to make love stay?*" (p. 4). More than ever before, marriage and committed relationships have become the center of intimacy and self-fulfillment. Nevertheless, all long-term relationships become somewhat habituated and therefore less sexually alluring. Many become downright mundane. In previous eras, this development didn't mean a whole lot. People stayed married no matter what. Gay people, having fewer ways in other times to meet new partners, were more likely to stay together once they found someone—fearing that they might never meet other appropriate people.

But now the centrality of sex in U.S. culture makes it hard for people to ignore a lack of sexual excitement, particularly when they are young. People are told that sex is at the center of identity and a good measure of relationship quality. That belief has enormous normative power in contemporary culture. When sex starts to wane, spouses feel they have to find some way to either reinvigorate their sexual relationship or recast the meaning of their marriage. Otherwise, one or both partners grow dissatisfied, worried that an important part of life is being truncated, worried that vital emotional rights are being trespassed, worried that the lesser quality or quantity of sex has dire implications for the relationship's viability.

Given the sexualization of contemporary culture, people who have grown up in it have a great deal of trouble making sex a secondary consideration. People who matured prior to the sexual revolution have less trouble with the concept—partly because their sexual needs have moderated, but also because they married under different norms, values, and expectations.

We shouldn't be surprised that even though the norm of monogamy and the b anctity of marriage is still strongly held, trespasses much of marriage as a joining of the flesh as well ends that render men and women more sexually r have tamed men's right to roam, so have these freedom to do so. The anonymous quality of city the workplace as a place to encounter potential tion of the Internet create possibilities for ticipation in extramarital sex that have never existed before. Opportunity plus an ideology of the right to sexual pleasure in marriage make extramarital sex almost a certainty for some number of people in our society. The challenge, as we mentioned at the beginning of this chapter, is to find a way to live a sensual life that is also as committed as both partners want it to be. Sexuality, burdened by gendered sexual scripts, can slow down, leading partners to romantic alternatives. But it doesn't have to, and we are optimistic that some committed relationships are making progress out of gendered sexual scripts.

Peer Marriage: Love Between Equals

As we have discussed, marriage is a location for reinforcing gendered norms and conventions. But it need not be. Does marriage also have the possibility to undermine gendered social norms and conventions? Although social norms are resistant to change, we offer a hopeful vision.

As we see it, the dilemma of unfulfilled sexual promise in marriage has much to do with the typical absence of equity in marriage. Power imbalance is at the heart of the enactment of gender difference; indeed, marital therapy researchers (who study troubled, rather than normal, marriages) observe that such imbalances are central to marital conflict (Jacobson 1989). However, marriage need not be the centerpiece of the institutionalization of gender difference. Research on egalitarian marriage, or **peer marriage** (Schwartz 1994), illustrates that the potential for power sharing, obligation sharing, and resource sharing in marriage is real, though not commonly enacted. Pairs with the ambition of egalitarianism often fall short, into the "near peer" category, but a few are making it.

The typical scenario is the couple who believes in equality but doesn't quite achieve it. Usually, the husband "helps" his wife with the children more, and the woman "helps" her husband make economic decisions. The husband still does the major earning, and the woman still is primary parent and support staff to the family.

In peer marriage, couples have organized their emotional, sexual, economic, and parenting functions with the idea that there are no prescribed jobs or responsibilities. The key to happiness, they believe, is to experience together, and in much the same way, all things marriage needs to accomplish. The model—whether characteri coparenting, job sharing, or acting as a parenting and workin not impossible, although it is still rare. Couples who are coprincipals of their own firm and who bring their child to work with them so that they can both give care may not be ordinary, but they do exist. These couples typically have a high level of companionship, mutual respect, and a notably minimal amount of anger. Equity has its rewards.

The gendered quality and power differences of marriage and intimate relationships can influence sexual and other social practices within marriage (like housework). But peer marriages are resolutely different sexually and socially from nonegalitarian pairing. Thus, there are few examples for couples to follow, and special attention must be given to creating and sustaining shared domestic and economic responsibility. The social world tends to reinforce traditional couples far more than nontraditional and peer marriages.

Although peer marriages are not particularly common, studying these couples helps us predict social change. The prediction is the following: Where gendered power differences are minimized and committed partnerships—whether heterosexual or homosexual—use equality rather than difference as the governing principle, then satisfaction, shared sexual roles, and commitment can be better sustained. It may be that passion still diminishes over time in such a relationship. After all, if passion is often inflamed by tension, fear, uncertainty, and the desire to bridge gaps between people, then equitable marriages will be less passionate. But that doesn't mean they will be less sexually satisfying. What remains is the desire to give and receive pleasure and love—which is more likely to continue when the relationship is reciprocal in all other ways. Equity in a sexual relationship, like equity in the rest of the relationship, is about comradeship, which might sound a little less than exciting on first blush but is really the highest and best hope for a union to last 50 years or more.

At this point, our prediction is yet to be thoroughly tested. The peer marriages that have been studied (Schwartz 1994) had greater satisfaction but they had less frequent sex than couples in **near peer marriages,** and far l--   ~uples in traditional marriages. However, the part-
ced on initiation, and there was more experimen-
~xual acts. For example, women in peer marriages
an women in traditional relationships. Both men
rriages said that when one of them did refuse, it
rejecting gesture. The reduced passion charac-
s seems to relate to the burdens of everyday life
les are subject to), intense work schedules, and

perhaps the way sexual imaginations and desires are shaped by our culture. The sexual imagery that people are raised with nearly always includes gender differences in power and social position. Even in an egalitarian marriage, participants continue to be constrained by the sexual traditions that are part of U.S. culture. Even when the mind says, "I want to find a person who regards me as an equal and does a fair share of everything," the erotic internal script might say, "I want to be 'swept away' " or "I like it when I feel strong and competent and my partner feels helpless and innocent." In time, as these old scripts fade, new imagery may become most exciting. For example, athletic, fit women are possible sex objects to men who also believe in physical fitness, even though such an image of female beauty has probably not existed before in modern history. Or people may fantasize about closing a business deal together, rather than taking care of someone or being taken care of. When such images become popular, we predict, passion will increase in peer marriages—perhaps surpassing passion in traditional marriage.

Conclusion

Marriage is a special category of intimate relationship; as it exists currently it seems to hinge on and amplify gender difference. The reason this is a problem isn't a theoretical one, because gender difference tends to mean power difference. Thus, men and women do not simply have different rules they're expected to play by when it comes to sex in marriage or infidelity or the use of force in intimate relationships. Men and women have different levels of power and different privileges in the social structure. The strategy that we think best for modifying sexuality within marriage and intimate relationships is not to erase sexuality, but instead to minimize power differences and create diverse new ways to experience sex in long-term relationships.

Note

1. This quotation is from an unpublished 1996 interview relating to parenting.

CHAPTER 5

The Politics of Sexuality

Sexuality in the United States is a political football. Sides team up, there's little compromise, and people love to watch the competition. Recall Supreme Court Justice Clarence Thomas's Senate nomination hearing in 1991. Thomas, one of the youngest-ever nominees to the Supreme Court, is a political conservative who had advanced to the heights of jurisprudence despite the disadvantages of being raised poor and black in south Georgia. But the hearing captured the country's attention because it focused on detailed allegations of sexual harassment. Law professor and former Thomas staff member Anita Hill reported that he had remarked to her that a hair in his soft drink might be a pubic hair. The allegation was one among many that demonstrated a pattern of sexual innuendo and improper advances that undermined Professor Hill's job performance and promotions. U.S. senators, on national television, invited the country to contemplate the significance of mentioning pubic hair. On the one hand, this case was a consciousness-raising event. New policies and statutes emerged in businesses and in government, and a new vocabulary for sexual issues in the workplace emerged.

But this episode had a striking downside: It humiliated almost everyone involved as political and media forces seized on the story and gave it round-the-clock coverage. The subject provided titillation that exceeded anyone's concern for sexual harassment in the workplace. For many, this bizarre scene also pitted race against gender. Thomas was among the few African Americans at the time who had surmounted many economic and cultural obstacles to climb to such heights in government. Although his politics are dissimilar to the more liberal views held by many African Americans, his accomplishment was still an affirmation of black achievement in the historically racist United

States. Anita Hill, who is also African American, found herself the "poster woman" for feminist outrage about men's many trespasses against women in—and out of—the workplace. Ultimately, many people felt the incident was a lose-lose situation. Thomas was confirmed amid skepticism, Hill's integrity was a matter of brutal public debate, and the gulf between men and women was confirmed in most people's minds. The popular image was a cartoon, a "he said, she said" split-screen reality.

If men and women see things so differently, sexuality—the most prominent of all the realms of gender difference—is always going to be potentially explosive. Scan the newspaper, and you'll see myriad stories relating to the topic. Sex sells. Political candidates use various kinds of sex scandals ("unfaithful husbands"; "sexual predators") to build a political base and, if possible, to make opponents look immoral.

What makes sexuality a political football is our culture's ambivalent obsession with sex:

> In the U.S., sex tends to be treated as a special topic, and there is much ambivalence: sex is romantic, but also sinful and dirty; it is flaunted but also something to be hidden. . . . American teenagers seem to have inherited the worst of all possible worlds regarding their exposure to messages about sex: movies, music, radio, and TV tell them that sex is romantic, exciting, titillating; premarital sex and cohabitation are visible ways of life among the adults they see and hear about; their own parents or their parents' friends are likely to be divorced or separated but involved in sexual relationships. Yet, at the same time, young people get the message good girls should say no. Almost nothing they see or hear about sex informs them about contraception or the importance of avoiding pregnancy. (Jones et al. 1985:59-61)

As suggested in the quotation above, political factions contradict each other, and cultural messages can be chaotic and confusing. Throughout this book, you have already read quite a bit about the **politics of sexuality**. Politics—regarding family and individual differences, social interaction, and human bodies—influence and shape every aspect of sexuality. Political institutions sustain the social structure's use of gender to justify and extend the control over sexuality in subtle and not-so-subtle ways.

The expression "war of the sexes," for instance, implies that blame for a social problem can generally be placed on one sex or the other. It suggests opposing sides in a battle for one winner and one loser. It gets played out in larger than life episodes, like the Clarence Thomas and Anita Hill case, and in everyday life as well. In either context the so-called war enforces the idea that gender differences are large and impassable. We are being asked to maintain distinct statuses for men and for women. The facts—of sexual assault or harassment, for example—are only part of the message. Indeed, part of the problem is that "facts" are almost impossible to know: negotiation about these truth claims is highly gendered.

In reality, much of the politics of sex and gender is about controlling women's bodies. One of women's few resources, historically, has been their sexuality. When women are obliged to protect this resource, they are treated as if their sexuality is what's most valuable to them as well as to fathers (mothers), husbands, and other men in their lives. Throughout this book, we have told the story of women either needing to worry about their virtue (as traditional rules of sexuality dictate) or waging a sexual revolution to obtain sexual and other kinds of freedom as early feminists suggested. In other words, sexual politics seem nearly always located in and around women's bodies. This chapter discusses two contemporary political issues that clearly involve women's control over their own bodies: teen sexuality and sexual assault. The core of the third issue discussed in this chapter, same-sex marriage, is different. Nevertheless, it is an important issue in contemporary sexual politics, in part because it disturbs the long tradition that calls for gender difference as fundamental to romantic and marital unions.

Debates Past and Present

Public debate over sexuality is not new. In fact, public debate about sexuality in North America is as old as—or older than—the United States. Every era has had its own definitions of sexual deviance and its own punishments. During the colonial era, sexual sinners were taken to court, and neighbors were encouraged to spy on one another to denounce misdeeds to a panel of "judges." Public humiliation was the reward for any sexual behavior beyond procreatively oriented intercourse by married couples.

During the nineteenth century, postmaster Arthur Comstock used Congress and the newspapers to rally popular and political support for his antipornography campaign. His target was any advertisement or advice regarding contraception. Women's movements of the period, including the social purity and women's suffrage movements (D'Emilio and Freedman 1988), rallied support for Comstock. They believed that sexual images, including those related to contraception, would demean women and that if procreation were not a possible consequence of sexual activity, women would be victims of more frequent nonrefusable sexual demands of their spouses. Comstock was enormously effective; the United States criminalized all access to and discussion of birth control from 1873 until 1936, when the anticontraception provisions of the Comstock law were finally rescinded. Sexually suggestive images hardly disappeared, however, even during Comstock's era, and movies and advertisements frequently used sex to sell consumer goods in the early part of the twentieth century. Antipornography groups organized to ban portrayals of sexuality, and in the 1930s, the Legion of Decency, led by the Catholic Church hierarchy, campaigned against "indecency" in the movies. In this period, Hollywood adopted many of its rules and rating systems (D'Emilio and Freedman 1988). Thus, the United States has a history of suppressing sexual imagery that some groups consider pornography, only to find sexuality expressing itself in new ways in new places, to be subject to conservative suppression yet again.

In recent decades, other controversies have taken center stage. For example, the ongoing demonstrations for and against abortion and the shocking assassinations of physicians and other personnel who provide abortion services riveted popular attention in the early 1990s. The issues have been framed as fetal rights versus women's rights. Who benefits from this perspective? For the political right, the issue devolves into a litany of blame for women who seek abortions. Meanwhile, the political left presents images of women victimized first by the lack of easily administered, safe, and automatic birth control methods and second, when birth control fails, by their harassment at abortion clinics. Politicians take their pro- or antichoice positions, and sexuality becomes the subject of heated and sensational debate. But little is actually done to improve access to birth control, to improve sex education for teens and communication between men and women, to empower women sexually, or to train men to take more responsibility for the consequences of their sexual acts.

In the controversy over gays and lesbians in the military, national security is pitted against nonnormative sexual desire and behavior. The issue for some is whether homosexuals have equal protection under the law. For others, the controversy provides an opportunity to wave the flag by linking patriotism to heterosexuality. Given the level of **homophobia** (fear of homosexuality and hatred of homosexuals) in our society and ignorance about homosexuality, an antigay politician can easily portray an opponent as antimilitary, antisecurity, and antifamily for taking any position short of authorizing a witch-hunt for homosexuals in the armed services. Yet no information has been found to support the contention that a homosexual is more likely than a heterosexual to reveal national secrets. In fact, in 1996 it was President Clinton's heterosexual political consultant, Dick Morris, who shared national secrets with a high-paid woman prostitute.

In addition to these issues, the "gendering" of sexuality has become conspicuous again. Conservative movements have sought to turn back the tide of sexual change that has marked the contemporary era. One of the central agendas of new conservative activists is to browbeat women back into traditional incarnations of womanhood by resurrecting the flagging double standard. Conservatives believe that sexuality outside of wedlock is immoral and unmarried childbearing even more horrific. One way to help contain illegitimacy is to stigmatize all those who have sex outside of marriage. But because women bear children, they are easier targets of scandal and criticism than are men. The conservative campaign against female sexuality aims to render the cost of sexual liberty so high that more girls and women will, as former First Lady Nancy Reagan suggested in the context of drug use, "just say no." By 1996, the fervor to control sexuality had become so politically acceptable that a town outside Boise, Idaho, dragged out old fornication laws from the nineteenth century and prosecuted unwed men and women for having sex. A 19-year-old woman, among others, was fined, put on probation, and forced to do community service for her "criminal" behavior. How did they find her? The police had been instructed to look for women with "big bellies and no wedding rings" (Tizon 1996).

Conservatives see nothing wrong with reestablishing women as gatekeepers of men's "uncontrollable sexual appetite." They believe that the reduction in gender-based sexual norms has led U.S. culture to, as they see it, "the horrible mess we are in today." One way to reorient women to their traditional role is to appeal to the idea of core, biologically based sexual identities, with gender-specific desires and behaviors. If sexuality is biologically based (and therefore gender specific), goes the view, then women are the gatekeepers of virtue and the "natural" caretakers of children. Contemporary feminists oppose this trend and reject biological arguments. They insist that sexuality has become a pawn in power struggles between competing political interest ·oups.

FIGURE 5.1

Trends in Heterosexual Experience among Teens

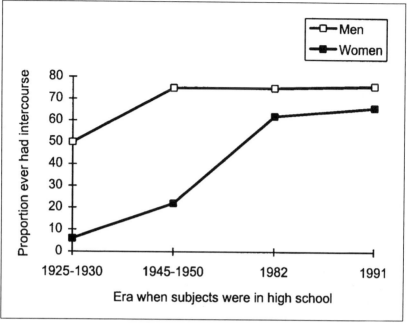

Source: Data from Laumann, Michael, and Gagnon (1994) and Modell (1989).

In all this debate, we wonder, is there room for the private experience of sexual pleasure? Or is sex necessarily part of a political tug of war over who shall incur what social obligations? Some continue to use gender as a tool for pathologizing youthful sexual expression. Others seek to increase autonomy in sexual expression and to enhance tolerance for sexual diversity. Thus, we turn to our first issue, teenage sexuality, with the observation that true progress has occurred in this arena even though it has become a favorite political football.

Teenage Sexuality

The publication of the Kinsey reports in the late 1940s stimulated anxiety that they would promote youthful, unconventional, nonmarital sexual experimentation. And, true enough, teens have embarked on sexual careers earlier and with greater freedom in the past century, as Figure 5.1 illustrates. Kinsey reported that fewer than 6 percent of American women who were teens in the 1920s or earlier had had premarital intercourse. By 1991, 66 percent of high school senior women and 76 percent of high school senior men had had sexual intercourse.

Notice in Figure 5.1 that the shift for women is much greater than the shift for men. Adult commentary has labeled teen sexuality a spontaneous, irresponsible, narcissistic, and ever younger trend that is massively out of control, but the alarm would seem to be associated with the greater increase in women's—not men's—sexual freedom. Teens are demonized as morally wayward—because women have been admitting to engaging in sex at levels that are increasingly similar to men's. The persistent "gender gap" in acceptance of women's and men's sexuality is what we have referred to as the double standard.

The double standard is not the only contradiction attending teen sexuality. Teens may be having sex earlier, but they did not create the seductive adult clothing made for preteens or the ad campaigns with seductive 13-year-olds. Calvin Klein ads for jeans, T-shirts, and fragrance, and a host of other seductive images, present teens as having the sexy bodies that everybody wants. From here, contradictions multiply. On the one hand, prosecutors press statutory rape charges on behalf of girls who look 30 but are in fact 15. On the other, the culture urges those same young girls to be as sexy as they can and tells fashion models they are over the hill at 21. Our vision of sexiness is essentially based on the barely pubescent body, and yet the barely pubescent body is taboo.

Adolescence and Families

If these adult-generated images of sexy teens seem novel, so is the life stage known as adolescence. Interestingly, teenage sexuality sur-faced as a public issue just as the phase of life known as adolescence was recognized. Over the past 150 years, the age of puberty for both boys and girls has dropped from around 17 to around 11 or 12 (Rutter 1995), as a consequence of improved health and nutrition among youth. Yet youths don't legally become adults until their late teens. The interval between puberty and adulthood—adolescence—is a stage of life that had not existed biologically or socially until the mid-twentieth century.

A unique feature of this stage of life is youths' sexual maturity without social maturity. The contrast is apparent when one observes the bedroom of a 12-year-old girl who looks 18. She might still treasure stuffed animals or posters of horses or doll houses. And yet this same ʰild is at least partly aware of the allure she holds for boys and men, ʼ she may be eager to test her new powers of enchantment. Not sur-ˑly, parents are appalled and scared at this turn of biology—especially when it comes with rebellion against the restrictions they deem appropriate for a 12-year-old. Some psychologists have observed that the presence of sexually mature youth living at home has itself produced negativity of parents toward their teens, and sometimes even parental depression (Steinberg 1994). In other periods of history, a child old enough to be sexually active would be married or betrothed and out of the household. But today, youth tend to remain at home well past puberty, often until their 20s, when they finally complete their education.

In contemporary society, because puberty comes earlier but marriage comes later, a youth may experience sexual and romantic longing with no "socially acceptable" outlet for quite a long time. As teens mature and begin to have sexual relationships, they tend to resent parental interference or constraint. Parental judgments and controls might not be too insufferable for the children (and the rebellion too difficult for the parents) if they lasted for only a short time before the launch into true independence. But many families experience severe challenges to parental authority. At the very least, parents tend to feel that when someone lives in their home, they need to follow house rules, both moral and practical (such as when the kids are due home at night). As guardians of their children, they are concerned for their teenagers' safety and well-being. And they also may find it threatening to lose control over their children. In response, adolescents tend to feel that these rules infringe on their right as human beings to live according to their own judgments and desires.

Some teenagers respect and honor their parents' wishes. They may agree that it is in their best interest to curtail sexual desire and wait to have sex until they are older or married. Some parents may respond to teens' emerging sexual curiosity with support and the information they need to remain safe and self-confident. But other families fight about sexuality with everything they can muster. Not surprisingly, many households with teenagers in them also harbor conflict and psychological distress.

In some families, competition between parent and child may arise. Adult insecurities can emerge as aging adults worry about being displaced as sexual beings by their younger, more sexy offspring and grieve over the loss of their own youth. Some research has shown that parents of a same-sex adolescent (fathers who have a son or mothers who have a daughter) experience a decline in psychological well-being and even temporarily lose sexual interest in their spouse (Steinberg 1994).

For a variety of reasons, then, many parents become ambivalent about teen sexuality. And the same ambivalence is present at the societal level. Teens are perceived as having great sexual opportunity and even feared or resented because of it. Ironically, however, teen sex tends not to be nearly so active as adults imagine nor nearly as pleasing as sex between more experienced adults.

The State of Teen Sexual Behavior

The early onset of adolescence and the increased autonomy of young people have left teens with little guidance regarding sexuality and relationships. The consequences are serious: Teenage childbearing undermines the futures of the mothers and the children; sexually transmitted diseases (STDs) undermine hope for a healthy adulthood for many sexually active teens. In addition, a compelling body of research indicates that teen sexuality is often experienced in negative ways, undermining teens' self-esteem, and that it frequently involves coercion or harassment.

The ability to address teenagers' needs has been undermined by adults' obsessive attention to teen sex and neglect of most other aspects of teen life. Ironically, contrary to many popular media stories, teens aren't having a great deal of sex. Often they will try intercourse once and then not try it again until they are older (Rubin 1990). Even teens who remain sexually active are generally not as active as adults, and they tend to be serially monogamous—one exclusive sexual relationship at a time—just like adults.

But sufficient numbers of teenagers get involved in sex and get pregnant to make their sexual behavior a social concern. Luker (1996) reports that 11 percent of women experience pregnancy before the age of 19. Although teens often believe that they can't get pregnant the first time they have sexual intercourse, they can—and they do. To state the obvious, pregnancy happens to women, not men, and thus generates a focus on changing teenage women's behavior rather than intervening with teenage men as well.

Much of the concern about teen sexuality has to do with the observation that more women are having children out of wedlock. In 1990, 31 percent of unwed mothers were teenagers (Luker 1996:199). Conservatives decry the perceived epidemic of teen motherhood, but the facts more complicated. In the United States and western Europe, there en what demographers call a major fertility transition or a subhange in fertility rates. The result has been a steady decline in the rate of reproduction to replacement or below-replacement levels. In North America, fertility has declined steadily since the early nineteenth century, with the exception of the post-World War II baby boom era. People have fewer children, causing the population of some groups— particularly better-educated, richer, and mostly white groups—actually to shrink. Teen pregnancy has declined, just like pregnancy rates among older women, but it simply hasn't declined as much. Therefore, teens represent a larger proportion of the total population of reproducers. In other words, adolescents are not having more babies, adults are having fewer. Furthermore, over half of teen mothers in 1990 were 18 or 19. Twelve thousand women 15 or under had a baby in 1990; over 330,000 women 18 or 19 gave birth (Luker 1996). In other words, the image of "children having children" applies to a small proportion of teenage women having babies.

Plenty of the people who are raising the alarm about teen pregnancy know that, in sheer numbers, there is no such thing as an epidemic of teenage pregnancy. But arousing an outcry over rising teen pregnancy rates is of political value. Mention teen mothers and numerous U.S. voters start paying attention. Politicians spark citizens' outrage and use it to get votes by associating teen motherhood with welfare and casting these women as producing unwanted children whom they cannot support economically.

Nevertheless, the rising proportion of teenage mothers who are not married may be a legitimate cause for concern. Parenthood out of wed-lock used to be so stigmatized that every pressure possible was applied by families on both sides to make sure a woman married the father of her child. The old phrase "shotgun wedding" was real enough in some parts of the country. But the ability to compel teenagers to marry evaporated as love triumphed over more pragmatic standards for choosing a mate, such as being "a good provider" and "a solid member of society." The sexual revolution and the women's movement were both preaching independence and individual decision making for women. Parents who wanted to force marriage on pregnant teens received little help from law enforcement agencies. Of course, forcing marriages does not promote the well-being of teen mothers or their offspring. Authorities are not particularly good at either helping establish paternity or making sure child support gets paid. Furthermore, poverty and unemployment make it difficult for young fathers to provide the support the government might like to see them deliver. The welfare system evolved to help support some of these young families to ensure that children did not suffer unduly for their parent's lack of preparation. But in the past three decades, the proportion of teenage mothers who weren't married changed from 25 percent to 75 percent of all teenage mothers (Luker 1996). In some communities, particularly those inhabited by the chronically poor, single motherhood became not simply common but normative. Thus, many began associating teen parenthood, young women involved in sex, single parenthood, and poor and minority women leaning on the state to assist with their progeny. Despite political rhetoric to the contrary, unwed, teen motherhood has not grown as a result of welfare to these needy young people. In fact, welfare has reduced in real value over the period when rates of unwed teen motherhood grew.

Although poverty is a common correlate for teenage motherhood, it isn't the only one. An influential 1994 book by Mary Pipher, *Reviving Ophelia*, shows how teenage women who become mothers are undermined early on by basement-level self-esteem. Although hopelessness and poverty are often experienced together, Pipher found that a future-orientation was not always associated with economic advantages. Regardless of their economic status, women who can see a future and who think well of themselves, profiled in several chapters of *Going All the Way* (Thompson 1996), are often able to abstain from sex or to protect themselves from unwanted pregnancy. But most teenage mothers, bereft of parental support or overwhelmed by the pleasure of romance in a life that has few other pleasures, look to their child for love and community.

And what about the fathers? Historically, and even today, young unmarried men have been given license to have sex. At the beginning of the sexual revolution, teenage men's rate of sexual experience was substantially higher than women's, as demonstrated in Figure 5.1. But although it has increased over the past several decades, it has not increased as much as women's. Perhaps in middle- or upper-middle-class homes, where parents fight to protect their child's future career and social status, a son's sexuality is seen as just as dangerous to his future prospects as a daughter's. But even in families where the future holds promise because of their social class, daughters, not sons, seem to receive the more dire warnings about sex outside of marriage. Regardless of class, the consequences of teen sexuality continue to be more ⁿstly for women than for men.

This imbalance may be changing somewhat—but not because of a ⁿ recognition that young men are and should be equal partners ¹ responsibility. Instead, conservative political forces have seen new possibilities for spreading moral blame and sharing social costs. An odd coalition of feminists and the "new right" have created an image of the unwed young father as a predatory young male, knowledgeable and malevolent, who is really to blame for all this teenage pregnancy and should be severely punished. He should be made to support his children. However, many of these young men, like the women they have paired with, have limited prospects in the job market (Lerman and Ooms 1993).

Another problem with this new focus on men's responsibilities is that it still emphasizes the helplessness of young women. Undoubtedly, sexual predators are out there. And as Chapter 3 pointed out, only 71 percent of women claimed to have wanted their first sexual experiences; 25 percent said it was unwanted and 4 percent said it was coerced. Nevertheless, many young women participate in sex with confidence and gusto. Some of these women are canny planners of their own lives—even if one doesn't agree with their values or goals—and not all teenage women are victims or potential victims of predatory young men. Like women in other age groups, some teenage women are attracted to older men; many find the interest of an older guy flattering. Some women know the young men with whom they have sex because they grew up together in the neighborhood and are friends. It is also important to remember that some of these older men are still teenagers or are barely in their 20s themselves. Finally, some young women reject seduction or receive the guidance necessary to contracept effectively.

The idea of raising social costs for the sexual activity of young men to induce them to abstain or use birth control is sensible. Everyone needs to take responsibility for the possibility of a child. But seeing men as predators is a simplification and in many cases an injustice. Feminist columnist Katha Pollitt (1996) made the point clearly: "Construing teen sex as all victimization seems more compassionate than construing it, like Newt Gingrich [Speaker of the House of Representatives], as all sluttishness. But do we really want to say that a 15-year-old girl is always and invariably incapable of giving consent to sex with her 18-year-old boyfriend?" (p. 9).

We can't assume that all young men somehow know more about what they are doing than young women do. Certainly, some men organize their lives to take advantage of women. Men ought to be accountable for sexual activity, but they ought not to be automatically vilified for being sexual any more than women should be vilified for the same behavior.

Our view is that a very real social concern—teen sexuality—has been used to advance the sex-negative and sex-punitive agendas of various religious and political groups. Of course, young men and women should not produce babies before they are ready to be parents, and young people should have a shot at an unfettered youth and productive adulthood. But the vision that teenagers should be nonsexual, especially in a hypersexualized society, is simply unrealistic. Abstinence may be a reasonable suggestion to the younger teenagers, particularly in conservative neighborhoods or in communities that are unified in their support of them, but in most U.S. and European urban areas, this stance is simply unrealistic.

Sexuality Education

Societies like Sweden, where sex education starts early with full public support, have much lower rates of teen pregnancy than we do. Admittedly, Sweden is different in other important ways: It has fewer people in poverty, it is more homogeneous ethnically, and it has a vast social safety net for all citizens. Sweden has a record of pro-family social policy along with a record of pro-sex education policies that emphasize that parenthood should be voluntary (Gauthier 1996). But in our country, people still act as if sex is the exclusive privilege of married people, even though everyone knows that unmarried people have sex. Sex education for youth would surely improve the sexual quagmire teens seem to be in today. Sex education for adults would help, too, so that citizens might understand that sex is neither dangerous nor shameful.

Remarkably, at the same time that teens are being blamed for unrestrained sexuality and an excess of illegitimate births, little in the way of comprehensive sex education or services for teens exists across the United States. For example, virginity for its own sake is still prized in many communities, especially for daughters. This moral code, somewhat more flexible for adults, is highly charged when it concerns teenage sons and daughters. Even though research (Kirby et al. 1994) indicates that the "just say no" and abstinence campaigns tend to increase, rather than decrease, sexual activity, powerful lobbies have installed many of these programs in churches and school systems. These programs tend also to be conservatively gendered, reconnecting female 'rginity with marriageability and presenting definitions of propriety are different for men than for women.

fairness to many conservative communities, abstinence move-
'e not all premised on the double standard. Many religious

groups preach abstinence for both sexes and apply sanctions equally. But, in general, social conservatives still see women as more vulnerable than men, see them as incapable of making sexual decisions, and believe that purity is the natural preference of and ideal for young women. Thousands of years of controlling of women's sexuality does not quietly fade away.

Even if conservatives did not take issue with sex education as a means for reducing pregnancy and delaying sexual initiation, they would have another argument against it. Conservatives believe that the family should be controlled by parents, not by government. Therefore, parents should decide what information a child should have about sexuality. Liberals, on the other hand, believe that all children deserve adequate information about sexual health, whether or not their parents elect to provide their children with it. This conflict is highlighted in debates regarding the media and censorship; conservative parent activist groups seek to influence broadcasting on the premise that sex and violence on television contributes to the corruption of children.

In contrast, sex education, from the public health point of view, ensures that young people who engage in sex will do so more safely. Public health professionals who believe in "healthy" sexuality emphasize the benefits of sex education to young people. They will have thought more about their own motives and goals and their responsibility to a partner and thus be prepared to act responsibly. Furthermore, sexuality education seems to reduce sexual abuses, including sexual harassment and coercion among teenagers. Groups taking this position—such as the Sexuality Information and Education Council of the United States (SIECUS); Planned Parenthood; and American Association of Sex Educators, Counselors, and Therapists (AASECT)—recognize that teens will continue to experiment with sexuality but believe education may delay some sexual experimentation. For many professionals, however, the main benefit of sex education is to teach young people how to communicate about sex. The goal is to help people treat one another humanely and to reduce the amount of shame, guilt, and manipulation in sexual relationships.

The comprehensive sex education side seems to be losing this debate. Although the number of sex education programs has increased since the 1970s, the goals have become more diverse, and program efficacy is undermined by a lack of consensus and, in some cases, a lack of quality materials or well-trained instructors (Yarber 1994). Policymakers have generally seen the growth in sexual activity among teenagers as a reason to limit services for sexually active young people. Although sex education is not the culprit for young women's increased sexual activity, nevertheless the fear persists that sex education legitimizes teen sex. Vocal bands of parents have succeeded in locking sex education courses out of many school districts. In some, they have substituted "chastity" programs, which are often programs based on religious ethics and traditional gender roles.

The sexual double standard has perhaps not surprisingly persisted for youth. For teenage men, having sex for the first time still counts as a coming-of-age ritual. Young men are often expected to have sex before late adolescence, and many families are relieved when they see some sign that a son has heterosexual capabilities and desires. These same accolades do not exist for young women: Not only do parents avoid direct or subtle approval of their daughters' sexual initiation, but the consequences of heterosexual sex for young women are more evident. Sexually active women are more vulnerable than men to STDs as well as to negative social reactions. Even liberal parents are more conservative for their daughters than their sons.

Ironically, teenage women, whom conservatives feel have more to lose sexually, still get little special instruction on how to negotiate the crosscurrents of their sexual environment. Some women in impoverished or other high-risk environments, where teenage women are more likely to get pregnant, may get special programs directed at controlling their fertility. But coping skills in such matters as negotiating with men about sex or avoiding health risks are rarely provided. When young women receive guidance, most programs assume that they and not their partners are and should be the sexual gatekeepers. Planned Parenthood is an exception: Local chapters often provide education for teenage men and women and their families. But Planned Parenthood reaches only a small percentage of at-risk young people, and its clinics and group meetings are disproportionately attended by young women and mothers.

Teen Health

The public debate on teen sexuality has focused squarely on teen pregnancy—as if sex were all that teenagers were doing with their spare 'ime (Dreyfoos 1990). Politicians and opinion leaders moralize about 'ithful promiscuity and the tax burden it entails for supporting the 's of unwed teen mothers. Worried parents are galvanized by office ` and political fund-raisers who tell them that each and every vulnerable to teen pregnancy unless their platform of moral renewal is adopted. Of course, the policymakers emphasize their compassion for teens, but it is instructive to note just how little attention they pay to other health costs of teenage sexuality besides pregnancy.

All the concern about teen sexuality has caused health institutions to provide reproductively focused health care to the exclusion of other kinds. Teens in the United States are enormously underserved (Dreyfoos 1990). Paradoxically, the fear of teen sexuality has reduced teen health services rather than sharpening them.

Even sex-related health problems are inadequately addressed by services to youth. STDs are growing among teens (Holmes et al. 1990). Untreated STDs, especially pelvic inflammatory disease (PID) and chlamydia, threaten women's fertility. PID can cause horrific pain as well as major complications, including damage to the urinary tract and the reproductive organs. Chlamydia may be asymptomatic, but it can end a woman's reproductive future. Although infertility rates in the population in general are declining (U.S. Office of Technology Assessment 1988), they are increasing among poor people and the youngest portion of the U.S. population (Scritchfield 1995). Perhaps it is cynical to think that more attention would be paid to PID and chlamydia if they affected men as much as they affect women.

Although the history of medicine can be said, without much distortion, to be the treatment of male problems (Ehrenreich and English 1978; Lorber 1997), an enormous amount of consciousness raising has changed a total blindness to the specific problems of adult women—if not to teens. A women's health movement grew up in the 1960s and 1970s, marked in part by the publication in 1973 of the first edition of *Our Bodies, Ourselves* by the Boston Women's Health Book Collective. (A revised edition was published in 1996, as well as an edition dedicated to women's health and aging.) Growing attention to women's health concerns such as breast cancer prevention, detection, and treatment continues presently.

Turning teenage sexuality into a political issue may be an inevitable consequence of the relatively new, extended stage of adolescence. Ambivalent and punitive attitudes toward youthful sexuality are useful to many politicians who stir up parental fears and then offer comforting but unrealistic promises that voting for them will turn back the clock. But rarely does any of this politicization translate into health and other services for young people. More often political solutions involve rolling back sexual trends and revitalizing dichotomized, gendered sexual scripts for teenagers.

Sexual Assault

Sexual assault is hardly a new issue. Although rape did not historically exist in some cultures, such as Polynesia, sexual assault of women is by and large a constant across many cultures and across time. What is new about sexual assault is not only greater public and political awareness but also a level of political activism that has changed the way people talk about it and define it, the way police departments react to it, and the way many women—and men—now regard their own vulnerability in sexual situations. In this section, we describe several political movements associated with sexual assault and then examine the issues surrounding accusations of assault and date rape.

Sexual assault is a difficult problem to study: Victims are not always willing providers of data because of the stigma and self-doubt associated with this crime. But we do know that sexual assault is not randomly distributed. Overwhelmingly, sexual assault involves men victimizing women. In this sense, it is a crime at the intersection of sexuality and gender. From an essentialist view, it is a consequence of men's predatory nature. From a constructionist view, it is a consequence of the social permission men have to dominate women and their need to reinforce that status. These interpretations do not "explain away" the problem. Instead, these approaches point to different strategies for reducing rates of sexual assault.

It is not always clear when or even whether efforts to reduce sexual victimization will have the desired effect. It is possible that the discourse on sexual threats maintains fearfulness among women (Hollander 1997). The specter of sexual assault does indeed render many women fearful of walking alone at night, even in statistically safe areas.

Feminist Versus Patriarchal Positions

The feminist movement is largely responsible for consciousness raising regarding the sexual assault of women. Since the late 1960s, feminist activists have struggled to obtain resources to aid victims of assault, legislation to aid the prosecution of sexual crimes, and legislation to define as crimes such acts as husband-wife rape and sexual harassment in the workplace. This cause has been well served by the efforts of such leaders as Catherine MacKinnon and Andrea Dworkin, who have worked to eliminate pornography, to increase awareness of how certain cultural images and practices foster violent attitudes, and to reduce misogynistic violence toward women. This faction holds the view that women must be protected from predatory men and that most men are potentially predatory. Other feminist groups, as we discuss below, disagree with MacKinnon's and Dworkin's emphasis on women as victims and take issue with attitudes that are often viewed as antagonistic to sexuality.

The feminist movement originally battled the status quo, or **patriarchy,** a system of power relations in which (some) men hold power at the expense of (some) women. The problem with patriarchy was even part of the sexual revolution. Whereas feminists in the early stages of the sexual revolution were committed to polymorphous and liberated sexuality for all adults, as time progressed, other feminists noticed that sexual liberation tended to maintain male sexual and social dominance (Seidman 1992). But divisions by gender are not the whole picture; sexual assault has also been more tolerated when women of color and poorer women are victims. The criminal justice system, from cops to courts, has been slow to abandon its entrenched skepticism regarding sexual assault and thus exemplifies the patriarchal status quo. Defense lawyers have, in the past, been free to use a woman's friendly behavior, past sexual history, or style of dress as evidence to contradict the claim of victimization.

A case from the 1980s illustrates the conflict between feminist and patriarchal perspectives. Andrea, aged 24, from Gardner, Massachusetts, was at a New Year's Eve party where a friend introduced her to David Partridge, her brother. David offered to drive his sister and Andrea home but dropped off the sister first. At Andrea's, he invited himself in for coffee, and then the evening took a dark turn. A *Time* magazine account continues:

> "I trusted [David's sister]. Why not trust him," Andrea says. "He had been so nice, so polite, all evening long." Once inside, Andrea alleges, he forced her to perform a variety of sex acts. She decided to prosecute. It turned out that Partridge had got out on parole on a rape conviction only six days before he met Andrea. People at the party testified for the defense that they had seen the couple talking that night and Andrea drinking. A jury acquitted Partridge. (Dowd 1983:28)

In this story, Andrea was brave enough to attempt to prosecute. Her courage was, no doubt, bolstered by an explicit feminist agenda to hold men accountable for sexual violence. But society's resistance to the agenda was also evident. The jury found that Andrea's ostensibly unguarded behavior mitigated criminal intent or behavior.

For feminists, the challenge has been to get judges and juries to listen to women and to believe their accounts of assault. Defenders, tapping the sentiments of patriarchy and the status quo, have been able simply to use a woman's gender to explain away the crime of sexual assault. The news article about Andrea's case went on to note that defense lawyers have been fond of using the nineteenth-century French writer Balzac's statement on rape: "One cannot thread a needle when the needle doesn't stand still" (Dowd 1983). From this point of view, by definition sex cannot possibly occur without a woman's consent. Furthermore, rape is seen as the biological act of penetration.

Since the early 1980s, however, feminist efforts have raised consciousness and prompted policy changes regarding sexual assault on college campuses, in local statutes, and in law enforcement policies and procedures. Additional movements relating to sexual assault against women have also emerged. Some of these reforms have been so successful that a counter-voice among feminists has emerged, expressing concern about a view on sexual assault (and sexual harassment and pornography) that appears too ready to define women as victims and sexuality as inherently dangerous.

The dilemma has been where to draw the line between seduction and coercion. When **emotional abuse** is included in the definition of sexual crime, the door is open for a range of interpretations. Emotional abuse is a real and damaging method of coercion that involves systematic humiliation, badgering, and control of one person by another. However, identifying what constitutes systematic humiliation or control is difficult. For some, the systematic humiliation of women starts with the culture at large, in which, for example, images of half-clothed women are used to sell everything from cigarettes to cars. However, because such images are so diffuse, cannot all women claim victimization? And if all women claim victimization, how can a legal system make judgments regarding relative seriousness?

This debate has fractured feminist advocacy. One faction, whom we refer to as **free-speech feminists,** takes issue with the continued identification of women as victims with little power or individual responsibility in social interactions that involve sex and gender. Betty Friedan is quoted on the "Feminists for Free Expression" Web site: "To suppress free speech in the name of protecting women is dangerous and wrong."

Free-speech feminism has been concerned with specific issues such as censorship of pornography and social trends that according to some free-speech feminists, involve casting women as perpetual victims; that is exactly what Friedan's quotation addresses. Although Friedan is a senior feminist, this issue has been taken up in a younger generation than the radical, free-love feminists of the 1960s and 1970s. Writers like Katie Roiphe (1993) began to wonder publicly whether some of the sexual assault and date rape reports weren't distorted, especially those that used very broad definitions of emotional abuse. Along with others, she noticed that some of the rhetoric of feminist activists seemed to highlight a pervasive oppression that didn't ring completely true to her. Widely publicized claims of cultural, sexist oppression by middle-class, privileged white women, Roiphe and others posited, tend to dilute the claims of the most severely victimized of women.

A generation earlier, feminists had promoted sexual liberation, yet activists had to contend with continued sexual violence against women. Thus, feminist movements had had to fight to convince law enforcement personnel to believe women and hear their accusations of sexual and domestic violence. Harkening back to more sex-positive, liberationist notions, free-speech feminists wondered if antiviolence movements were exaggerating the problems of sexual violence. Roiphe and others believe that some quarters of feminist efforts were using rape as a political tool, and they wondered about the limits of credulity, particularly regarding accusations of date rape. Roiphe wondered if women should always be believed any more than men should always be believed. The skepticism of free-speech feminism has polarized feminist communities, and of course, it is the polarization of feminism that has captured popular attention, thus siphoning off concern about reducing sexual assault. Feminist writers and activists have found themselves in the odd position of battling one another rather than advancing feminist causes. Notably, the rates of rape (as reported in the section "Consent and Coercion" in Chapter 2) persist in lifetime prevalence around 20 percent. Furthermore, mainstream institutions such as the United Nations and the U.S. armed forces continue to be exposed as venues for sexual harassment and coercion.

Although the disputes among women's movements tend to eclipse men's voices regarding sexual assault, there are several distinct men's movements. A number have arisen since the mid-1980s as a response to feminism. Some, such as the mytho-poetic movement led by Robert Bly, resent the suggestion that masculine sexuality is defined by power (Bly 1990). The men in this movement feel increasingly powerless and persecuted and tend to think that their powerlessness is as salient as women's vulnerability to sexual violence. Through mythology and group activities, these men attempt to "reclaim" their masculinity, which they believe has been eroded by feminism.

Other men's movements, such as Men against Violence, seek to reduce the problem of domestic violence and sexual assault. Some of these groups recognize men's accountability and the influence of a historically patriarchal culture. They seek to change cultural practices that tend to be associated with sexual violence and promote policies that adequately punish sexual violence.

Other groups, however, see men as sometimes being unavoidably, essentially violent, and for them the struggle against violence is much like a struggle for a cure to a medical (rather than social) problem. Although these men cast themselves as pro-feminist, they present a dilemma to the politics of feminism. These men see masculine violence as a medical or psychological problem, one that is developed on an individual level and that requires individual solutions, like psychotherapy or self-help groups. For most feminists, however, violence against women is a social problem. Of course, individual perpetrators ought to be held accountable for crimes against women, but these crimes are bound to emerge in a patriarchal social context.

Strange Bedfellows

Not only have multiple battles flared up among seemingly natural allies within feminist communities, but surprising alliances between feminists and others have also sprung up. The American mainstream was not transformed by feminist efforts in the 1960s and 1970s, but in recent years the mainstream has begun to share the feminist concern with protecting women from violence. In the 1980s, the Reagan administration forged an unlikely alliance with some feminists around anti-pornography efforts. These disparate communities are brought together by an essentialist view of sexuality: Men are fundamentally predatory, women should be protected, and women should shield themselves from men.

The common ground of these two groups is well illustrated by the Reagan administration's Meese Commission on Pornography. As part of a pledge to the Christian Right, which helped him get elected in 1980 and 1984, Ronald Reagan appointed U.S. Attorney General Edwin Meese to chair a group examining the connections between pornography and sexual violence against women. The group set aside the findings of a 1970 report by the U.S. Commission on Obscenity and Pornography, which found that exposure to pornography had little or no relationship to crime or deviance (Seidman 1992). Among the witnesses for the Meese Commission was Andrea Dworkin, the antipornography feminist who has advocated the abolition of all sexually explicit materials. This odd coalition abandoned concerns for First Amendment rights to free speech and ignored research that did not support the beliefs of antipornography advocates. It reported that men exposed to sexually explicit material and entertainment were likely to become sexual victimizers. The conservatives were interested in protecting the "virtue" of women, for whom they felt virginity and sexual purity are paramount. The antipornography feminists were interested in making the streets safe for women by means of punitive and far-reaching legislation against pornography.

Like a mirror image, some factions of the men's movement have joined free-speech feminists in another opportunistic (although less high-profile) alliance. Those in the men's movement who emphasize men's feelings of powerlessness and their own victimization at the hands of unfeeling fathers and castrating mothers hardly feel like sexual threats. Thus, they resist the antiporn feminists' blanket condemnation of men as potential sexual predators who get stoked up by sexually explicit material. They have found common cause with a faction of feminists who believe there is more harm in censorship than in pornography. Feminists who want to protect pornography under the mantle of free speech are not enthusiastic about most commercially available sexual materials; they simply believe the First Amendment requires support.

How well does this political maneuvering advance the cause of reducing sexual assault? It depends on whom you ask. Some feminists believe the debate has merely ensured that women's stories will be heard and believed. However, free-speech feminists are alarmed at the potential for women's claims to be exaggerated and fear the resulting antifeminist backlash will undermine sympathy and legal support for women who have been horribly threatened, attacked, or coerced.

Moreover, men and women who are concerned for individual civil liberties are worried about how uncritically women's claims should be taken. We are obliged to protect the rights of individuals who are unjustly accused. But even if women's claims are ever distorted or exaggerated, we need to address the real problem of sexual assault. Sexual assault persists, even if some people misrepresent themselves.

False Prophets, False Accusations, and True Lies

In the 1960s and 1970s, researchers made many advances in the study of sexual assault and sexual abuse and generally raised consciousness about perpetrators, victims, and the consequences of the crime. In the 1980s, acquaintance rape became recognized as a rampant problem; in 1987, Miller and Marshall published a study that indicated that 27 percent of college women experienced coerced or forced intercourse during their college career. By the late 1980s and 1990s, a new issue surfaced: "false accusations" of assault. In a study of a small midwestern city, one researcher determined that 42 percent of the allegations of sexual assault were subsequently recanted by the claimants as false allegations (Kanin 1994); the recanting rate is similar in cases of college campus assault.

The incidence of recanting does not necessarily provide evidence of false accusations, although it does invite consideration of this potential problem. Women may recant for many reasons—for instance, because they lose the courage to face an impersonal legal system or because of community pressure to protect the accused, especially when they know the alleged perpetrator. Recanting can also reflect women's feelings of guilt and shame about their sexual victimization.

Unfortunately, we do not have enough data on the frequency of outright lying about sexual assault to evaluate the impact, and issues of misperception are extremely hard to measure. Thus, researchers face two dilemmas. The first dilemma is to establish the authenticity of the information we have about sexual assault. As with all research, one can question the representativeness of the sample or the method for collecting the data. Or one can speculate about variables that were not accounted for in the survey. For example, a skeptic might wonder under what conditions a claimant recanted. Was there coercion to recant? Or encouragement? These questions ought to be raised about any information presented as fact. In this case, however, the manipulation of data can have serious consequences such as undermining protective services for women or, on the other hand, encumbering the civil liberties of individuals falsely accused.

Another dilemma researchers face is how to interpret their data. If we can agree that, yes, in some undetermined number of cases false accusations of assault are made, how do we use this information? In a search for the "truth" about sexual assault, politics cloud our efforts. Antiviolence feminists are defensively skeptical about the magnitude of the false accusation problem, because they fear it will be inflated or used to downplay the quite dire and still largely hidden problem of sexual assault against women. Civil libertarians, anxious to see justice served from the point of view of "innocent until proven guilty," are skeptical of claimed rates of sexual assault and therefore likely to take at face value reported incidents of false accusations. They are concerned about accepting crime reports with little or no investigation.

The question, as we see it, is how social institutions and individuals can cope with ambiguity—or even false accusations. They are abhorrent, but we must remember that even some false accusations constitute the truth as the victims of sexual assault see it. In other cases, false accusations of a particular act, at a particular time, represent a woman's overwhelming sense of general abuse, powerlessness, and anger at being used. From this point of view, a lie about the man's behavior is not to be tolerated, but at the same time it has a context that should not be ignored or discounted. Many women have less power, less opportunity, and even less sexual freedom than men have, thanks to culture and social structures. Women need a sense of power and efficacy to reduce the gendered quality of interaction. This will alleviate anger and bitterness that can fuel attempts to equalize power differences. Above all, the discussion of sexual assault and false accusations of sexual assault has the unintended consequence of distracting from the central issue: preventing sexual assault. Some see the central issue as the civil rights of the accused.

In the end, efforts to reduce violence against women sputter ahead. Some feminists seek to ensure that women's stories of abuse will be heard and believed; other feminists fear that if some women's claims are exaggerated, legitimate claims will be disbelieved, like the story of the boy who cried wolf. However, both groups agree about the seriousness of sexual violence.

For our purposes, the political divisions on this issue are interesting because of the different theories implied by the approach to sexual assault and false accusations. Those who recognize the power of social institutions and culture to form gendered sexual styles focus on institutional change; those who posit that biology and evolution drive the gendered sexual system focus on ways to refine "natural" roles for men and women to reduce sexual violence. Few people believe women or men should be made sexually compliant against their will (although some still do).

Our position is that sexual assault has to be understood in this context of real and perceived male domination. Sexual assault highlights a gendered sexual system where men in general have more power than women. But the gender system that gives men and women different sexual power is also responsible for those unhappy instances where men and women interpret the same "facts" terribly differently. Simultaneously, a man might think he was invited and that sex was mutual while a woman might feel helpless, overwhelmed, and coerced. In the gendered sexual system, such misunderstandings between men and women are viewed as normal and natural. Thus, popular views regarding false accusations of sexual assault seem based on a polarized sexuality that casts men as essentially predatory and women as responsible for avoiding trouble. As long as gender difference is considered fundamental to sexuality, some aggression will be cast as "misunderstandings" and some "misunderstandings" will be cast as aggression.

Same-Sex Marriage

Although the politics of teenage sexuality and sexual assault is mostly about what happens to women's bodies, homosexual marriage is sexual politics of a different sort. Instead of being about women's sexuality, the central, thorny dilemma is about the importance of gender difference to normative sexuality. Gender difference is so central to traditional visions of acceptable sexuality that some people abhor and fear a sexuality that is not defined by having a man and a woman participating.

The political debate over **same-sex marriage** is about whether gay and lesbian partners can have the same access to social and legal support of their unions that heterosexuals gain by entering the social contract of marriage. The underpinning of the debate is the gendered status of marriage within the Judeo-Christian traditions. Heterosexual marriage is a sexual union that requires gender difference because of what is seen as the purpose of marriage: reproduction and child rearing. Homosexual marriage, by eliminating gender difference and hence reproduction by the married partners, challenges many people's religious beliefs and inflames the dialogue about changing the rules.

Political distress over same-sex marriage underscores a notion we have emphasized throughout this book: Gender difference is central to the social control of intimacy. Indeed, homosexual marriage provides the perfect experimental design. Only one crucial variable—gender—

has been altered, and all others remain constant (love, commitment, concern for property, union of two families). Varying gender in the context of marriage, it turns out, is a highly provocative innovation.

Precipitating Events

Same-sex marriage became a front-page issue in 1996 as a consequence of two events. First, three same-sex couples penetrated the previously unfriendly legal system. After the validity of their marriages was rejected at lower levels of Hawaiian courts in 1993, including the state appeals court, they found an unexpectedly friendly state supreme court in 1996. Stating as their basis of consideration the Equal Rights Amendment to Hawaii's constitution, the Hawaii Supreme Court said that unless the lower court could show "clear and compelling" evidence why prohibiting same-sex marriage was not a form of sex discrimination, then same-sex marriage should be legalized. Following a trial in September 1996, the right to same-sex marriages was upheld in the State of Hawaii (although legislation and litigation related to it continue).

Almost out of the blue, the United States (and western European countries, too) has been confronted with the demand that marriage and all of its social, legal, and economic benefits be accorded to couples who are not heterosexual. Across the country, lawyers, politicians, and laypeople have expressed concern about the implications of the Hawaii case. If Hawaii has same-sex marriage, are all states obliged to recognize same-sex marriage? The question raises issues of autonomy and local rights embedded in the U.S. Constitution as well as practices of state-to-state legal reciprocity. The conundrum is that each state has the right to set its own statutes about marriage, which could prevent the recognition of Hawaiian same-sex marriages. On the other hand, reciprocity has always been extended to make marriages constituted in one state legal in another. Thus, a same-sex marriage, made legal by a Hawaii Supreme Court judgment, would become valid in all other states of the United States. If Hawaiian same-sex marriages do not receive reciprocity, reciprocity on heterosexual marriages could also be invalidated. Many states created laws to eliminate reciprocity for homosexual marriage, but affirm cross-sex marriages. These laws will be appealed by gay activists, state by state, prompting countless new headlines that will keep this issue in the public eye.

The second event bringing homosexual marriage to the political forefront was the presidential election of 1996. The "family values" lobby of the Republican party used the threat of same-sex marriage to tap homophobia, proclaiming it as a new assault on traditional values and trying to smear the Democrats as the party that would countenance such an outrage. Senator Robert Dole, running for president, cosponsored a bill in the U.S. Congress known as the Defense of Marriage Act (DoMA), designed to deny federal recognition to gay marriages. President Bill Clinton, recanting earlier support for gay and lesbian civil liberties, was advised that he should not support same-sex marriage because his (modest) support for gays in the military had started out his presidency with great controversy. When DoMA was presented to him, he and his advisers had already concluded that this political bomb needed to be lobbed back over the fence. Polls had indicated that the voters were not ready to accept gay marriage and a liberal position on this issue might help lose the election for Clinton. Thus, Clinton said he was not in favor of gay marriage and would sign DoMA.

DoMA, now a federal law, is an attempt to deny recognition and federal benefits to same-sex couples and thereby prevent any obligation of reciprocity by other states when the Hawaii case came out in support of gay marriage. The bill received much popular and political support, although many legal scholars and practitioners believe it is unconstitutional. Legal scholars such as David Chambers observe that the law is designed to curtail the rights of one special group, because it takes powers clearly given to the states (e.g., marriage and divorce law) and gives them to the federal government.

Meanwhile, European Union countries are confused about the status of same-sex marriage, because they, too, have reciprocal rights and obligations. Member country Denmark established domestic partner rights in 1988, and Holland offers many rights to heterosexual and homosexual cohabitors, with more formal legitimization of gay partners pending. The fear among some Europeans is that the practices in Denmark and Holland will require other member nations to also accord these rights. In Europe as in the United States, the intimate partnerships of gay and lesbian couples have become a hot political topic.

Pro and Con Positions

Public opinion on same-sex marriage in the United States is divided, but it is more negative than positive. In December 1995, a Roper poll showed that 56 percent of Americans disapproved of gay marriage and only 30 percent approved. The rest were undecided ("Family: Time to Legalize" 1995). On the other hand, 85 percent of those polled thought gay people should have equal access to jobs. Obviously, homosexuality is more threatening in some domains than in others. Furthermore, something about marriage brings out special territorial feelings.

The politics of same-sex marriage are complicated. There are several positions regarding same-sex marriage—even among homosexuals. Mainstream heterosexual political leaders tend to reject same-sex marriage, but not all of them do; some gay and lesbian activists and political leaders support same-sex marriage, but others reject it. The reasons for these positions are hardly uniform.

The fact that gays and lesbians are on both sides of the debate seems counterintuitive. However, some gays and lesbians prefer not to be involved with the state or to follow mainstream definitions and rules about intimacy. A vocal minority of gay and lesbian activists speak strongly against same-sex marriage—and only a minority of gays and lesbians are actively pursuing it (Rotello 1996). Gay and lesbian opponents of same-sex marriage see it as a problematic, patriarchal institution. They feel gays and lesbians have been lucky to escape the strictures of gender roles and religious dogma about marriage and prefer not to be subjected to what is, in their estimation, a sexist and inequitable institution, as Vaid wrote in *Virtual Equality: The Mainstreaming of Gay and Lesbian Liberation* (1995). Gays and lesbians who are vocal in the campaign to receive marriage equity include couples who want the various legal benefits of marriage. In addition, some homosexual civil libertarians may not want to get married themselves but feel that gay people should be vested with all the rights and obligations of heterosexual citizens.

These people join heterosexual supporters who believe that there is no God-given or "natural" shape to marriage and that same-sex marriage is in no way a sacrilege. Their position relies on the constructionist idea that social institutions, such as marriage, are created by society and therefore appropriately manipulated by society. Barring some groups from enjoying the benefits of marriage is discrimination that ought to be remedied through social engineering. In essence, courts and legislators should lead the country away from prejudice against homosexuals and away from the religious ideology penetrating social institutions. Separation of church and state, in other words, means that religious ideas about marriage cannot be the basis for barring gays and lesbians from marriage.

Despite fairly strong public opposition to same-sex marriage, the constructionist argument concludes that judges and elected officials should do the fair thing and support same-sex marriage. There is powerful civil rights precedent: slavery, which was not abolished by popular demand. Abolition was unpopular and unsupported in the South and some of the North, and religion was often used to justify discrimination based on "natural and spiritual" differences between the races. Abolitionists eventually triumphed by encouraging the government to recognize that abolition was fair in law and consistent with the mandate of the U.S. Bill of Rights. Like abolitionists, gay activists know they cannot win a popularity contest. By using arguments of "constitutional right" and legal consistency, however, they hope to give gay citizens all the same opportunities and rules that other citizens have automatically.

Nonetheless, opponents of same-sex marriage cloak their argument in moral terms. Conservative factions claim that marriage is the cornerstone of morality and the guide to a country's ethos and social plan. Their opinion leaders hold symposia and speak in churches and on campaign trails about how same-sex marriage will degrade the sacred institution of marriage and therefore corrupt society. Like the biological essentialists, these stakeholders claim that, by God's (and nature's) plan, marriage is for procreation. Two biological sexes were designed to perpetuate the species. Nature, therefore, ordains the pairing of men with women. God created two sexes to create family and, from family, create society.

This model has some unintended irony. In reality, modern marriage is not primarily a procreative institution. A growing proportion of heterosexual, married couples do not have children (they are having fewer children later in life, or none at all). Furthermore, same-sex couples can have children, either through a temporary heterosexual alliance, fertility technology, or adoption. Opponents fear that children raised by homosexuals will suffer discrimination and even perversion; however, no evidence supports this position. In fact, research demonstrates that children of homosexuals are no worse or better off than children of heterosexuals (Golombok and Tasker 1996; Patterson 1992; Green 1987; Bozett 1987). There is, in fact, reason to think that children will benefit from legitimizing same-sex unions. Stable parenting pairs are endangered among all classes and subcultures in the United States. Nonetheless, the belief in marriage as an essentially procreative institution and the fear that gay parenting is worse than heterosexual parenting have been a cornerstone of the state's argument in Hawaii's same-sex marriage case. And it was on this point that the state lost and the plaintiffs won the right to same-sex marriage in Hawaii.

Legal Precedent

Providing social support for motivated parents, whether they are homosexual or heterosexual, can only benefit children. An estimated 10 percent of lesbians have custody of children (Demo and Allen 1996), and a smaller number of gay males have custody of children.

Without laws to safeguard the rights of both parents in a homosexual union, children's lives are often disrupted when one parent is disabled or dies. In a recent case, the grandparents obtained custody of their eight-year-old grandchild after their daughter died unexpectedly in an accident. The child's second parent, the lesbian partner of the deceased woman, had been a mother to the child all her life. In this case, the child liked the grandparents but was distraught over the loss of not only her biological mother but her nonbiological parent as well. After many appeals and several years, the child was returned to the psychological parent, the lesbian mother. In another case in the late 1980s and early 1990s, a Virginia state court ruled that Sharon Bottoms was guilty of violating an old statute against sodomy in that state by virtue of her lesbian sexual orientation—and therefore an unfit mother. After a long battle, the courts awarded the child to the mother's mother, with highly restricted visitation by the child's biological mother. Custody was restored to the biological mother, at last, in 1994 ("Custody Restored to Lesbian" 1994). It is hard to see how these battles or uncertainty about parental rights could be in the best interest of children. Heterosexual couples have a recognized biological right and adoption procedures that solidify their children's future. The issue of procreation pales when real children, with real attachments to parents who are performing well in their obligations, suffer disrupted homes and perhaps tragic loss of a beloved parent.

In addition, the notion of marriage as procreative has been explicitly rejected by the highest court of the United States. The Supreme Court decided in the case of *Griswold v. Connecticut* that laws prohibiting married people from using contraceptives were antithetical to the constitutional notion of privacy (Eskridge 1996). According to this precedent, and according to the cultural shift that the Court recognized, marriage is not a procreative institution but a private one created for whatever emotional and social purposes its partners choose. This precedent, however, was ignored in the Hawaii case by the attorney for the state, who gave little or no credence to the right of individuals to institutional protection for their relationship or for their children. The plaintiff's side called many witnesses who testified that marriage confers certain emotional and psychic benefits that same-sex unions, with or without children, deserve. Paradoxically, the state ended up arguing against marriage as an important institution for maintaining sentiment and commitment.

The discrimination argument relies on yet another legal precedent. Proponents of same-sex marriage note parallels between the gay marriage ban and the miscegenation laws, which until 1967 prohibited marriages between individuals from different races. The premise of a ban on gay marriage is the same. A biological imperative ordains some pairs but not others. Of course, such bans on marriage are also a tool of social control based on prejudice. In the 1967 decision *Loving v. Virginia*, the ban against interracial marriage was finally lifted. Miscegenation laws were thus still in force until fairly recently, illustrating the persistence of prejudices about race, religion, and gender. Laws that recognize the inalienable rights of humans are apparently not as easily agreed on as traditions based on prejudices, fears, economic systems, and class structures.

Although marriage confers many economic and social benefits, it is far from an ideal institution. We noted in Chapter 4 that marriage tends to reinforce traditional, gendered social practices. And it has some undesirable aspects, as eighteenth-century social commentator Samuel Johnson noted: "It is so far from being natural for a man and woman to live in a state of marriage, that we find all the motives which they have for remaining in that connection and the restraints which civilized society imposes to prevent separation, are hardly sufficient to keep them together." Gays and lesbians who seek to break away from social sexual norms may be excused for their ambivalence toward marriage. Some questions are as yet unanswered: If gay marriage is allowed, will gay and lesbian pairs who do not step up to the altar be stigmatized for abstaining from participating in this institution? And will marriage bring with it gendered performance norms that confuse rather than aid same-sex couples?

As for the public's ambivalence about same-sex marriage, we join other commentators in observing that it is rooted in **homophobia,** the intense hatred and irrational fear of homosexual behavior and individuals, which, in turn, is related to ambivalence about sexual pleasure. Marriage is about intimacy and pleasure as much as it is about children. This is a radical and upsetting notion to many people. However, the case for same-sex marriage is unfolding as we write.

Conclusion

We have pointed out some remarkable political battles about changes in sexual behavior and attitudes. In some ways, liberalizing forces have prevailed: People's opportunities for sexual expression have increased. At the same time, however, gendered sexuality continues to predominate in the political debate. And this debate has focused more on women's, rather than men's, bodies.

Historian John Modell, who documents social change and continuity in *Into One's Own: From Youth to Adulthood in the United States 1920-1975*, observes that "so substantial was the repositioning of sexuality within American culture that theorists have suggested that its expression, rather than its repression, came to lie near the core of the energy that structures the society" (p. 308). In other words, sexual expression has increased over time and with it the political battles regarding sexual expression. The question is whether freedom of sexual expression, for both men and women, has advanced unimpeded by political and media attention to sexuality or whether the attention has sidetracked desirable changes in sexual desire and sexual behavior. We believe that there has been progress but that nongendered sexual freedom has been resisted and diverted by the numerous political debates about sexuality. Clearly, much of the political controversy continues to be focused on women's bodies or, in the case of same-sex sexual politics, the fear of the feminization of men's bodies and the masculinization of women's bodies.

Have the sexual privileges and responsibilities of women and men changed nevertheless? Yes. Have these changes brought the experiences of being a man and of being a woman closer, or allowed for greater diversity? Somewhat. And there is reason for optimism. The public debate over sexual issues constitutes an opportunity to revise tired notions of masculinity and femininity. However, it is merely an opportunity. Social traditions—as much as biological realities—are neither immutable nor completely pliant. Political and media attention can reinforce gender differences, which may in the end be explained as a combination of social and biological forces. But this attention may also be an opportunity to promote diversity, rather than polarities, in sexual expression.

Promoting diversity in sexuality and sexual expression has not been a gentle process, nor will it be any time soon. Political battles over teen sexuality, sexual assault, and same-sex marriage continue even as we write, and sincere advocates on all sides press on with their agendas. Young people's feelings about sex are intense, caught up in their allegiance to their parents' values, their fleeting system of personal identity—in sum, who they are and who they want to be. Conservatives express alarm about nonmarital sex. Liberals feel just as strongly that their very liberty is linked to unfastening the short leash conservatives and traditionalists have imposed on sexuality—especially women's sexuality—and personal choice. These fights aren't intellectual; they are part of people's heart and soul. No wonder they sometimes end in long, expensive court fights that the losing side never takes as a final answer—or even end in bloodshed.

Even while sexuality is the product of social processes, it is so personal that people can have trouble moderating opinions on the subject. We forget that there are many different orientations toward sexuality and even choices out there. In the political arena, people forget that sexuality is a positive force as well as one with potential pitfalls, and that men's and women's propensities are arranged along a continuum of desire and behavior, rather than at dichotomous poles.

But the sexual world is less polarized by gender than we often think it is, and we encourage you to be wary of positions on sexuality that rely on hidden or explicit assumptions regarding gender differences in matters sexual or otherwise. And so in the next chapter we evaluate a few very important questions about personal and social aspects of sex. The chapter will provide you with examples of how sexual issues are about similarity as well as difference and show you how to identify gendered assumptions in everyday quandaries regarding sexuality.

CHAPTER 6

Answers and Questions

No book ever answers all the questions people have on any given subject. We have addressed the "big issues" of gender and sexuality in this book and provided you with a framework for answering questions about sex and gender. More important, we hope we have provided a framework you can use to raise new questions about the issues.

As is often the case with the topic of sex, people want to know more. When we discuss sex with students, colleagues, and friends, they have endless questions about their sexuality and experiences. Indeed, after studying many of the topics that are addressed in this book, a class of college seniors was asked what they wanted more information on. Here are 11 of their questions related to sexual orientation, sexual harassment and violence, and sexual function, along with our responses.

Sexual Orientation

1. *I still don't know where homosexuality originates. Where do you think it begins? Do you think it is really different for men and women?*

Determining origins of homosexuality is extremely difficult. Remember, we still have people arguing over the origin of the species. Too many people are invested in competing theories—and the theories all come loaded with political implications.

This question isn't debated just in the halls of academia. The popular media debate it. In churches, temples, and synagogues the issue is debated. Even around the dinner table in some households, it is debated.

Before we review the arguments regarding the origins of homosexuality, we'd like to ask why the origins of homosexuality are of concern.

From our point of view, debates about homosexuality have much to do with the importance of gender difference to sexuality. That is, even though sex typically gets done in private, people judge one another in terms of whether they conform to norms of masculinity and femininity and to the heterosexual "dos and don'ts" that are attached to being male or female. If one doesn't know the origins of homosexuality, one also doesn't know the origins of heterosexuality. Still, that is hardly ever the question that gets raised. Why is that? For many people, the origins of heterosexuality aren't questioned because it appears to be natural and rooted in the imperative to procreate.

From a theoretical point of view, the debate over the origins of homosexuality is tied to whether one is an essentialist or a social constructionist. But the consequences of these abstract theoretical per-spectives are quite practical. The essentialist position would suggest that homosexuals and heterosexuals are born and not made. But if so, essentialists' discrimination against homosexuality seems cruel and unjust, like discrimination based on race, size, or able-bodiedness.

What if social constructionists are right, and homosexuality is not a natural, genetic trait? Does that then mean that it is a choice? Not necessarily. People can choose how they behave but have far less control over how they feel or what they desire. People do not necessarily choose to feel homosexual or heterosexual attractions.

These two theoretical perspectives produce three popular hypothe-ses regarding homosexuality's origins: (1) that it is biological, caused by hormones, chromosomes, and genetic information; (2) that it is sociological, learned through lifestyle and sexual opportunity, which can happen throughout a lifetime; (3) that it is the result of various kinds of early childhood identification with men's and women's experience, formed prior to any adolescent sexual encounters. The people who say homosexuality is biological and the people who say it is the result of early childhood identification believe homosexuality is not voluntary. Homosexuals no more control the direction of their sexual desires than heterosexuals do: They just experience them.

Those who have a sociological point of view are much more divided on the question of choice. Those who disapprove of homosexuality say that people decide to be gay or lesbian, and therefore deserve no protection against discrimination, because they are not a special group so much as a lifestyle. People who favor gay rights argue that even if gay and lesbian people establish their identities through everyday experiences and choose to follow their desires, the final product is no less legitimate a choice than heterosexual persons' becoming whatever they become. Becoming homosexual is not volitional for most: It just evolves, through a complex array of everyday choices and environmental circumstances. Furthermore, even if some choice is involved, so what? We choose our religion, and that is a protected right, no matter what we choose.

There is some support for all of these theories. In fact, many scientists believe there is more than one way to become gay or lesbian. Dean Hamer's work on the inheritance of a "gay gene" (discussed in Chapter 1), which shows up through the maternal line of gay men and is far more common among gay men than chance would predict, convincingly shows that for at least some gay men, homosexuality may be an inherited trait, or predisposition. LeVay's (1993) work on brain samples, showing different brain construction, has more critics, but there is still strong evidence that some gay men may be physiologically different from heterosexual men. Fred Whitman's (1983) cross-cultural data showing that certain kinds of behaviors appear in gay men but not heterosexual men the world over fuels the biological argument.

And yet some homosexual men and women, who have no genetic marker, still feel that they were homosexual from their very first sexual stirrings. There is no explanation for these early feelings; they begin young and are very distinct. Some psychologists believe these feelings have been reconstructed from hindsight, but some parents report that their children, early on, have strong same-sex crushes and a greater identification with the other sex.

Some people are attracted to both sexes. Somewhere along the line they may find themselves attracted to the same sex, with no prior homosexual attractions in their young or adolescent life. Some men were happily married or dating women until midlife and then find their attractions to other men steadily growing. Or even more numerous are the women who never found women sexually alluring and then fall in love with a specific woman and sexualize that person (Schwartz and Blumstein 1976). They are as surprised as anyone else. A case in point is a woman who was married her entire adult life, had three children, but then fell in love with a woman colleague. They were both 60 at the time; neither had had a sexual fantasy about women prior to their own love affair.

Any gender difference in the origins of homosexuality is likely to be this: Women seem to be able to sexualize whomever they love; men tend to love whom they sexualize. In gay and lesbian sex surveys by the *Advocate*, 29 percent of lesbians say that they thought their sexual orientation was in part a choice, but only 4 percent of gay men indicated that they thought it was a choice (Lever 1994a, 1995). This outcome is as likely a product of gendered social processes, not fundamental gender differences. Girls, whether homosexual or heterosexual, are raised to be more relationally focused than boys are, and this learning is embedded in social structures that influence how girls and boys grow up to be sexual adults. The difference between a gay sexual orientation and a lesbian sexual orientation, then, is related to social experience that treats boys and men one way and girls and women another.

2. *I have been told that in the absence of prejudice, everyone would be bisexual. Does society impose so many rules against homosexuality because people are afraid of their own bisexuality?*

Is everyone, at core, bisexual? Some people think so. But probably a whole continuum of sexual desire exists, with some people no more able to sexualize same-sex people than they can a bowling ball and some people no more able to sexualize other-sex people than they can a basketball. Still others can be turned on to either—and even to bowling balls or basketballs, depending on the circumstances.

Society imposes many constraints on bisexuality. For example, many religious groups interpret their scriptures as prohibiting all same-sex sexuality. Governments, influenced by religious beliefs, show little tolerance for same-sex sexual activity. Many parents, even liberal ones, are nervous or panicked if their child has any kind of sexual play with a same-sex friend. It is hard to know what kind of bisexual behavior would exist in a more open society.

In many countries around the world, bisexual conduct is more tolerated and even more expected than it is in the United States. Boys in many parts of the world are not allowed to get near girls until they marry, and many boys may wait to marry until they are older and richer. Under these circumstances, same-sex experiences are expected. Other countries, such as Greece and other European and African Mediterranean countries, allow men more license with each other. American men are often shocked to see men kissing each other and holding hands in the affectionate way that women are allowed in this country. The range of same-sex contact is much broader in other parts of the world than it is in the United States.

It has also been observed in the United States that if access to the other sex is cut off, people who had no previous desire for same-sex partners develop it. The most common place this situation is noted is in prisons and reformatories. Men may take a male partner for the duration of their stay, and perhaps cease same-sex affiliation on their release. Or they may merely use another man sexually, denying that the act is homosexual. They insist that if they are the one penetrating the other sexual partner, then they are still playing the heterosexual part. And many books have noted the quasi-family and marital arrangements that girls in reform schools arrange. Some are sexualized, and some are not. It is easy, it seems, for women to love each other when necessity or opportunity presents itself.

This evidence doesn't prove that anyone can have bisexual desires or that if they have it they have equal desire for both sexes. In fact, the latter is empirically uncommon. Most people who describe themselves as bisexual still state a preference for one sex. Or they have had significant love affairs with both sexes over a lifetime and define themselves more strongly in terms of the person they are in love with now. A smaller group of men and women, however, have claimed the right to be seen as truly bisexual, retaining the ability to sexualize both sexes throughout the life cycle and not be seen, by either homosexuals or heterosexuals, as denying their true preferences.

What is so interesting about the question of bisexuality is that some gay, lesbian, and heterosexual communities have problems with the notion of bisexuality. Gays and lesbians may feel that a person claiming bisexuality is reserving the option to be heterosexual and thereby gain the perks of being a sexual conformist. Heterosexuals may feel the same homophobia toward bisexuals that they feel toward gays and lesbians. What marks bisexuals as different from both homosexuals and heterosexuals is the fundamentally "sex positive" approach to sexuality that bisexuality seems to represent. Homosexuals and heterosexuals run the gamut in terms of sexual freedom and sexual expressiveness; however, bisexuals are seen as sexual outlaws by both straight people and gay people.

So, to answer the question, more bisexuality would probably occur if we had fewer sanctions against homosexuality. But for bisexuality to be accepted by the larger culture, another shift would need to occur: a reduction in ambivalence or negativity regarding sexual expression and sexual freedom. Slow but steady steps are being made toward accepting homosexuality as a legitimate form of sexual expression and family building. However, the sex-positive attitudes associated with bisexuality are further behind.

3. I understand why lesbians might want children, but what about gay men? Wouldn't gay men be dangerous to their own boy children?

This question might appear offensive to many readers, but well-meaning people continue to ask it. The question reflects their skepticism about gay male sexuality—and even beliefs about the dangers of heterosexual male sexuality. However, the question unfairly maligns gay men. There is no evidence that being gay is in itself associated with child molestation, or pederasty. Both heterosexual and homosexual men have molested children. We are not sure why more men than women have the desire to sexualize young children and to pressure them into sexual activity. As we've mentioned, some researchers suggest that men who aren't involved in the care of infants more easily sexualize those children as they grow up. Also, men's sexual imagination is influenced by cultural and commercial emphasis on young and nubile women's bodies.

We are more interested in why gay men have been associated with pederasty. Pederasty is actually much more common among men who live heterosexual lives. It is assumed that when men sexually abuse boys this must be a homosexual act. But in fact pederasts (people who sexualize children) tend to like both boys and girls and often are equally likely to victimize either. Of course, there are homosexual predators, but they seem to be remembered for their awful deeds out of proportion to their numbers.

The other side of the coin is that the literature on gay parenting is positive. In the 1996 trial on gay marriage in the state of Hawaii, opponents of the law tried to make the point that gay men might not be fit parents, to convince the court that gay men ought not to be allowed to marry. However, all the **empirical** evidence presented at the trial indicated that gay men who choose to parent are as qualified as heterosexual or lesbian parents. They may tend to be somewhat more structured (disciplinarian, scheduled) than other households and perhaps have more playtime with their children, but in most ways, they are similar to other kinds of parents.

There are more data, however, on heterosexual and lesbian parents. Lesbians are much more likely to have children from a previous relationship or have a personal script that guides them to motherhood even if they have no wish to be heterosexually married. Gay men, on the other hand, cannot be pregnant and often have no model of fatherhood outside of a marital union. Nevertheless, an increasing number of gay men have recently begun to consider single fatherhood or fatherhood with a gay partner. Currently, however, most gay men with children are noncustodial parents with visitation rights from a previous marriage and so the data on them are not entirely comparable to these other family forms.

There is no reason to believe that gay men will not be good fathers with all the same loving and protective feelings about their children that other parents have. Most adults do not see children, especially their own, as sex objects. Gay men are no exception to this rule.

Sexual Harassment and Violence

4. *Aren't some charges of sexual harassment trumped up—maybe just because the guy has a better job than the woman? Can't the woman's acts be responsible for a sexual encounter some of the time?*

The short answer to this question is, yes, of course a woman can instigate a sexual encounter. If we were responsible for mediating or adjudicating claims of sexual harassment, the woman's behavior would be an important part of the perspective we would use to make decisions. Still, a question like this suggests that publicity about exceptional sexual harassment cases has left some people with the wrong impression about sexual harassment laws. Sometimes those laws may seem to have become a justification for abridging free speech or for punishing people who may be awkward or inept but are not malicious or intent on undermining another person's chances to succeed.

Skepticism regarding sexual harassment claims is labeled "backlash" by those concerned about sexual harassment, and, as we described in Chapter 5, the polarization of the issue tends to take precedence over the problem itself. Keep in mind that the cases that receive the most publicity are not a random sample of sexual harassment cases. The popular media typically pick the anomalous or exceptional cases, such as reverse sexual harassment or seemingly frivolous claims. Sex sells, and exceptional sex sells better than ordinary sex.

Sexual harassment is a hot topic partially because the law has become involved and partially because complaints have finally sifted through university and corporate bureaucracies and through the courts. Legitimate cases of sexual harassment are, or should be, beyond society's tolerance. They are really an abrogation of a woman's right to work; to be in charge of her own body; to be able to do her job without insult, humiliation, bullying, or self-doubt. Both women and men have been found guilty of demanding sexual favors from unwilling and shocked coworkers or employees, but rate of incidents by men is much greater than the rate of incidents by women. However, many women feel that the reaction has been too long coming and not swift or widespread enough. Many women observe that they continue to suffer indignities and threats. Relatively few actually file suit—and then only when life is unbearable. The widespread sexual harassment of women army recruits by their male training officers, which was uncovered in 1996, suggests that the problem of sexual harassment persists more than people want to believe.

Some men and women feel that sexual harassment lawsuits are used as clubs by spurned women or guilty women who are not taking responsibility for their own seductive behaviors. They may readily condemn quid pro quo harassment, where a woman is given the choice to comply with sexual requests to obtain or advance in a job. But the question gets a little complicated when the scene shifts into grayer areas, like men telling sexual jokes or displaying photos of nude women—things that are tasteless but not necessarily dangerous. The charge of sexual harassment is also questionable when a consensual love affair ends. Some people feel a love affair between two people of wildly different statuses and power relationships—such as a professor and a student or a military instructor and a trainee—cannot be consensual. On the other hand, many people observe that power inequalities are extremely erotic to both parties, and were we to outlaw them, we would be unraveling many relationships.

Perhaps the issue is most clearly framed as a sociological rather than a legal question. Under what circumstances does a person have free will? When does consent seem freely given? And when does it seem coerced either directly or indirectly? We know a five-year-old can't say no to a date. But what about a woman of 20 who accepts a date with her professor? Is she free and capable of saying no? This is the kind of case that raises controversy.

The subtleties of the interactions that may be deemed sexual harassment are difficult to verify in a legalistic setting. Sociologists Judith Howard and Jocelyn Hollander used a scene from the David Mamet play *Oleanna* to highlight the dilemma in their book, *Gendered Situations, Gendered Selves* (1996). The play opens with an undergraduate woman waiting to meet with her male professor. He proposes that she spend more time with him to improve her grade. He also keeps her waiting a very long time. Howard and Hollander point out that the power difference between the student and the professor places her in an impossible situation, even before anything explicitly sexual or romantic becomes involved. As the play evolves, the student experiences the instructor's acts (such as suggestions to work alone and requests to make accommodations to his personal life) as improper and indicative of his abuse of his power over her, and she files a complaint of sexual harassment. Whether a "pass" has been made is never clear in the play, and it is certainly not clear to the professor. The complaint renders the professor at risk of losing his job and his good reputation. One of the observations that the playwright is making is that the student now appears to have power over the instructor. But, of course, the power gained in prosecuting a sexual harassment case is merely winning a battle. The student is still confined to a subordinate and sexualized position. Moreover, even though the professor didn't recognize the coercion involved in interaction with the student, the power difference loaded the situation with potential for manipulation. The professor's obtuseness regarding the power difference led directly to bitterness on the part of the student.

Of course, women can and should be held accountable for their own acts, whether they constitute aggressive sexuality or merely adult consent. We do not see women as always the victim. A woman who has sex with a man and who later regrets it is still accountable for her acts. On the other hand, a woman's acting sexy is not license for "open season." And women who interact with powerful people, such as a student directly working with a Ph.D. adviser, should be as alert as their mentors that if a sexual relationship starts, they should alter the power relationship to maintain their free will.

Nevertheless, real life offers few clear, cut-and-dried examples. Individuals have mixed agendas, and they have their own levels of self-awareness. Ideally, that self-awareness should involve awareness about power as part of gauging sexual propriety. Most people reinterpret events to their advantage. We hope that flirting, jokes, and good-natured, but not hostile or abusive, sexual remarks will still be allowed. Playful sexual exploration makes life pleasant for many people. But sexual harassment persists, and will persist into the twenty-first century. We think after a period of long-needed protection (and perhaps now a few cases of overreaction), we will reach an understanding that sexual bullies should be consistently and swiftly punished but that awkward sexual behavior should merely be corrected.

5. *What is sadomasochistic sex about? Is it always a reflection of the desire to dominate?*

There are two kinds of sado-masochistic sex (S and M): playful, mutual experimentation with the eroticism of power and its evil twin, the real thing. Because domination is part of the heterosexual sexual script, which tends to provide greater privilege to men than to women, there's good reason to think about S and M from a gendered perspective. Be mindful, though, that just because S and M plays on gendered notions of power and submission in sexuality, it isn't necessarily bad. S and M can indeed reinforce gendered power relationships, but people who try S and M are not necessarily submitting to such tired scripts; in fact, S and M can be a disruption or rejection or reversal of such scripts.

Playful sado-masochism is not necessarily a degrading or sexist experience. As described by many writers in the interesting book *Pleasure and Danger: Exploring Female Sexuality* (Vance 1984), sado-masochism can be an eye-opening excursion into submission and domination. One person tries out being powerful and gets turned on by the ability to direct all the action. The paradox is that because this is a mutual act, the person can only "order" what the other person really wants to do. So the "sadist" has to understand the script that the "masochist" seeks, including what the masochist experience excludes. If the sadist and masochist don't both understand the boundaries, the fantasy is broken. To do a "play" in which both people like the part they have, the script has to be subtly negotiated and the ritual has to be one that is reassuring to both.

The sadist may have to dress right (leather, knee-high boots, other commanding sorts of paraphernalia) and follow a set script of commands. The masochist also has to communicate to the dominant actor what acts he or she wants to experiment with so that each person's fantasies are fulfilled.

What is the appeal of this particular fantasy? For masochists, it is the loss of ego, responsibility, and resistance. They want to be directed and humbled (but only during the play). The masochist may want rough sex but indicates what is too rough. It is a challenge to achieve the thrill of submission without the risk. The sadist gets to feel omnipotent, gets exactly the sex acts that he or she wants, and knows that the partner feels pleasure in submission. Each person's fantasy nicely folds into the other person's need. One person likes to be spanked, and the other person wants the sensation of turning someone on by inflicting light pain. Such acts may not be appealing to some tastes, but so long as partners have complementary desires, a good match has been made.

But that's the play version. In the darker variant of S and M, the masochist really wants to be significantly humiliated, beaten, or frightened. Some people really get aroused by being treated as contemptible and by being abused. If they find a true sadist to oblige them, they may be in grave jeopardy. It is one thing to be tied up by someone whom you trust and who will untie you immediately if you become scared. It's quite another to be tied up by someone who really wants you to panic. The panic makes the person feel all the more worthless, far beyond what he or she needs to be sexually aroused.

Even the game may be a problem when it too clearly mirrors gender reality. When gay men or lesbians play S and M games, they need not worry about mirroring the gendered reality in the everyday world, although gender is not the only source of power difference in couples. But when heterosexual men and women play them, they risk strengthening real domination. If the man dominates the woman in real life, dominating her even more in play may be psychologically brutalizing to both parties. The man becomes a tyrant and respects the woman even less. The woman becomes merely a shadow of herself and loses her sense of worth and peer status. If, however, the two are equals in real life they can "afford" this type of play, or if they reverse roles they can have fun experimenting with the partner's position and perks. Men may enjoy being directed rather than always being the director. Women may be turned on by literally as well as figuratively being on top.

As with all explorations, S and M sex requires the players to know why they are going somewhere and what they want to happen when they get there. If the couple likes experimentation and play, S and M doesn't have to be personally or politically dangerous. But if one person has a real need to dominate and humiliate and if the other is passive and has low self-esteem, then sadomasochistic sex is not fantasy but exaggeration. And then it's not fun.

6. *Are all men potential rapists? Is the proclivity to rape wired in?*

The short answer is no. The long answer is that these certainly aren't unreasonable questions, given that rape is overwhelmingly gendered: 99 percent of sexual assault cases involve a male perpetrator. Furthermore, sex offenders, including rapists, child molesters, and exhibitionists, are very, very difficult to rehabilitate. In other words, sex offenders do not, in general, get better through psychiatric or psychopharmaco-logical treatment, or even imprisonment.

Nevertheless, sexual violence may have its origins in a culture that privileges men. Patriarchal norms and individually held beliefs about men's sexual entitlements make rape and other sexual violence more likely. Thus, rehabilitating the culture to reduce gendered beliefs, sexist imagery, and the romance of sweeping a woman off her feet seems like a crucial element in reducing men's sexual violence toward women. Similarly, restructuring institutions that confer different entitlements to men than to women can further help to reduce misogynistic acts.

A small subgroup of sex offenders may in fact have a genetic or physiological basis for their pathology. Research on psychopathology in serial killers and serial rapists suggests that a very small proportion of men may be organically different from others and are truly incorri-gible. They feel no remorse and are prepared to do whatever is neces-sary to get their next victim. These men tend to have been abuse victims themselves as children, and sometimes they have suffered a head injury at an early age, but sometimes they have completely uneventful back-grounds. In either case, this very small subset of rapists has displayed the pathology of having no remorse from a very early age. Even for these "biologically different" cases, however, culture, learning history, and social structures are nevertheless the more likely culprits for why they are fixated on victimizing women, or engaging in sexual victimi-zation rather than other kinds of victimization.

Sexual Function

7. Sex is supposed to be such an important part of a man's life. What if sex isn't great or important to him?

Remember the bell curve we introduced in Chapter 2? Both men and women exhibit a wide range of sexual desire, sexual frequency, and other sexual behaviors. For the most part, men and women are far more similar than they are different on various dimensions of normal sexual appetite. There is no right or wrong amount of sexual desire or activity.

We have so glorified sex in our culture that a man who doesn't think about it and do it 24 hours a day feels that he is somehow deflating the national average, letting down the team, and abandoning his own claim to normality. Men, in particular, have been designated as being always sexually available. Empirically, we know that men aren't always in the mood and ready for sex. But many a man who has not wanted casual sex or who has had relatively limited sexual desires has been made to feel unmasculine.

Women have a similar problem. For a long time, women who seemed to have much interest in sex were considered abnormal. But today the woman who says "No, maybe later" or "I'm only interested twice a month" may be carted off to a counselor.

Unfortunately, all our statistics may lead us to presume a "right" amount of sex in a relationship instead of accepting that a unique pattern is appropriate for each person. That statistical norm may not even be valid, because many of the people surveyed are inflating the number of times they say they have sex so they will look good to themselves and to the interviewer.

The thing to remember is that sex is like any other appetite: It can change by circumstance and over the life cycle. It can also depend on what, if any, relationship you are in. Some people are more interested in sex than others. Likewise, some people really savor food, and others can take it or leave it. But we don't pathologize that difference unless someone is grossly over- or underweight. On the other hand, sex is supposed to be experienced a certain way and so we chastise anyone who is brave enough or honest enough to say, I can take it or leave it. We use psychiatric problems or trauma as an explanation, even though the person's difference may not be associated with trauma or pathology, but simply with his or her own learning history. Thus, we have created a catch-22. We criticize men and women for too much sexual interest, and we send them to therapy for too little. The bottom line is, you don't need help unless your level of interest is so different from your partner's that you have to work on a compromise to preserve the relationship.

8. *Can a woman really have a "male type" sexuality and not suffer for it?*

Throughout most of history, women have been punished for adopting the sexual prerogatives of men or, for that matter, even exceeding the narrow constraints of female sexuality. However, that stance is changing. Slowly but surely society's ideas about goodness and virginity, even sexual scarcity and worth, are becoming more liberal. Perhaps even more important for the change is the availability of more dependable birth control. Women cannot have sex at will without feeling they are protected from pregnancy and the lifelong consequences a mistake might entail.

Sociobiologists believe that concern about motherhood and children creates a different sexual drive for women than for men. But the data belie a biological explanation. Most women want sex only in the context of love or the hope of a further relationship; for many, that relationship has to be marriage. Some women, however, have a very male kind of sexuality. Before she became a mother in 1997, the pop icon Madonna certainly made it part of her act to show her ability to have sex for pleasure, often and under varied circumstances. (And after she became a mother she talked about giving birth and motherhood in starkly conventional terms.) Other female "sexual outlaws," women who have sex for curiosity or for pleasure rather than for love or commitment, definitely exist. Some women who are not prostitutes have had hundreds of lovers and, if they have been lucky enough not to catch a sexually transmitted disease (STD), have no regrets.

How can we explain the sexuality of these women? How can these women engage in free-and-easy sex without ruining their lives? First of all, they have to be smart enough or lucky enough to avoid medical complications (as do men). Women are more at risk for many STDs than men are. Moreover, complications from those diseases can compromise a woman's fertility and make her more vulnerable to cancers. To escape the health consequences of a liberated sexuality, women have to be fastidious about birth control and careful to avoid STDs.

The women who do not suffer for liberal sexuality usually have many other social advantages that cause them to be exempt from the ordinary rules of the culture and the influence of social structures. They are attractive and successful professionally and therefore able to control their own destiny. They have sufficient charisma so that men don't care about their prior sexual experience. In the same way that women have idolized certain men and accepted their previous experience as just part of their power, there are now men who want to be the one who captures these women's hearts or respect. Think for a minute of the very successful, beautiful, and rich women stars, directors, and heads of studio in Hollywood. Cher, Barbra Streisand, Jessica Lange, and others have had widely publicized affairs with other famous people, and they still remain a "catch." They, like their male counterparts, are loath to settle down, feel good about being independent, and have no problem going from one exciting relationship to another.

To do that, a woman has to be able to shuck off old images of female purity, be able to separate physical attraction from love, be confident enough to see men as companions rather than husbands, and enjoy sex for its own sake. Not too many women want to do that or can do it. But it is possible.

One important point. Most men aren't "sexual outlaws" either. Most men want sex in the context of love or attachment or commitment. Their reputation may not suffer as a woman's would for a significant history of sexual experiences, but most men want more than just a no-attachment, no-strings, no-future kind of liaison. A "male type" sexuality is less common for both men and women than the polarized, gendered view of sexuality suggests.

9. *Does beginning sex at an early age affect sexuality in good or bad ways? Might its effect be different for boys and girls?*

There is some evidence that the younger a girl is when she has sex the more likely she is to have been victimized. Somewhere between the ages of 11 and 18 or so, a girl may have a woman's body but a girl's ignorance. She would have trouble understanding what an older male's intentions are or what sex is about and what the consequences of early sex might be. These mature-looking girls, and even girls who still look immature, are often flattered to have an older male's attention (even if he is only six months older). If they haven't been taught some self-protective responses, they are likely to accede to any demands—only to be shocked and disappointed.

Young boys are less commonly preyed on sexually by older girls, but they are often pushed into sex earlier than they want by peer opinion. They may also be tempted into premature sex by a girl who makes herself available so that she will be liked or given some attention. Boys aren't supposed to refuse sex of this type even if they would like to; thus, they have sex before they have much desire and often under duress. Sex of this type is disappointing, guilt producing, and altogether an alienating experience.

Of course, some young people start young, like sex a lot, and keep at it. For some boys and girls, sex is a recreational skill, and they seem to believe that the sooner you start, the better you get. Disappointments seem to roll over them without crushing them, and they gain a sense of mastery and power by their conquests. Again, this is much more culturally available to boys, who are encouraged to revel in their sexual accomplishments. But increasingly there are girls who love sex, also see experimentation as their right, and feel no shame or guilt.

Most parents, most institutions (like churches and schools), and more conventional teens don't believe that kids can like sex or know what they are doing. As a culture, we are not comfortable with early sexuality. Some cultures may assume that with puberty comes sexual encounters, but ours likes to delay sexuality as long as possible, envisioning all kinds of bad consequences (both physical and psychological) from early experience. We are particularly unwilling to think that our teenage daughters can cope with sexuality. Although some data indicate that early intercourse is dangerous and damaging for some boys and girls, many other data suggest that the real problem is not sex itself but rather the individual maturity, responsibility, and self-knowledge of the person in question. Some people benefit from early sexual experience, some people suffer.

10. *Why do men and women sometimes not use contraception, even when it is obviously necessary?*

First of all, for many sexual acts and in many situations, contraception is not necessary. Gay men and lesbians need not be concerned about contraception. Heterosexual couples who engage in comasturbation, oral sex, and other kinds of nonintercourse sexual play that leads to orgasm don't need contraception. Of course, all these groups do need protection from STDs.

When heterosexual couples are having sexual intercourse, they are usually motivated by love or passion. In the spirit of the moment, partners may be tentative about using contraception or protection, or they may be just plain irrational. It is hard, in the heat of love or lust, to modify one's behavior—even, amazingly enough, if one's future is at stake. One part of the brain is saying "Better watch out" and the other part is saying "Don't worry this time." That is the power of desire talking: to cast one's fate to luck and do something that has obvious possibilities for disaster.

Given human nature, perhaps the surprising thing is that anybody does use contraception or protection. The passion of the moment and the awkwardness of slipping on a condom at the last moment might be deterrents. Gender plays a role, too. Some young girls are taught that it is sexy to submit to men, that men like women who give men more pleasure and less aggravation—in this case, by having sex without a condom. Young women especially think it is their role to submit when a boyfriend asks. At the same time, women have been given all the responsibility for contraception and protection and have been made the gatekeepers for sexual intercourse—as if they are the only ones who have something to lose if things go wrong. So the very people who are less likely to feel comfortable directing the action or to be dominant in decision making, especially when young, are given all the responsibility for preventing pregnancy and STDs. Throughout life, it is women more than men who are put in a position of being pressured to abdicate these responsibilities.

However, both women and men find themselves unequipped to make contraception and protection a natural part of sexuality. Boys as well as girls feel awkward about talking about sex. Discussing contraception and protection, much less planning for them, takes a high level of social skill and comfort with the mechanics of sexuality. And because few sexuality classes cover the topic, nearly everyone learns "on the job." The first time one is usually faced with the situation is right in the middle of a passionate clinch. This is spot training, and it usually doesn't work. Grownups and adolescents alike are unprepared to deal with contraception and protection in a way that feels practiced and not embarrassing.

This lack of preparation explains why the United States continues to have a higher rates of teenage pregnancy than other Western countries where sex education is more common. Teens are new to sex and unlikely to be able to articulate their own interests or to enforce them. They are too embarrassed to introduce a condom, too inexperienced to use it right, and too young to realize how much they will lose if they get a disease or get pregnant. In fact, they have a certain fascination with the idea of seeing if their bodies actually work—if their sperm can actually impregnate someone, if their ovaries work and a baby will form. They pay a high price for finding the answers to those questions.

Many people refuse to believe that education about sex and training in communication skills will actually reduce negative consequences. But research indicates that teen pregnancy rates decline when communication skills are learned and reinforced by practice in sex education programs. Unfortunately, few teens have access to such programs, and most of the programs that do exist aren't long enough to cause lasting changes in behavior. Until we teach people how to use condoms as a normal and sexy part of lovemaking, until we teach them that safe sex is better sex and that lovers naturally contracept, we can expect depressing statistics on pregnancy and disease transmission.

In the meantime, improving bonds and understanding between men and women (partners in same-sex relations as well) will help people learn to show they care by taking responsibility for contraception and simple health care. Sure, some people will still refuse to use contraceptives and protection; some will refuse to compromise sensation; still others will believe they are invulnerable. But changing cultural beliefs about contraception and safe sex could get most people to take precautions and have a happy, safe sex life.

11. *I know my grandparents must have had sex when they were young. But now they are in their late 70s, and it is hard for me to think of them "doing it." Is the sex drive still alive in older people?*

We didn't spend much time in this book talking about sex and aging, but we predict that the issue is going to become much more prominent in the next two decades as those in the baby boom generation reach their 60s and 70s.

Masters and Johnson studied older as well as younger people. They came to the conclusion that many elderly people can and do have an active sex life way into their 80s—but only under these two conditions: They must be in reasonably good health, and they must have had a continuous sex life over their lifetime.

Health is an important consideration. Not only does bad health cause depression and otherwise diminish sexual interest, but a lot of the medications prescribed for the common diseases of older people (such as late-onset diabetes, high blood pressure) tend to suppress sexual interest or inhibit male sexual performance or female lubrication. Even without medication, natural aging processes can cause physical and psychological complications. Men, in particular, get upset when they experience longer time needed to get an erection, when the refractory period between ejaculations lengthens, and when their erections aren't as hard as they used to be. These extremely common changes may be expected, but some men get so depressed about them that they experience psychological problems that lead to temporary or sustained erectile failure.

Another big contributing factor for men is prostate problems. The prostate is a gland that surrounds the urethra as it exits the bladder; it secretes part of the seminal fluid. Over time it becomes looser, or "boggy" as physicians like to describe. Thus, ejaculation occurs with less force. More than half of all men have had a significant prostate problem; by their 80s, almost 80 percent have had a problem. Surgery to ameliorate the problem is not uncommon. A significant number of men get prostate cancer, and in about half of these cases removal of the gland or chemotherapy is necessary. A significant number of men have trouble with erection after the operation.

Obviously, women escape this particular problem. But other facts of aging influence their sexuality. Increased risk of breast cancer, hormonal changes, and increased risk of heart disease and high blood pressure after menopause can all depress sex drive. After menopause, women may lose some ability to produce natural vaginal lubricant, but commercial lubricants like K-Y Jelly are a handy substitute. In addition, society's image of the sexy and desirable woman is young, not old. Older women—as well as older men—have to adjust to the idea of being sexual in a less than idealized body.

Despite these potential problems, older people can still enjoy sex. Masters and Johnson found that the single strongest predictor of continued sexual activity was past behavior. Older women lubricated more and older men had fewer erectile problems if they had continued to have sex at least every so often through life and had never stopped for a long time. Their conclusion: "Use it or lose it." In other words, sometimes physical disability may follow from sexual behavior (or lack of sexual behavior) rather than cause it.

Part of the reason older people sometimes stop having sex is because they think they should. We tend to stereotype passion as a prerogative of the young. We even stigmatize sexually interested elderly persons as "dirty old men" or "ridiculous old ladies." A continuing interest in sex can even be considered evidence of senility or mental instability. There are many documented cases of nursing home personnel locking older people in their rooms so that they cannot visit each other's beds. Nursing home personnel have complained to family members that their parent masturbated or masturbated too much and that steps should be taken to stop such behavior.

If older people are lucky enough to control their own destiny, to have access to a partner, and to be reasonably healthy, the data suggest that they like sex, albeit less frequently than younger folks. Some data indicate that sexual intercourse varies in married elderly persons from about once a week to about once a month, but that isn't the only nor necessarily the best measure of sexual activity. A decrease in the capacity for erection or ejaculation in men doesn't necessarily mean low sexual interest or less capacity to be a good sexual partner. Quite the contrary, older women often voice pleasure in their partner's new attention to foreplay, touching, and longer, gentler sexual sessions.

Many older people have sexual fantasies and needs. Unfortunately, they have few chances to find a partner. Heterosexual women, especially, find partners scarce, because women live several more years on average than men do (which may explain why, as the figures we provided earlier in the book indicate, sexual activity among older men is more common than among women). Lesbians are more fortunate, because they are seeking partners among other women rather than men. Lesbian sex tends to be less genitally focused than gay or heterosexual sex, and so their sexual experience may be more continuous.

In general, then, although the fire of sexuality among older people may be embers more than a raging conflagration, there is still heat. Even people with severe medical problems, such as a serious heart condition, still maintain a sex life. In fact, some have made news by dying while "in the act." For example, the former New York State governor Nelson Rockefeller died during a tryst with a much younger woman, disobeying the orders of heart specialists—who usually say that sex is fine if it is with your spouse, but with others it could be too exciting.

So don't discount your grandparents' sexuality until they are gone. And be happy for them if they are sexually active and continue to enjoy one of the delights of being alive.

Conclusion

We have come to the end of our discussion of gender and sexuality. We hope that the questions raised in this book will inspire you to ask even more questions about the social organization of sexuality. We hope you'll wonder about hidden assumptions and explicit norms regarding the role of gender in how individuals, groups, and whole nations "do" sex.

One of the questions we've raised is, why is gender such a powerful influence over the organization of sexuality? To understand this, we have looked to assumptions that sexuality is naturally gendered and rooted in biology, that men and women are different sexually, and that this difference is consistent and universal across societies. In a simple sense, you have seen that sexual rules for men and women vary by society and region, they vary from one historical era to another, and they vary under the influence of social institutions.

Of course, not only does what appears "natural" in one society differ from other societies, but the whole idea that sexuality has a well-defined set of rules that are identified as natural tends to serve political purposes that advance the social control of sexuality. The biological, or natural, assumption is powerful. But can change occur? Inroads at contesting assumptions about gender and sexuality can be seen in the visibility and modest success (as we write) of efforts to legalize same-sex marriages. The campaign to block same-sex marriage on the grounds that marriages require a gender difference has the unintended consequence of provoking the question of "Why do marriages require gender difference?" For most of the opponents of same-sex marriage, this is not a natural question—but has been implicated as a central issue to the opposition.

We have also looked to the everyday experience of sexuality. The rules of sexuality are not simply writ large in institutions like religions, governments, or even sexuality education programs in schools. By examining sexuality in relationships, and sexual attitudes that individuals carry around and express in their behavior, we've tried to help you see how gendered sexuality gets inscribed and reinscribed in daily lives of ordinary people going about their business. This individual level is powerful, but it is powerful for challenging norms as well as for reinforcing them.

A great example comes from a story told by a college professor we know. She told the story of how in grade school, her teacher, a Catholic nun, had instructed her class on "the birds and the bees." The teacher was explaining that when a man's hand touches a woman's breast, that the woman responds sexually. Our colleague recalls, "I wondered, how does the breast know it's a man's hand?" She didn't take the assumption that sex requires two genders for granted, nor did she take for granted that sexual bodies "naturally" know the social rules for gendered sexuality.

By calling the book *The Gender of Sexuality,* we challenge you to think about how even things that people tend to consider biological, like reproduction, are influenced enormously by the social processes that determine what motherhood is all about and how motherhood is different from fatherhood. In the movie *Junior* (1995), Arnold Schwartzenegger plays a husband who becomes pregnant, thanks to the scientific creativity of Danny DeVito. The biological anomaly—a man rather than a woman incubating a baby—is only a prop for a movie full of jokes about how a man's producing a baby is a social anomaly, a twist on the cross-dressing comedies like *Mrs. Doubtfire* (1993) (in which Robin Williams dresses like a older woman to become nanny to his estranged children after a nasty custody battle that isolated him from his children), or *Tootsie* (1982) (in which Dustin Hoffman acts and dresses like an insipid matron for a part on a soap opera). The movie *Junior* suggests that even if men were biologically capable of producing babies, socially they are ill prepared for primary caretaking of children.

Biology or, more simply stated, bodies are mechanisms for passionate experience, even if that experience happens only in the brain (in the absence of actual sensations in the skin or other sexual organs). In this sense, biology is a crucial context for sexuality. However, we know that interpersonal, biographical, social, and political contexts influence sexuality, and interact with biology in surprising ways. Bodies are also mechanisms for sending cues to others about whether the person is male or female, masculine or feminine. But how people use bodies to signal gender is learned rather than biological.

From our perspective, sexuality and gender are powerful social constructs. But we hope that this message has not been delivered in strictly ominous tones regarding the machinations of social forces. Sexuality as it intersects with gender produces great fun—both in one's imagination and in sexual or social activity. Breaking sexual rules, playing with gendered rules, even following rules or norms can be amusing and meaningful, as cross-dressing or sexual role-playing are but obvious examples among the many.

What makes sexuality and gender more than just amusement and fun is the presence and perpetuation of power differences that is at the center of gendered sexual practices. Institutional and individual contexts continue to promote power differences—such that heterosexuals have more privileges than homosexuals; such that men have more privilege than women in marriage; such that social class and ethnicity and race confer different sexual rules and opportunities for different groups depending on social resources.

So, what now? Ask questions. When someone supposes sexual similarities, look for difference. When someone supposes sexual difference, look for similarity. And be mindful of power differences and how gender and sexual norms support those, and how power differences can be reduced.

REFERENCES

Abbey, A. 1982. "Sex Differences in Attributions for Friendly Behavior: Do Males Misperceive Females' Friendliness?" *Journal of Personality and Social Psychology* 42:830-38.

Angier, N. 1995. "Does Testosterone Equal Aggression? Maybe Not." *New York Times,* June 20, p. A1.

Bailey, J. M., R. C. Pillard, M. C. Neale, and Y. Agyei. 1993. "Heritable Factors Influence Sexual Orientation in Women." *Archives of General Psychiatry* 50:217-23.

Bancroft, J. 1978. "The Relationship between Hormones and Sexual Behavior in Humans." Pp. 493-519 in *Biological Determinants of Sexual Behavior,* edited by J. B. Hutchinson. New York: Wiley.

———. 1984. "Hormones and Human Sexual Behavior." *Journal of Sex and Marital Therapy* 10:3-21.

Bancroft, J., D. Sanders, D. Davidson, and P. Warner. 1983. "Mood, Sexuality, Hormones, and the Menstrual Cycle: III. Sexuality and the Role of Androgens." *Psychosomatic Medicine* 45:508-24.

Barbach, L. 1975. *For Yourself: The Fulfillment of Female Sexuality.* Garden City, NJ: Doubleday.

Bartell, G. D. 1971. *Group Sex: A Scientist's Eyewitness Report on the American Way of Swinging.* New York: Wyden.

Blumstein, P. and P. Schwartz. 1983. *American Couples: Money, Work, and Sex.* New York: William Morrow.

Bly, R. 1990. *Iron John: A Book about Men.* Reading, MA: Addison-Wesley.

Boeringer, S. B., C. L. Shehan, and R. L. Akers. 1991. "Social Contexts and Social Learning in Sexual Coercion and Aggression: Assessing the Contribution of Fraternity Membership." *Family Relations* 40:50-64.

Boston Women's Health Book Collective. 1973. *Our Bodies, Ourselves.* New York: Simon & Schuster.

Boswell, J. 1994. *Same-Sex Unions in Pre-Modern Europe.* New York: Villard.

Bozett, F. 1987. *Gay and Lesbian Parents.* New York: Praeger.

Briere, J., and N. M. Malamuth. 1983. "Self-Reported Likelihood of Sexually Aggressive Behavior: Attitudinal versus Sexual Explanations." *Journal of Research in Personality* 17:315-23.

Bright, S., ed. 1988. *Herotica: A Collection of Women's Erotic Fiction.* Burlingame, CA: Down There.

Brines, J. 1994. "Economic Dependency, Gender, and Division of Labor at Home." *American Journal of Sociology* 100:652-60.

Brown, M. and A. Auerback. 1981. "Communication Patterns in the Initiation of Marital Sex." *Medical Aspects of Human Sexuality* 15:105-17.

Brownmiller, S. 1975. *Against Our Will: Men, Women and Rape.* New York: Simon & Schuster.

Bumpass, L., J. A. Sweet, and A. J. Cherlin. 1989. "The Role of Cohabitation of Declining Rates of Marriage." *Journal of Marriage and the Family* 53:913-27.

Burt, M. R. 1979. *Attitudes Supportive of Rape in American Culture.* Rockville, MD: U.S. Department of Health and Human Services.

Buss, D. 1994. *The Evolution of Desire: Strategies of Human Mating.* New York: Basic Books.

————. 1995. "Psychological Sex Differences: Origins through Sexual Selection. *American Psychologist* 50:164-68.

Call, V., S. Sprecher, and P. Schwartz. 1995. "The Incidence and Frequency of Marital Sex in a National Sample." *Journal of Marriage and the Family* 57:639-50.

Cherlin, A. 1992. *Marriage, Divorce, Remarriage.* Rev. ed. Cambridge, MA: Harvard University Press.

Chia, M. and D. A. Arava. 1996. *The Multi-Orgasmic Man: Sexual Secrets Every Man Should Know.* New York: HarperCollins.

Cochran, S. D. and V. M. Mays. 1990. "Sex, Lies, and HIV." *New England Journal of Medicine* 322:774-75.

Coltrane, S. 1997. *Gender and Families.* Thousand Oaks, CA: Pine Forge.

Comfort, A. 1972. *The Joy of Sex.* New York: Simon & Schuster.

————. 1974. *More Joy.* New York: Simon & Schuster.

Coontz, Stephanie. 1992. *The Way We Never Were: American Families and the Nostalgia Trap.* New York: Basic Books.

Copenhaver, S. and E. Grauerholtz. 1991. "Sexual Victimization among Sorority Women: Exploring the Link between Sexual Violence and Institutional Practices." *Sex Roles* 24:31-41.

"Custody Restored to Lesbian." 1994. *National Law Journal,* July 4.

D'Emilio, J. D. and E. Freedman. 1988. *Intimate Matters: A History of Sexuality in America.* New York: Harper & Row.

Demo, D. H. and K. R. Allen. 1996. "Diversity within Lesbian and Gay Families: Challenges and Implications for Family Theory and Research." *Journal of Social and Personal Relationships* 13:417-36.

Dowd, M. 1983. "Rape: The Sexual Weapon." *Time,* September 5, pp. 27-29.

Dreyfoos, J. 1990. *Adolescents at Risk: Prevalence and Prevention.* New York: Oxford University Press.

Dutton, D. 1988. *The Domestic Assault of Women: Psychological and Criminal Justice Perspectives.* Newton, MA: Allyn & Bacon.

Dutton, D. and A. Aron. 1974. "Some Evidence for Heightened Sexual Attraction under Conditions of High Anxiety." *Journal of Personality and Social Psychology* 30:510-17.

Dworkin, A. 1991. *Woman Hating: A Radical Look at Sexuality.* New York: Dutton.

Ehrenreich, B. and D. English. 1978. *For Her Own Good: 150 Years of the Experts' Advice to Women.* Garden City, NY: Anchor/Doubleday.

Ellis, B. J. and D. Symons. 1990. "Sex Differences in Sexual Fantasy: An Evolutionary Psychological Approach." *Journal of Sex Research* 27:527-55.

Eskridge, W. N. 1996. *The Case for Same-Sex Marriage: From Sexual Liberty to Civilized Commitment.* New York: Free Press.

Faderman, L. 1981. *Surpassing the Love of Men: Romantic Friendship and Love between Women from the Renaissance to the Present.* New York: William Morrow.

"Family: Time to Legalize Gay Marriage." 1995. *Newsweek,* December 11, p. 82.

Finkelhor, D. 1984. *Child Sexual Abuse: New Theory and Research.* New York: Free Press.

Finkelhor, D. and K. Yllö. 1985. *License to Rape: Sexual Abuse of Wives.* New York: Free Press.

Fisher, H. E. 1992. *Anatomy of Love: The Natural History of Monogamy, Adultery, and Divorce.* New York: Norton.

Forman, B. 1982. "Reported Male Rape." *Victimology: An International Journal* 7:235-36.

Foucault, M. 1978. *A History of Sexuality: Vol. 1. An Introduction.* New York: Pantheon.

French, M. 1977. *The Women's Room.* New York: Summit.

Friday, N. 1973. *My Secret Garden.* New York: Pocket Books.

———. 1991. *Women on Top.* New York: Pocket Books.

Friedan, B. 1963. *The Feminine Mystique.* New York: Norton.

Friedan, B., M. Carrow, C. Harrison, A. Kimbrell, F. Pittman, S. Quinn, K. Roiphe, and A. Roiphe. 1996. "Overcoming the Scars and Frustrations of Old Sex Roles, Sexual Politics and Backlash." A panel sponsored by Mount Vernon College, March 21, Washington, DC.

Gagnon, J. H. and W. Simon. 1973. *Sexual Conduct: The Social Sources of Human Sexuality.* New York: Aldine de Gruyter.

Gauthier, A. H. 1996. *The State and the Family: A Comparative Analysis of Family Policies in Industrialized Countries.* Oxford: Clarendon.

Glass, S. P. and T. L. Wright. 1992. "Justification for Extramarital Relationships: The Association between Attitudes, Behavior, and Gender." *Journal of Sex Research* 29:361-87.

Goffman, E. 1977. *The Arrangement between the Sexes."* *Theory and Society* 4:301-31.

Golombok, S. and F. Tasker. 1996. "Do Parents Influence the Sexual Orientation of Their Children? Findings from a Longitudinal Study of Lesbian Families." *Developmental Psychology* 32:3-11.

Goode, W. 1969. "The Theoretical Importance of Love." *American Sociological Review* 34:38-47.

Gottman, J. M. 1994. *What Predicts Divorce?* Hillsdale, NJ: Lawrence Erlbaum.

Gray, L. A. and M. Saracino. 1991. "College Students' Attitudes, Beliefs, and Behaviors about AIDS: Implications for Family Life Educators." *Family Relations* 40:258-63.

Green, G. D. 1987. "Lesbian Mothers: Mental Health Considerations." Pp. 188-98 in *Gay and Lesbian Parents,* edited by F. W. Bozett. New York: Praeger.

Greenhalgh, S. 1977. "Hobbled Feet, Hobbled Lives: Women in Old China." *Frontiers* 2:7-21.

Guttentag, M. and P. P. Secord. 1983. *Too Many Women? The Sex Ratio Question.* Beverly Hills, CA: Sage.

Hamer, D. H. and P. Copeland. 1994. *The Science of Desire: The Search for the Gay Gene and the Biology of Behavior.* New York: Simon & Schuster.

Hatfield, E. and R. L. Rapson. 1993. *Love, Sex, and Intimacy: Their Psychology, Biology, and History.* New York: HarperCollins College.

———. 1996. *Love and Sex: Cross-Cultural Perspectives.* Needham Heights, MA: Allyn & Bacon.

Hawthorne, N. 1947. *The Scarlet Letter.* New York: Rinehart.

Heiman, J. R. 1977. "A Psychophysiological Exploration of Sexual Arousal Patterns in Females and Males." *Psychophysiology* 14:266-74.

Hess, B. B. and M. M. Ferree (eds.). 1987. *Analyzing Gender: A Handbook of Social Science Reserach.* New bury Park, CA: Sage.

Hite, S. 1976. *The Hite Report: A Nationwide Study of Female Sexuality.* New York: Dell.

Hollander, J. 1997. "Discourses of Danger: The Construction and Performance of Gender through Talk about Violence." University of Washington. Ph.D. dissertation.

Holmes, K. K., P.-A. Mardh, P. F. Sparling, and P. J. Wiesner. 1990. *Sexually Transmitted Diseases.* 2d ed. New York: McGraw-Hill.

Hoon, P. W., K. E. Bruce, and B. Kinchloe. 1982. "Does the Menstrual Cycle Play a Role in Sexual Arousal?" *Psychophysiology* 19:21-27.

Howard, J. A. and J. A. Hollander. 1996. *Gendered Situations, Gendered Selves: A Gender Lens on Social Psychology.* Thousand Oaks, CA: Sage.

Hunt, M. 1974. *Sexual Behavior in the 1970s.* Chicago: Playboy.

Huston, M. and P. Schwartz. 1995. "The Relationships of Lesbians and Gay Men." In *Under-Studied Relationships: Off the Beaten Track,* edited by J. T. Wood and S. Duck. Newbury Park, CA: Sage.

Jacobson, N. S. 1989. "The Politics of Intimacy." *The Behavior Therapist* 12:29-32.

Jacobson, N. S. and A. J. Christensen. 1996. *Integrative Couple Therapy: Promoting Acceptance and Change.* New York: Norton.

Jones, E. F., J. Darroch-Forest, N. Goldman, S. K. Henshaw, R. Lincoln, J. I. Rossoff, C. F. Westoff, and D. Wulf. 1985. "Teenage Pregnancy in Developed Countries: Determinants and Policy Implications." *Family Planning Perspectives* 17:53-63.

Jones, J. C. and D. H. Barlow. 1990. "Self-Reported Frequency of Sexual Urges, Fantasies, and Masturbatory Fantasies in Heterosexual Males and Females." *Archives of Sexual Behavior* 19:269-79.

Kanin, E. 1994. "False Rape Allegations." *Archives of Sexual Behavior* 23:81-92.

Kaplan, H. S. 1979. *Disorders of Sexual Desire.* New York: Simon & Schuster.

Kinsey, A. C., W. B. Pomeroy, and C. E. Martin. 1948. *Sexual Behavior in the Human Male.* Philadelphia: W. B. Saunders.

Kinsey, A. C., W. B. Pomeroy, C. E. Martin, and P. H. Gephard. 1953. *Sexual Behavior in the Human Female.* Philadelphia: W. B. Saunders.

Kirby, D., L. Short, J. Collins, D. Rugg, L. Kolbe, M. Howard, B. Miller, F. Sonenstein, and L. S. Zabin. 1994. "School-Based Programs to Reduce Sexual Risk Behaviors: A Review of Effectiveness." *Public Health Reports* 109:339-60.

Klawitter, M. M. and V. Flatt. N.d. "The Effects of State and Local Antidiscrimination Policies for Sexual Orientation." University of Washington. Unpublished.

Kollock, P., P. Blumstein, and P. Schwartz. 1985. "Sex and Power in Interaction: Conversational Privileges and Duties." *American Sociological Review* 50:34-46.

Kolodny, R. C., W. H. Masters, and V. E. Johnson. 1979. *Textbook of Sexual Medicine.* Boston: Little, Brown.

Koss, M. P., T. E. Dinero, C. A. Seibel, and S. L. Cox. 1988. "Stranger and Acquaintance Rape: Are There Differences in the Victim's Experience?" *Psychology of Women Quarterly* 12:1-24.

Koss, M. P., L. A. Goodman, A. Browne, L. F. Fitzgerald, G. P. Keita, and N. F. Russo. 1994. *No Safe Haven: Male Violence against Women at Home, at Work, and in the Community.* Washington, DC: American Psychological Association.

Koss, M. P. and K. E. Leonard. 1984. Pp. 213-32 in *Pornography and Sexual Aggression,* edited by N. M. Malamuth and E. Donnerstein. New York: Academic Press.

Kreuz, L. E., R. M. Rose, and J. R. Jennings. 1972. "Suppression of Plasma Testosterone Levels and Psychological Stress: A Longitudinal Study of Young Men in Officer Candidate School." *Archives of General Psychiatry* 26:479-82.

Laumann, E. O., R. T. Michael, and J. H. Gagnon. 1994. *The Social Organization of Sexuality: Sexual Practices in the United States.* Chicago: University of Chicago Press.

Lawson, A. 1988. *Adultery: An Analysis of Love and Betrayal.* New York: Basic Books.

Leland, J. 1996. "Bisexuality." *Newsweek,* July 17.

Lerman, R. I. and T. J. Ooms. 1993. *Young Unwed Fathers: Changing Roles and Emerging Policies.* Philadelphia: Temple University Press.

LeVay, S. 1993. *The Sexual Brain.* Cambridge: MIT Press.

Lever, J. 1994a. "The 1994 Advocate Survey of Sexuality and Relationships: The Men." *The Advocate: The National Gay & Lesbian Newsmagazine,* August 23, pp. 17-24.

———. 1994b. "Viewpoint: Bridging Fundamentals of Gender Studies into Safer Sex Education." *Family Planning Perspectives* 27:172-74.

———. 1995. "The 1995 Advocate Survey of Sexuality and Relationships: The Women." *The Advocate: The National Gay & Lesbian Newsmagazine,* August 22, pp. 22-30.

Lorber, J. 1997. *Gender and the Social Construction of Illness.* Thousand Oaks, CA: Sage.

Luker, K. 1996. *Dubious Conceptions: The Politics of Teenage Pregnancy.* Cambridge, MA: Harvard University Press.

MacKinnon, C. 1987. *Discourses on Life and Law.* Cambridge, MA: Harvard University Press.

Malamuth, N. M. 1984. "Aggression against Women: Cultural and Individual Causes." Pp. 19-52 in *Pornography and Sexual Aggression*, edited by N. M. Malamuth and E. Donnerstein. New York: Academic Press.

Malthus, T. R. [1798] 1929. *An Essay on the Principle of Population as It Affects the Future Improvement of Society.* New York and London: Macmillan.

Masters, W. H. and V. E. Johnson. 1966. *Human Sexual Response.* Boston: Little, Brown.

Masters, W. H., V. E. Johnson, and R. C. Kolodny. 1995. *Human Sexuality.* 5th ed. New York: HarperCollins College.

McCall, N. 1995. *Makes Me Wanna Holler.* New York: Random House.

McCormick, N. B. 1994. *Sexual Salvation: Affirming Women's Sexual Rights and Pleasures.* Westport, CT: Praeger.

Messner, M. 1997. *The Politics of Masculinities: Men in Movements.* Thousand Oaks, CA: Sage.

Meuwissen, I. and R. Over. 1992. "Sexual Arousal across Phases of the Human Menstrual Cycle." *Archives of Sexual Behavior* 2:101-19.

Miller, B. and J. C. Marshall. 1987. "Coercive Sex on the University Campus." *Journal of College Student Personnel*, January, pp. 38-47.

Modell, J. 1989. *Into One's Own: From Youth to Adulthood in the United States 1920-1975.* Berkeley: University of California Press.

Morgan, S. P., D. N. Lye, and G. A. Condran. 1988. "Sons, Daughters, and the Risk of Marital Disruption." *American Journal of Sociology* 94:110-29.

Muehlenhard, C. L. 1988. " 'Nice Women' Don't Say Yes and 'Real Men' Don't Say No: How Miscommunication and the Double Standard Can Cause Sexual Problems." *Women and Therapy* 7:95-108.

Muehlenhard, C. L., D. E. Friedman, and C. M. Thomas. 1985. "Is Date Rape Justifiable?" *Psychology of Women Quarterly* 9:297-310.

Muehlenhard, C. L. and L. C. Hollabaugh. 1988. "Do Women Sometimes Say No When They Mean Yes? The Prevalence and Correlates of Women's Token Resistance to Sex." *Journal of Personality and Social Psychology* 54:872-79.

Muehlenhard, C. L. and M. L. McCoy. 1991. "Double Standard/Double Bind: The Sexual Double Standard and Women's Communication about Sex." *Psychology of Women Quarterly* 15:447-61.

Muehlenhard, C. L. and J. S. McNaughton. 1988. "Women's Beliefs about Women Who 'Lead Men On.' " *Journal of Social and Clinical Psychology* 7:65-79.

Nordhoff, C. and J. N. Hall. 1932. *Mutiny on the Bounty.* Boston: Little, Brown.

"Parents End Battle, Agree to Share Custody of Girl." 1996. *Los Angeles Times*, October 18, p. A-21.

Patterson, C. J. 1992. "Children of Lesbian and Gay Parents." *Child Development* 63:1025-42.

Patterson, D. G. 1995. "Virtual In-Laws: Kinship and Relationship Quality in Gay Male Couples." University of Washington. Unpublished master's thesis.

Patterson, D. G. and P. Schwartz. 1994. "The Social Construction of Conflict in Intimate Same-Sex Couples." In *Conflict in Personal Relationships,* edited by D. D. Cahn. Hillsdale, NJ: Lawrence Erlbaum.

Peplau, L. A., Z. Rubin, and C. T. Hill. 1977. "Sexual Intimacy and Dating Relationships." *Journal of Social Issues* 33:86-109.

Perper, T. and D. L. Weis. 1987. "Proceptive and Rejective Strategies of U.S. and Canadian College Women." *Journal of Sex Research* 23:455-80.

Pipher, M. 1994. *Reviving Ophelia: Saving the Selves of Adolescent Girls.* New York: Putnam.

Pittman, F. 1989. *Private Lies: Infidelity and the Betrayal of Intimacy.* New York: Norton.

Pollitt, K. 1996. "Motherhood and Morality." *Nation,* May 27, p. 9.

Quackenbush, D. M., D. S. Strassberg, and C. W. Turner. 1995. "Gender Effects of Romantic Themes in Erotica. *Archives of Sexual Behavior* 24:21-35.

Reiss, I. L. 1967. *The Social Context of Premarital Sexual Permissiveness.* New York: Holt, Rinehart & Winston.

———. 1980. *Family Systems in America.* 3d ed. New York: Holt, Rinehart & Winston.

Risman, B. J., C. Hill, Z. Rubin, and L. A. Peplau. 1981. "Living Together in College: Implications for Courtship." *Journal of Marriage and the Family* 43:77-83.

Robbins, T. 1980. *Still Life with Woodpecker.* New York: Bantam.

Roiphe, K. 1993. *The Morning After: Sex, Fear, and Feminism on Campus.* New York: Little, Brown.

Rose, R. M., J. W. Holaday, and I. S. Bernstein. 1970. "Plasma Testosterone, Dominance Rank, and Aggressive Behavior in Male Rhesus Monkeys. *Nature* 231:366-68.

Rosen, R. and L. Rosen. 1981. *Human Sexuality.* New York: Random House.

Roth, P. 1967. *Portnoy's Complaint.* New York: Random House.

Rotello, G. 1996. "To Have and To Hold: The Case for Gay Marriage." *Nation,* June 24, pp. 11-18.

Rubin, L. B. 1976. *Worlds of Pain: Life in the Working-Class Family.* New York: Basic Books.

———. 1990. *Erotic Wars: What Happened to the Sexual Revolution?* New York: HarperCollins.

Russell, D. E. H. 1984. *Sexual Exploitation: Rape, Child Sexual Abuse, and Work.* Beverly Hills, CA: Sage.

Rutter, V. 1995. "Adolescence: Whose Hell Is It?" *Psychology Today,* January/February, pp. 54-66.

———. 1996. "Who Stole Fertility?" *Psychology Today,* March/April, pp. 44-70.

Schmidt, G. and V. Sigusch. 1970. "Sex Differences in Response to Psychosexual Stimulation by Films and Slides. *Journal of Sex Research* 6:268-83.

Schwartz, P. 1994. *Peer Marriage: Love between Equals.* New York: Free Press.

———. 1995. "When Staying Is Worth the Pain." *New York Times,* April 29, p. B1.

Schwartz, P. and P. Blumstein. 1976. "Bisexuality in Women." Pp. 154-62 in *The Social Psychology of Sex,* edited by J. Wiseman. New York: Harper and Row.

Scritchfield, S. 1995. "The Social Construction of Infertility." Pp. 131-46 in *Images of Issues,* edited by J. Best. New York: Aldine de Gruyter.

Seidman, S. 1992. *Embattled Eros: Sexual Politics and Ethics in Contemporary America.* New York: Routledge.

Sexuality Information and Education Council of the United States. 1995. *A Report on Adolescent Sexuality.* New York: SIECUS.

Shakespeare, W. 1983. *Macbeth.* New York: Penguin.

Shorter, E. 1975. *The Making of the Modern Family.* New York: Basic Books.

Simpson, J. A. and S. W. Gangestad. 1991. "Individual Differences in Sociosexuality: Evidence for Convergent and Discriminant Validity." *Journal of Personality and Social Psychology* 60:870-83.

Sprecher, S., E. Hatfield, E. Ptapova, A. Levitskaaya, and A. Cortese. 1992. "Sexual Miscommunication: Saying No When Meaning Yes and Saying Yes When Meaning No." Manuscript submitted for publication.

Sprecher, S. and K. McKinney. 1993. *Sexuality.* Thousand Oaks, CA: Sage.

Stanislaw, H. and F. J. Rice. 1988. "The Correlation between Sexual Desire and Menstrual Cycle Changes." *Archives of Sexual Behavior* 17:499-508.

Stark, R. 1996. *The Rise of Christianity: A Sociologist Reconsiders History.* Princeton, NJ: Princeton University Press.

Steinberg, L. 1994. *Crossing Paths: How Your Child's Adolescence Triggers Your Own Crisis.* New York: Simon & Schuster.

Struckman-Johnson, C. 1988. "Forced Sex on Dates: It Happens to Men, Too." *Journal of Sex Research* 24:234-41.

Symons, D. 1979. *The Evolution of Human Sexuality.* New York: Oxford University Press.

Thompson, S. 1996. *Going All the Way: Teenage Girls' Tales of Sex, Romance, and Pregnancy.* New York: Hill & Wang.

Tiefer, L. 1995. *Sex Is Not a Natural Act and Other Essays.* Boulder, CO: Westview.

Tizon, A. 1996. "Idaho County Fights Teen Sex Using Old Fornication Law." *Seattle Times*, July 15, p. A1.

Todd, J. 1986. *Sensibility: An Introduction.* London: Methuen.

Tucker, M. B. and C. Mitchell-Kernan. 1995. *The Decline in Marriage among African Americans: Causes, Consequences, and Policy Implications.* New York: Russell Sage.

Twine, W. 1996. "Heterosexual Alliances: The Romantic Management of Racial Identity. In *The Multiracial Experience: Racial Boundaries as the New Frontier,* edited by M. P. P. Root. Thousand Oaks, CA: Sage.

U.S. Office of Technology Assessment. 1988. *Infertility: Medical and Social Choices.* Publication No. OTA BA 358. Washington, DC: U.S. Congress.

Updike, J. 1960. *Rabbit Run.* New York: Knopf.

Vaid, U. 1995. *Virtual Equality: The Mainstreaming of Gay and Lesbian Liberation.* New York: Anchor.

Valins, S. 1966. "Cognitive Effects of False Heart-Rate Feedback." *Journal of Personality and Social Psychology* 4:400-8.

Vance, C. S. 1984. *Pleasure and Danger: Exploring Female Sexuality.* Boston: Routledge & Kegan Paul.

Waterman, C. K., L. J. Dawson, and M. J. Bologna. 1989. "Sexual Coercion in Gay Male and Lesbian Relationships: Predictions and Implications for Support Services. *Journal of Sex Research* 26:118-24.

Whitehead, B. D. 1994. "The Failure of Sex Education." *Atlantic Monthly,* October, pp. 55-80.

Whitman, F. 1983. "Culturally Invariable Properties of Male Homosexualities: Tentative Conclusions from Cross-Cultural Research. *Archives of Sexual Behavior* 12:207-26.

Williams, T. 1947. *A Streetcar Named Desire.* New York: New Directions.

Wright, L. 1995. "A Reporter at Large: Double Mystery. *New Yorker* 8/7:44-50.

Wu, F. C., T. M. Farley, A. Peregondon, and G. M. Waites. 1996. "Effects of Testosterone Enanthate in Normal Men: Experience from a Multicenter Contraceptive Efficacy Study." *Fertility and Sterility* 65:626-36.

Wyatt, G. E. 1992. "The Sociocultural Context of African American and White American Women's Rape." *Journal of Social Issues* 48:77-92.

Yarber, W. I. 1994. "Past, Present, and Future Perspectives on Sexuality Education." Pp. 3-28 in *Promoting Healthy Sexuality in Young People.* New York: SIECUS.

Zelnick, M. and F. K. Shah. 1983. "First Intercourse among Young Americans." *Family Planning Perspectives* 15:64-70.

About the Authors

Pepper Schwartz is Professor of Sociology at the University of Washington. She is the author of many books, among them *American Couples* (with Philip Blumstein) and *Love Between Equals: How Peer Marriage Really Works*. She is past president of the Society for the Scientific Study of Sex and a columnist for *American Baby, Glamour* (with Janet Lever) and *One Click Away* on the Microsoft Network. She lives on a horse and llama ranch in Snoqualmie, Washington.

Virginia Rutter is working toward her Ph.D. in sociology at the University of Washington with a focus on gender and families. Prior to joining academia, she worked as a journalist and in public affairs in Washington, D.C., and she continues to write for general audiences about a variety of issues pertaining to relationships, gender, and sexuality and is author of *The Love Text* (with Pepper Schwartz). She also has a master's degree in 18th-century British Literature from the University of London. She teaches writing for sociology to undergraduates at the University of Washington.